DJs do Guetto

33 1/3 Global

33 1/3 Global, a series related to but independent from **33 1/3**, takes the format of the original series of short, music-based books and brings the focus to music throughout the world. With initial volumes focusing on Japanese and Brazilian music, the series will also include volumes on the popular music of Australia/Oceania, Europe, Africa, the Middle East, and more.

33 1/3 Japan

Series Editor: Noriko Manabe

Spanning a range of artists and genres—from the 1970s rock of Happy End to technopop band Yellow Magic Orchestra, the Shibuya-kei of Cornelius, classic anime series *Cowboy Bebop*, J-Pop/EDM hybrid Perfume, and vocaloid star Hatsune Miku—33 1/3 Japan is a series devoted to in-depth examination of Japanese popular music of the twentieth and twenty-first centuries.

Published Titles:
Supercell's *Supercell* by Keisuke Yamada
Yoko Kanno's *Cowboy Bebop Soundtrack* by Rose Bridges
Perfume's *Game* by Patrick St. Michel
Cornelius's *Fantasma* by Martin Roberts
Joe Hisaishi's *My Neighbor Totoro: Soundtrack* by Kunio Hara
Shonen Knife's *Happy Hour* by Brooke McCorkle
Nenes' *Koza Dabasa* by Henry Johnson

Forthcoming Titles:
Yuming's *The 14th Moon* by Lasse Lehtonen
Yellow Magic Orchestra's *Yellow Magic Orchestra* by Toshiyuki Ohwada
Kohaku utagassen: The Red and White Song Contest by Shelley Brunt

33 1/3 Brazil

Series Editor: Jason Stanyek

Covering the genres of samba, tropicália, rock, hip hop, forró, bossa nova, heavy metal and funk, among others, 33 1/3 Brazil is a series devoted to in-depth examination of the most important Brazilian albums of the twentieth and twenty-first centuries.

Published Titles:

Caetano Veloso's *A Foreign Sound* by Barbara Browning

Tim Maia's *Tim Maia Racional Vols. 1 &2* by Allen Thayer

João Gilberto and Stan Getz's *Getz/Gilberto* by Brian McCann

Gilberto Gil's *Refazenda* by Marc A. Hertzman

Dona Ivone Lara's *Sorriso Negro* by Mila Burns

Milton Nascimento and Lô Borges's *The Corner Club* by Jonathon Grasse

Racionais MCs' *Sobrevivendo no Inferno* by Derek Pardue

Naná Vasconcelos's *Saudades* by Daniel B. Sharp

Forthcoming Titles:

Jorge Ben Jor's *África Brasil* by Frederick J. Moehn

Chico Buarque's *Chico Buarque* by Charles A. Perrone

33 1/3 Europe

Series Editor: Fabian Holt

Spanning a range of artists and genres, 33 1/3 Europe offers engaging accounts of popular and culturally significant albums of Continental Europe and the North Atlantic from the twentieth and twenty-first centuries.

Published Titles:

Darkthrone's *A Blaze in the Northern Sky* by Ross Hagen

Ivo Papazov's *Balkanology* by Carol Silverman

Heiner Müller and Heiner Goebbels's *Wolokolamsker Chaussee* by Philip V. Bohlman

Modeselektor's *Happy Birthday!* by Sean Nye

Mercyful Fate's *Don't Break the Oath* by Henrik Marstal

Bea Playa's *I'll Be Your Plaything* by Anna Szemere and András Rónai

DJs do Guetto by Richard Elliott

Forthcoming Titles:

Los Rodriguez's *Sin Documentos* by Fernán del Val and Héctor Fouce

Massada's *Astaganaga* by Lutgard Mutsaers

Nuovo Canzoniere Italiano's *Bella Ciao* by Jacopo Tomatis

Czesław Niemen's *Niemen Enigmatic* by Ewa Mazierska and
     Mariusz Gradowski

Amália Rodrigues's *Amália at the Olympia* by Lila Ellen Gray

Ardit Gjebrea's *Projekt Jon* by Nicholas Tochka

Vopli Vidopliassova's *Tantsi* by Maria Sonevytsky

Édith Piaf's *Recital 1961* by David Looseley

Iannis Xenakis' *Persepolis* by Aram Yardumian

DJs do Guetto

Richard Elliott

Series Editor: Fabian Holt

BLOOMSBURY ACADEMIC

NEW YORK · LONDON · OXFORD · NEW DELHI · SYDNEY

BLOOMSBURY ACADEMIC
Bloomsbury Publishing Inc
1385 Broadway, New York, NY 10018, USA
50 Bedford Square, London, WC1B 3DP, UK
29 Earlsfort Terrace, Dublin 2, Ireland

BLOOMSBURY, BLOOMSBURY ACADEMIC and the Diana logo are
trademarks of Bloomsbury Publishing Plc

First published in the United States of America 2022

"Library of Congress Cataloging-in-Publication Data
Names: Elliott, Richard, 1971 June 28– author.
Title: DJs do guetto / Richard Elliott.
Description: [1st.] | New York : Bloomsbury Academic, 2022. |
Series: 33 1/3 Europe | Includes bibliographical references and index. |
Summary: "Uses the 2006 compilation DJs do Guetto as a central document of
Afro-diasporic music in 21st-century Lisbon and as a case study of postcolonial
encounters in global popular music"–Provided by publisher.
Identifiers: LCCN 2021043538 (print) | LCCN 2021043539 (ebook) |
ISBN 9781501357831 (hardback) | ISBN 9781501357848 (paperback) |
ISBN 9781501357855 (epub) | ISBN 9781501357862 (pdf) |
ISBN 9781501357879 (ebook other)
Subjects: LCSH: DJs do guetto (2006) | Electronic dance music–Portugal–
Lisbon–History and criticism. | Popular music–Portugal–Lisbon–2001–2010–
History and criticism. | Blacks–Portugal–Lisbon–Music–History and criticism.
Classification: LCC ML3540.5 .E48 2022 (print) | LCC ML3540.5 (ebook) |
DDC 781.64809469/42–dc23
LC record available at https://lccn.loc.gov/2021043538
LC ebook record available at https://lccn.loc.gov/2021043539"

ISBN: HB: 978-1-5013-5783-1
      PB: 978-1-5013-5784-8
      ePDF: 978-1-5013-5786-2
      eBook: 978-1-5013-5785-5

Typeset by Newgen KnowledgeWorks Pvt. Ltd., Chennai, India
Printed and bound in the United States of America

Series: 33 1/3 Europe

To find out more about our authors and books visit www.bloomsbury.com
and sign up for our newsletters.

Contents

Acknowledgements viii

1 PR001 1

2 Uprouted beats 17

3 Close encounters 37

4 Quinta do Mocho 47

5 Looped encounters 61

6 The making and unmaking of a DJ crew 73

7 Nobility 87

8 Strange futurity 101

9 Translation 111

10 An ending 123

Bibliography 133
Discography 140
Index 143

Acknowledgements

I would like to thank Fabian Holt, the editor of the 33 1/3 Europe series, for his encouragement in proposing this book and for his subsequent comments on the proposal and the manuscript. I am also grateful for the comments received from anonymous reviewers during the early stages of the project. Thanks to Leah Babb-Rosenfeld and the editorial and production teams at Bloomsbury Academic for their support throughout. Much of my thinking about the music discussed in this book and about contemporary global pop more generally has been worked out in the 'Global Pop' module I have taught at Newcastle University since 2016 and I have benefitted from the insights of my students on this and other modules at Newcastle. Thanks in particular to Nanette de Jong for offering me an opportunity to contribute a session on Portuguese urban musics to her 'Understanding World Music' module each year. In Lisbon, I was able to meet with DJ Marfox to discuss *DJs do Guetto* and much more and I would like to record my thanks to André Ferreira at Filho Único for setting this up and to Marfox for being so generous with his time. Kally Meru showed me around Quinta do Mocho and discussed its history, residents and culture, as well as acting as translator during my interview with Marfox; thank you, Kally, I learned so much from our meetings. I had the opportunity to present my research on Lisbon batida at the 'Iberian Sound Cultures' symposium in London in 2018 and at the IASPM UK & Ireland conference in 2020 and I'm grateful to the organizers and participants of those events. With IASPM-UKI 2020 being an online event, I received some stimulating feedback in the comments sections; engaging with these questions and comments in a text-based forum informed the final draft of this book, so my thanks go out to Ruth Adams, Maria Perevedentseva, Mimi Haddon and Ivan Mouraviev. As with my previous books I remain eternally grateful for the support I receive from my family. In particular I want to thank Maria Mata for her patience, support, advice and love. Finally, this is the first book project I have undertaken since the passing of my mother, Angela Elliott, in 2017 and I would like to dedicate it to her memory.

1 PR001

On 10 February 2013, a post appeared on the website of the Lisbon-based record label Príncipe Discos advertising a new release. Under the heading 'PR001 – V/A – Dj'S Do Guetto Vol. 1' was artwork for what looked like a record or CD cover (see Figure 1.1). It had the familiar look of the covers that adorned the limited-edition records previously released by Príncipe, all painted by Márcio Matos. This release, however, was marked as 'digital only', accompanied by a brief message in Portuguese and English – 'Original release in September 2006, re-release in February 2013' – and links to free downloads via the file-sharing sites Zippyshare and MediaFire.[1] Clicking on one of the links took the user to their chosen download destination, where they would find a zipped file of 160 MB entitled 'Djs Di Guetto Vol. 1 (2006 Reed. 2013 Príncipe Discos)', uploaded on 9 February 2013. Downloading and unzipping this file revealed two folders (labelled '#1' and '#2'), two PDFs ('Artwork 2013' and 'Original Artwork') and two rich text format (RTF) documents ('Dj's do Guetto Vol. 1 ENG' and

---

[1]From March 2019, the Zippyshare site became unavailable to users in the UK (where I live), with any attempt to access it from a conventional virtual private network (VPN) returning a '403 Forbidden message'. The MediaFire link continued to work. At the time of writing (mid-2021), both links are still listed on the Príncipe website: https://principediscos.wordpress.com/2013/02/10/pr001-va-djs-do-guetto-vol-1/, accessed 2 August 2021.

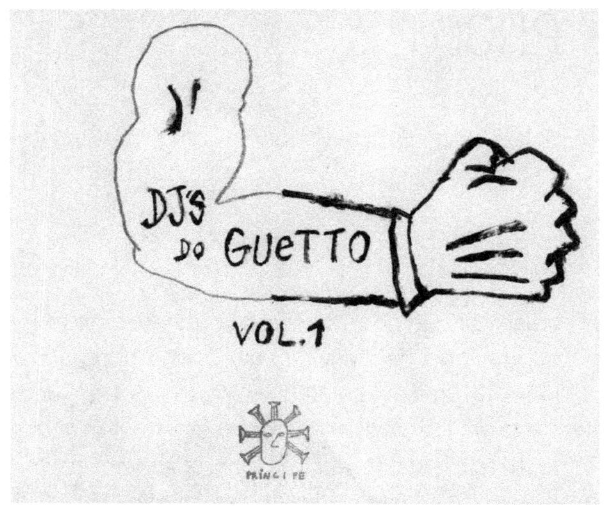

Figure 1.1 *Cover of the reissued DJs do Ghetto album, released by Príncipe Discos, 2013. Cover designed by Márcio Matos.*

'Dj's do Guetto Vol. 1 PT'). In the first folder were nineteen MP3 files, while the second contained eighteen more. As the texts in English and Portuguese explained, these thirty-seven tracks comprised the two CDs' worth of material of the *DJs do Guetto* (*DJDG*) compilation and were originally released by the eponymous crew as downloadable files in September 2006. This collection – also known by its creolized title, *DJs di Guetto* – was the material that had taken the DJs Nervoso, N.K., Marfox, Fofuxo, Jesse and Pausas from local renown in their neighbourhoods to wider fame in the dance music scene of Lisbon and beyond. It was an early taste of a sound that would come to be known as batida (from the Portuguese for 'beat') and that combined international variants of house and techno with Afro-Portuguese styles such as kuduro, tarraxinha, funaná and kizomba. In the years to come, these sounds would become ever more familiar on dance floors around the world as Marfox and others established batida as Lisbon's hottest new musical export, taking it from the rooms and the streets of the projects to trendy metropolitan nightclubs and music festival stages. They would also come to be known by consumers of the recorded artefacts released by Príncipe and other labels (including Enchufada, Warp and Lit City Trax) and users of digital platforms such as SoundCloud, Mixcloud, Bandcamp and YouTube.

This was the music that Príncipe had been set up to serve and promote and 2013 was a good time for the label to offer its growing audience a history lesson. The liner notes accompanying the reissued tracks underscored the historical importance of the music for the contemporary Afro-Portuguese dance music scene, the intensity of its sound and the precocity of its creators (all DJs were under twenty-one when the music was created). They also recognized the strangeness and futurity of the sounds:

> The precision and care with … the sound is impressive,
> millimetrically controlled in order to maximize the brutality
> of rhythm in any set of speakers. It is rhythm that is the
> essence of these compositions and the element that is all-
> transforming (alarm sirens, horror movie keyboards, kalimbas,
> cut-up voices, which are mutilated and cut-up again). Ranging
> in vibe and territory through universalist epics, works of pure
> percussive and amelodical austerity or grinding attacks that
> might provoke dizzy spells and cardiac problems, there is
> a clear feeling here of wanting to imagine a music for your
> friends but also for a planet that is as yet untravelled.[2]

[2]Uncredited liner notes to the 2013 reissue of *DJs do Guetto*, Príncipe Discos, accessible via links provided at https://principediscos.wordpress.com/2013/02/10/pr001-va-djs-do-guetto-vol-1/, accessed 2 August 2021.

This is as good a description as any of the music that Príncipe has been publishing since late 2011, when the label put out DJ Marfox's EP *Eu Sei Quem Sou* as its inaugural release. It gets at the precise, rhythm-heavy fragmentary yet coherent nature of the batida sound and highlights the tropes of strangeness and futurity that would feature in critics' responses to the music, as the work of Marfox and other Lisbon DJs found increasing coverage in publications such as *Pitchfork*, *Fact*, *Vice*, *Resident Advisor*, *Dazed* and *SPIN*. It also hints at the variety of sounds that would be associated with the genre, making it questionable whether 'genre' was even an appropriate term to use to describe this network of artists, sounds and methodologies. Furthermore, the understanding of this music as simultaneously in-this-world ('music for your friends') and signalling beyond ('a planet that is as yet untravelled'), which is linked to context and also removed from it, is crucial to the conception of batida I want to develop here.

The Príncipe liner notes go on to describe the precarious existence of the music, created as it was by young DJs working outside the music industry and therefore reliant on what they could make, keep and share on the computers they had access to. With their goals set on the present and what they could create for a local community of listeners, posterity was not the prime motive. Like mixtapes and playlists, the collecting of these tracks was meant primarily as a functional endeavour rather than a lasting artistic statement. It wasn't a collection designed to be revisited, let alone rereleased, several years later, which left the Príncipe team with limited sources to work from: 'This free digital reissue contains the files that survived PCs which have tragically passed away, the WAV files and Fruity Loops (amongst other software) projects from where this music was born out of apparently lost forever. Being as it is, we tried to find the files with the best audio quality for each MP3 we now make available to you.'[3]

***

This opening account of how the reissue of *DJDG* appeared to those who were tuning in to the Lisbon batida scene in early 2013 highlights a set of related points that recur in various forms throughout this book. What appears of the moment is often the result of prolonged and detailed labour (this is as true of writing as it is of making electronic dance music [EDM]). What might seem to hit instantaneously may echo for years. What appears at your fingertips one minute may become inaccessible or even vanish the next. What is to hand is often embedded in multiple fragile or permablocked layers, searchable but unreachable. Yesterday's easy download is tomorrow's prohibited content. Digital media relies on inbuilt obsolescence: it moves fast because it is so perishable, and it is endlessly perishable because it moves so fast.

This begs the question of whether it is appropriate to make a thing out of something so intangible. Can we really consider *DJDG* as an 'album', a fixed thing? Is it lasting enough as a statement to justify a book (another fixed or fixing thing)? I argue that we can and that it is. *DJDG* fixed a time and place in a permanent enough fashion to have acted, over the years and in different formats, as a statement of intent, a business card, a CV, a functional commodity, a shareable pleasure, a historical marker, a compilation of the sounds of one community that has travelled on to connect to other communities. As something to gather around – and I mean that both in the sense of a soundtrack for an event and a focal point for an

---

[3] Ibid.

extended discussion – *DJDG* does what many other albums do. It may not (yet) have taken on the tangibility of a physical item that can be placed in a record shop – it's not *that* kind of a functional commodity – but that is hardly a prerequisite for an album in the first decades of the twenty-first century.

The fact that *DJDG* blurs the lines of what we might historically consider to be an album is one of the many things that, for me, marks it as interesting and worthy of discussion *as* an album, and hence as an entry in this book series. I therefore approach it as I would any album I wished to discuss, by considering it as a relatively fixed and bounded object that encourages questions about its contents, its sounds, its makers, its history and the cultural context in which it emerges and which it reflects. My use of 'object' here refers not to the physical tangibility of a record or CD – or even to decks, mixers, speakers and resonant spaces, vital as all of these are – but rather to a thing that is graspable in other ways, something which demands its own label and importance, something without which something else could not have happened. Much has been written in music studies about the need to think of music as a process rather than a thing, to not get bogged down in the objects that accompany 'musicking', and this would seem to be especially important for a genre such as EDM, geared as it is towards dancing bodies and gathering communities.[4] But, just as objects are always in process (subject to the kinds of

[4]For 'musicking', see Christopher Small, *Musicking: The Meanings of Performing and Listening*, Music/Culture (Hanover, NH: University Press of New England, 1998). The amount of literature which applies and expands Small's concepts into popular music studies is voluminous. For a collection of essays that explores the kinds of music technologies relevant to EDM in relation to musicking, see Paul D. Greene and Thomas Porcello, eds, *Wired for Sound: Engineering and Technologies in Sonic Cultures*, Music/Culture (Middletown, CT: Wesleyan University Press, 2005).

change and loss discussed above with regard to digital media), so do processes rely on objects. For dancing and gathering to happen, there need to be things to dance to and gather around. Like other collections of EDM recordings released as albums, playlists or mixes, *DJDG* offers these services even as it wears its object status lightly.

In this book, I use *DJDG* as an object to launch a series of explorations, discussions and encounters, approaching the compilation from a number of angles. The idea of 'encounter' provides the main conceptual thread for this book and will be deployed in several interconnected ways. There are, for example, encounters between countries in spatial and temporal relationships; between the colonial past, the postcolonial present and the future (that strange space from which this music is often heard to emanate); between different communities of Lisbon (the segregated centre and the periphery); between global styles (with Lisbon as a site of encounter for the Lusophone Black Atlantic and its diaspora, and as a mediating centre between Luanda and London, but equally between São Paulo and Paris); and between mainstream and underground. By discussing these connected forms of encounter, I want to situate this book within a broader field of work on hybridity, diaspora, postcolonialism and cultural globalization. It will also connect to work being done on 'aesthetic cosmopolitanism' in global popular musics.[5]

---

[5]On aesthetic cosmopolitanism, see Motti Regev, *Pop-Rock Music: Aesthetic Cosmopolitanism in Late Modernity* (Cambridge, UK: Polity, 2013). Other works which have informed my thinking about batida, and with which I wish to place this book in conversation, include Jace Clayton, *Uproot: Travels in Twenty-First-Century Music and Digital Culture* (New York: Farrar, Straus and Giroux, 2016); Theresa Beyer, Thomas Burkhalter and Hannes Liechti, eds, *Seismographic Sounds: Visions of a New World* (Bern, Switzerland: Norient, 2015); Thomas Burkhalter, 'Sound Studies across Continents: A Multidisciplinary Research

I also mix in some of my own encounters as a listener/consumer of batida; with the music of Portugal more generally; with DJ Marfox and the Lisbon neighbourhood of Quinta do Mocho; and with the texts of music journalists who have written about this music. While this book is much more about the music than my position with regard to it, I have kept in mind my perspective as a mostly distant observer and listener-in and tried to recognize the affordances and limitations that such a position entails. My attempts to get closer to the makers of the music during the later stages of writing this book were curtailed, as so much was, by the restrictions brought about by the Covid-19 pandemic, making the tail end of the project one of forced remoteness. Responding to this in as positive a way as I can, I have tailored the book to reflect some of the many different encounters a listener can have with music, whether near to or far from its most obvious contexts. I have also considered the music as a prime example of 'World Music 2.0' and contemporary digital culture more generally, noting the ways in which, and the speed with which, sound travels across the networks of the twenty-first century.[6]

I have invoked some contexts into which this music might be placed, but I also want to think about a variety of de- or recontextualizing strategies. I've already mentioned one of

Approach', in *Sound as Popular Culture: A Research Companion*, ed. Jens Gerrit Papenburg and Holger Schulze (Cambridge, MA: MIT Press, 2016), 89–95.
[6]On 'World Music 2.0', see Clayton, *Uproot*; Burkhalter, 'Sound Studies'; David Novak, 'The Sublime Frequencies of New Old Media', *Public Culture* 23, no. 3 (2011): 603–34; Michael Gallope, 'World Music Without Profit', *Twentieth-Century Music* 17, no. 2 (June 2020): 161–95. Wayne Marshall has been writing and speaking about the concept for well over a decade; see his 'Sounds of the Wide, Wired World', *The National*, 29 October 2010, https://www.thenationalnews.com/arts-culture/music/sounds-of-the-wide-wired-world-1.516526, accessed 2 August 2021, as well as the extensive resources available via his website, Wayne & Wax (https://wayneandwax.com/).

these, which is the strategy of thinking of *DJDG* as an album that can be downloaded onto a device and played as one would play any other album. This is a recontexualization because it removes the music from its most obvious context of the nightclub or party and from any consideration of it as a DJ set (already aided by the fact that these are individual tracks, not mixed together) and places it as a set of tracks to listen to wherever the listener chooses. But we can go further with this. There is also the process referred to by Johannes Ismaiel-Wendt as 'sonic delinking', whereby music is liberated 'from an outdated ethno-musicological world map' in favour of 'an alternative world-view activated by musical forms'.[7] Ismaiel-Wendt's concept, building on the work of Walter Mignolo, relies on a recognition of the popular music track as 'a compositional mode of thought' that describes 'both individual sound-tracks and the mix of sound-tracks or the completed musical object', one that 'does not imagine a fixed entity … does not know a single order of events … lacks a hierarchy between melody, sound, and rhythm … is polymorphous and free from the sole task of representation'.[8] This idea is invoked by Philipp Rhensius in a way that explicitly connects it to the batida scene. Writing about the batida artist Nídia (also known earlier in her career as Nídia Minaj), Rhensius argues against those critics who instinctively refer to Nídia's roots and who 'associate the identitary with origin and not with the place of residence'. In contrast, he cites Ismaiel-Wendt's work and argues that Nídia's music is 'radically

[7]Johannes Ismaiel-Wendt, 'Track Studies: Popular Music and Postcolonial Analysis', in *Postcolonial Studies across the Disciplines*, ed. Jana Gohrisch and Ellen Grünkemeier (Amsterdam, The Netherlands: Rodopi, 2013), 102–3.
[8]Ibid., 98–9.

synthetic … free from anthropomorphic inadequacies, but also from localizations'.[9]

This approach resonates with that taken by Kodwo Eshun in his influential 1998 book *More Brilliant than the Sun: Adventures in Sonic Fiction*. Eshun's concept of sonic fiction challenges the common practice of connecting Black musics (from blues and jazz through soul, r and b, funk, hip-hop and techno) as connected to tradition, soul or the street, counteracting with an insistence on the fictive nature of the music under question. Wishing to highlight the importance of technology in creating alternative sonic worlds, Eshun writes that 'Sonic Futurism doesn't locate you in tradition; instead it dislocates you from origins. It uproutes you by inducing a gulf crisis, a perceptual daze rendering today's sonic discontinuum immediately audible'.[10] This way of conceiving of music has a significant appeal, especially for a style like batida that has often been written about in terms of futurity and strangeness. These tropes remove it from common contexts, or rather they set up a new range of increasingly common contexts from which to translate the music into something more familiar. We might say, extending some of the ideas at play in Eshun's framework, that music heard as alien should be written about as though from an alien or post-human perspective.[11] Some of Eshun's solutions to this are to create neologisms (see 'uproutes' above), to write against what he calls 'traditional Brit prose … so matey,

[9]Philipp Rhensius, 'Dance Away Your Origin: Nidia', *Norient* (19 September 2017), https://norient.com/stories/nidia, accessed 20 April 2021.
[10]Kodwo Eshun, *More Brilliant than the Sun: Adventures in Sonic Fiction* (London: Quartet Books, 1998), -001.
[11]For an analysis of Afrofuturism in relation to humanism and post-humanism, see tobias c. van Veen, 'Vessels of Transfer: Allegories of Afrofuturism in Jeff Mills and Janelle Monáe', *Dancecult* 5, no. 2 (2013): 7–41.

and so blokish, and so bluff and no-nonsense', and instead to try 'to engineer a kind of sensory alteration'.[12] While sensory alteration is not something I have dedicated myself to in the writing of this book, I do occasionally approach the sounds of batida as if from a naive perspective, as if encountering them for the first time. I also attend to the ways in which other writers have responded to batida by evoking strangeness and alterity.

For all the appeal of an approach that focuses on sonic fiction, sonic delinking and recording strangeness, I still feel the story of *DJDG* requires a situation in time and place and a connection to the humans involved in the project. Rather than ditching context in the name of a purely post-human approach (if such a thing is even possible at the moment), I aim instead for a two-deck technique that crossfades between text and context, mixing sonic fiction with biography, history and geography. As will become clear, people and places matter a great deal to those involved in the batida scene and, in many ways, the stories of people and places need to be recognized right now more than one critic's interpretation of a set of texts. What marks those people and places out as different from, as well as part of, the rest of the global EDM scene is as much the point as the sounds that come to us through the otherwise anonymous channels of contemporary digital distribution. Philipp Rhensius recognizes this even as he argues for sonically delinking Nídia's music, noting that it 'would probably not have been heard without the romanticization of post-migrant ghetto life'.[13] Such is the double bind in which much under-represented music finds itself. But there are other arguments

[12]Eshun, *More Brilliant*, 189.
[13]Rhensius, 'Dance Away'.

for reattaching context to music first encountered as strange, as we will see later when looking at some of the work that has been done on 'World Music 2.0', where writers such as Jace Clayton and Wayne Marshall have argued for the necessity of lingering and learning about global pop styles to avoid the dangers of turning them into passing trends.

In the following chapters, then, I flip between my interpretations of some of the tracks on *DJDG*, other people's interpretations or explanations and the story of how *DJDG* came to be made, as told to me by DJ Marfox and with additional details drawn from other published sources. My approach to the musical materials is also a mixed one, in that at times I attempt an alienating or 'semi-naive' encounter with the sounds at the heart of the album, while at others I give in to the inevitability of recognizing myself as a situated auditor with a listening biography and a pile of contextual baggage that it would be foolish to pretend I could dump. The semi-naive approach is designed (knowingly, and therefore *anaively*) as a way of not letting the sounds and the strangeness of *DJDG* get lost in other contextual framings. At the same time, I recognize this as another kind of sonic fiction as I reintroduce my own contextual signposts. I am, after all, writing about these tracks away from their obvious home on the dance floor, and I embrace this as another way of finding strangeness in the music. I am hardly alone in doing so; it's how many of the reviewers of this music write about it and how curators such as Príncipe sometimes frame the sounds for consumption as physical or digital objects via platforms like Bandcamp. But it's also what most of the music producers of the batida scene do as they labour on their music in their homes. When I visited Marfox in his Quinta do Mocho bedroom studio, I asked about this potential split between the producer concentrating on the business of constructing beats via the digital audio workstation (DAW) interface and the DJ and dancers working together in the physical communion of the nightclub. Although Marfox didn't wish to make too much of this, noting that he always dances while making music in his room, there was a clear sense of the labour involved in constructing beats and sets. One of the things I learned watching Marfox work and hearing him explain his music was that the music itself is transcontextual and connective: it's the thing the DJ makes and plays, the thing that dancers move to, the thing that we all talk about and write about. Everybody does their bit and this requires different spaces of production, consumption and reflection. Moving between them can sometimes seem bumpy and alienating, but it is possible to dance where you write and write where you dance.

If I were to fashion my account of batida from what Eshun terms a 'Postsoul' perspective or to take what others have identified as a post-humanist approach, I would probably not include biographical information about DJs or historical and geographical details of Lisbon's suburban housing projects.[14] This book has a bit of all of these, even as it wishes to sometimes hear batida more abstractly. Perhaps it has something of the stop–start dynamic that typifies much batida, an analogous mixture of the abstract and the representational. However clumsy my cross-fading may be at times, and however much it may feel like a refusal to commit to either a post-human or a humanist discourse, I am content to mix and match as I go in the interest of foregrounding encounter. At the centre of the encounters I evoke is the strange and interesting object that is *DJDG*, an object that raises questions and invites approaches.

[14]On 'Postsoul', see Eshun, *More Brilliant*, 005.

I see the writing of this book as a way of testing some of these out. And I see writing as another encounter. If my hearing of batida tracks was no longer really a naive one by the time I sat down to write this book, the attempt to write about them certainly was. What we meet in the act of writing is as strange and informative as anything we may have conceived of during our initial research and analysis. And, to make another analogy between this kind of writing and beat-making, that sense of discovery-in-process is a massive part of the enjoyment of composing sounds, as it is of words. As important as – perhaps more important than – the attempt to get down something you had in your head prior to opening the DAW are the countless things you discover as you try out different sounds: chopping, stretching, pitch-shifting, distorting, combining, hearing and feeling what happens when one loop encounters another, when the whole becomes something greater than the sum of its parts.

***

A note on names and orthography. For consistency and convenience, I am using the title *DJs do Guetto* and the abbreviation *DJDG* for the compilation that is this book's subject. The compilation is listed in other sources (including press features, academic studies and DJ bios on digital platforms) variously as *DJs di Guetto*, *DJs do Ghetto* and *DJs di Ghetto*, while references to the name of the DJ crew also vary. The reissue of the compilation by Príncipe in 2013 uses the title *Dj'S Do Guetto Vol. 1* on its cover but uses 'DJ's di Guetto Vol. 1' in the artist tag of each MP3 file and as the title for the zipped files containing the tracks. Similarly, orthography is not always consistent in terms of capitalizing the title 'DJ' or names such as 'N.K.' (who is sometimes referred to as 'N.k.' and 'Nk').

This shifting of signifiers seems apt in relation to an artefact that blurs the definitions of what an 'album' or a formal release might be, and also to a group of musicians who blurred similar lines and existed more as an idea than a formally designated band or crew.

2   Uprouted beats

While my account of *DJs do Guetto* (*DJDG*) and the scene for which it became a touchstone follows many others in referring to the music as 'batida', it's worth saying a bit more about this ambiguous term in relation to other genres and styles. On one hand, batida should not really be thought of as a genre; the word simply means 'beat' in Portuguese. Just as we wouldn't expect to be able to designate strict boundaries from the various Anglophone genres that have placed an emphasis on beats (from jazz to big beat), neither should we expect to from their Lusophone equivalents. And just as we do not expect the various artists who have used 'beat' in their name (from that beat combo the Beatles through the British ska group and the US power pop outfit both known as The Beat) to have anything to do with each other or to a single idea of what 'beat' might mean, neither should we be surprised to find a Portuguese group called Batida whose music overlaps, to an extent, with the loosely configured 'batida' scenes in Angola, Portugal and elsewhere.[1] On the other hand, the term does undeniable

[1]Batida (with a capital B) is a project established by the Huambo-born, Lisbon-raised musician, radio broadcaster and DJ Pedro Coqenão as a way of exploring links between Angola, Portugal and further afield (see https://batida.bandcamp.com/, accessed 2 August 2021). This is the 'Batida' referred to in Pedro Schacht Pereira's '"Dance Is a Disguise": Batida and the Infrapolitics of Dance Music in Postcolonial Portugal', in *Challenging Memories and Rebuilding*

categorical work. While musicians the world over invariably attempt to shrug off tags and designators to avoid being put in 'boxes', those who follow their work and talk and write about it generally find some shared vocabulary useful. I will have more to say about sharing through translation and negotiation at other points in this book; here, I give some space to discussing loose relationships and distinctions between some of the musical worlds referred to in the growing literature on Lusophone electronic dance music (EDM).

One obvious reference point for most of the key figures connected to the Lisbon scene is kuduro, the EDM genre that emerged from Angola in the early 1990s. Accounts differ as to where and who created kuduro, though few would deny its essential newness as a millennial sound that sought to fuse the EDMs of the later twentieth century – particularly North American and European house and techno – with rhythms and instrumental textures associated with African styles. Dance, sound and lyrics are all vital elements to kuduro, though they come into play at different moments in the genre's evolution. The term 'kuduro' itself designates a dance style, named for the 'hard ass' (*cú duro* in Portuguese) moves created by Tony Amado. Amado took his influence from a scene in the 1989 film *Kickboxer* in which Jean-Claude Van Damme moves from a drunken dance into a fight sequence. The sense of the body being simultaneously

Identities: Literary and Artistic Voices that Undo the Lusophone Atlantic, ed. Margarida Rendeiro and Federica Lupati (New York: Routledge, 2020), 121–38. The 'fruity batidas' referred to in an article by Garth Sheridan, meanwhile, refer to the beats produced by Angolan kuduro producers: see Garth Sheridan, 'Fruity Batidas: The Technologies and Aesthetics of Kuduro', *Dancecult* 6, no. 1 (2014): 87–8. I sometimes use the term 'Lisbon batida' in this book to avoid confusion, but, where I don't, I trust the context will make it clear which kind of batida I am referring to on each occasion.

out of and in control became crucial to the evolution of the kuduro dance style, which at times has placed emphasis on the restrictions as well as the versatility of the physical body. Along with Amado, Sebem was an early popularizer of kuduro and his track 'Felicidade' became a staple sound of turn-of-the-millennium Lusophone club nights. Initially, the focus was on dancing and it was in the nightclubs of downtown Luanda that what Marissa Moorman describes as 'DJ-driven music: techno mixed with Latin beats' became the batida sound that young middle-class Angolans craved.[2] As Moorman notes, kuduro quickly distinguished itself from other Angolan forms such as semba (the pre-eminent modern Angolan popular music prior to the 1980s), kizomba (a slower, sensual dance music influenced by Caribbean zouk of the early 1980s) and the *carnaval* musics popular in many parts of the country by being a harder, techno-based music aimed at individuals rather than couples:

> Popular Angolan musical and dance genres from the late
> nineteenth century *rebita* (danced in a circle to live music),
> to semba and kizomba, and to the 1990s and early 2000s
> *tarraxinha* [a slower, more sensual form of kuduro], are
> intimately related and mutually constitutive. But Kuduro is
> distinctive. Unlike the other genres, it is not a partnered social
> dance, though it is a social event with spontaneous *desafios*
> (challenges) between dancers that usually draw a crowd. It is
> danced in the streets by children and young adults, in middle-
> class homes during parties, and at the weddings and public
> birthday celebrations of political elites. Despite its origins in

[2]Marissa J. Moorman, 'Anatomy of Kuduro: Articulating the Angolan Body Politic after the War', *African Studies Review* 57, no. 3 (December 2014): 29.

downtown discos, today its creative soul is in the musseque,
home to the majority of studios and kuduristas [kuduro artists].[3]

Musseques are the informal housing settlements, or shanty towns, that sprawl across the outskirts of Luanda; they were already well established during the Portuguese colonial rule and later became home to millions of people and their descendants who were displaced during Angola's long civil war (1975–2002). These areas are marked by poor infrastructure: unpaved streets, makeshift buildings and lack of electricity and water. It is here that the second generation of kuduristas established themselves, building on the genre's early 'instrumental' phase to add lyrics voiced by MCs influenced by Jamaican-style toasting and US hip-hop. Writing about the changing aesthetics of kuduro across three generations of artists, Sheridan argues that the lack of vocals on earlier tracks was partly due to a lack of studio resources for recording them. But, he argues, like the hardware restrictions that led early kuduro producers to stick to short, looped arrangements (due to limited storage on 1990s sequencers), the choices were also aesthetic in that the sounds mapped onto the minimal techno being produced elsewhere at the time. By the early 2000s, however, other technologies were becoming more widely available, most notably home computers and music sequencing programmes such as FruityLoops (later rebranded as FL Studio). Hacked and pirated software spread through the musseques, along with the ability to more easily record vocals; even if a kudurista didn't have access to all of this in their own home, there was a

[3]Ibid.

greater likelihood that they could work with someone in the musseques who did.[4]

While much of the Anglophone scholarship on kuduro has focussed, understandably, on the role of music in reflecting the broader social and historical contexts of a country that, until 2002, had been in a state of war for forty years (thirteen years of anticolonial struggle against Portugal followed by twenty-seven years of civil war), Sheridan's work offers a useful account of how aesthetic choices have evolved the genre not only in its native country, but also in its spread to Portugal.[5] Sheridan notes that, by the time of the second generation of Angolan kuduristas (from the start of the 2000s), the genre was already making an impact in Portugal, especially in the capital Lisbon. This was partly through the movement of thousands of Angolans to Portugal during the civil war and its aftermath, but also to the thriving market for imported music available on cassettes and recordable compact discs (CD-Rs) that could be purchased in Lisbon's street markets, especially the African market at Praça de Espanha.[6]

[4]Sheridan, 'Fruity Batidas': 88.
[5]Garth Sheridan, 'Hard Ass: Representation, Diaspora and Globalisation in Kuduro', PhD thesis (RMIT, 2014). For other works on kuduro in Angola, see Moorman, 'Anatomy of Kuduro'; Stefanie Alisch and Nadine Siegert, 'Angolanidade Revisited: Kuduro', *Norient*, 6 June 2011, https://norient. com/academic/kuduro, accessed 2 August 2021; Jayna Brown, 'Buzz and Rumble: Global Pop Music and Utopian Impulse', *Social Text* 28, no. 1 (2010): 125–46; António Tomás, 'Becoming Famous: Kuduro, Politics and the Performance of Social Visibility', *Critical Interventions* 8, no. 2 (4 May 2014): 261– 75; Hershini Young, '"Sound of Kuduro Knocking at My Door": Kuduro Dance and the Poetics of Debility', *African American Review* 45, no. 3 (2012): 391–402.
[6]Kalaf Epalanga, a writer and a musician associated with the record label Enchufada and the group Buraka Som Sistema, describes the process of sourcing cassettes and CD-Rs from Angolans travelling to Portugal and from markets and stores in Lisbon in his book *Também Os Brancos Sabem Dançar: Um Romance Musical* (Alfragide, Portugal: Caminho, 2017).

DJ Marfox has spoken of how formative it was to hear these imported sounds as a teenager and particularly the productions of the Angolan DJ Znobia. Znobia was one of the second-generation kuduristas whose use of FruityLoops to create high intensity, often overdriven, beats would be influential for the batida producers in Lisbon, even if it wasn't always the most fashionable sound in Luanda. Based in Bairro do Rangel, on the outskirts of the capital, Znobia had started out as a kuduro dancer but changed career in order to find an audience; as he told Edwin Houghton in a 2008 interview, 'DJing happened out of necessity – to make my music reach the people. If it wasn't me playing my productions, no one would'.[7] If Znobia's approach was yet to become a popular one in Angola, in Lisbon the harder styles of kuduro were mainly relegated to the peripheries of the city, where most of the Luso-African community were based. In the trendy downtown nightclubs, African diasporic music tended either to stick to more traditional forms (especially those most associated with couple dances, such as kizomba and tarraxhinha) or to be mixed with Euro-American house music as a way of making it more cosmopolitan. An influential figure in this respect was DJ Amorim, who would mix kuduro from Angola with Eurodance and house tracks, one example being a megamix that mashed Sebem's 'Felicidade' with 'Rhythm Is a Dancer', a 1992 hit for the German Eurocance band 'Snap!' Starting in 1997, Amorim released several megamix CDs that proved popular with Portuguese audiences, particularly his 'Kumix' series.[8]

[7]Edwin STATS Houghton, 'Ghetto Palms: DJ Znobia/Angolan Kuduro', *The Fader* (11 June 2008), http://www.thefader.com/2008/6/11/ghetto-palms-dj-znobia-angolan-kuduro, accessed 19 April 2021.
[8]The Sebem/Snap mix can be heard on DJ Amorim's *Kumix 3*. CD. Sons D'África CD336, 2000.

Amorim is praised by Kalaf Epalanga in *Também Os Brancos Sabem Dançar*, his 2017 work of auto-fiction, as a pioneer in the popularizing of kuduro in Lisbon, while Znobia also cites Amorim as an influence on DJs in Luanda. For Epalanga, who was born in Angola and emigrated to Portugal at a young age, hearing kuduro in his new location enabled him to reconnect with his roots while also providing inspiration for his own subsequent work with the band Buraka Som Sistema.[9]

In Epalanga's account, despite the presence of kuduro in the Lisbon of the early 2000s, the genre didn't quite fit with other Luso-African sounds or the broader context of Portuguese popular music of the time. This take is supported by the journalist and cultural commentator Vítor Belanciano, who reflects that 'it was evident that the whole of Portuguese society would have difficulties embracing kuduro as its own music. But it was also clear that, for Afrodiasporic Portuguese, it was challenging to accept kuduro simply as Portuguese popular music'.[10] Belanciano argues that, for an older generation of immigrants, the music that connected them to Africa was from earlier traditions, whereas for their descendants there was more interest in globally dominant forms of popular music, such as US-dominated hip-hop, house or techno. Kuduro was

[9]Epalanga, *Também Os Brancos*, 35–44. Amorim, like Epalanga, had moved from Angola to Portugal. Znobia's comments on Amorim's influence can be heard in an interview he gave as part of the 'Terra Irada' series of events staged by Lisbon's MAAT (Museu de Arte, Arquitetura e Tecnologia) in December 2020; see https://www.maat.pt/en/event/kuduro-axis, accessed 2 August 2021. A video of the interview (moderated by Pedro Gomes of Príncipe Discos and also featuring DJ Marfox and Nazar) with English subtitles was uploaded to YouTube by MAAT on 12 December 2020, https://www.youtube.com/watch?v=T0ZLOwqbgDw, accessed 2 August 2021.
[10]Vítor Belanciano, *Não Dá Para Ficar Parado: Música Afro-Portuguesa: Celebração, Conflito e Esperança* (Porto: Edições Afrontamento, 2020), 65. My translation from Portuguese.

too modern and disconnected from tradition for the older generation, too 'African' for many of the younger generation. When I met DJ Marfox, he mentioned that the stripped-down kuduro of DJ Znobia and those like him *did* have an audience, but it was one restricted to the *noites africanas* or parties taking place on the periphery of the city and that these were close-knit affairs that did not influence the broader musical culture.

The extent to which kuduro and related sounds were transmigrating – being uprooted and 'uprouted' (to use Kodwo Eshun's term), cross-pollinating and extending influence – can be heard on compilations released in Europe in the 2000s. A Portuguese compilation produced by DJ Amorim and released as *African Dance Music* – with the subtitle 'New Beat of Angola 2006' – contains a range of approaches: tracks which combine instrumental textures such as semba guitar figures or traditional vocals with kuduro-inflected beats and 'global' English language vocal interjections (Amorim's 'Hot Africa' and 'Kumystic Dance', Joca Moreno's 'African Style', Viriato Muata and China's 'Angola Salé Salé'); Angolan MCs singing, toasting or spitting over hard and fast kuduro beats (DJ Kadu's 'É Para Sacudir', featuring Zoca Zoca, Yuri da Cunha and Pai Diesel); first-generation style kuduro, with brief sung refrains but no developed lyrical narrative (Victor Black's 'É a Nossa Tradição', featuring Virgilio Fire); Jamaican dancehall influences (Joca Moreno); bleep techno/acid house (Infrarave and Mix Mc's 'Acid Live in Two Days'); and stripped-down FL-style loops mixed with novelty sound effects (Znobia's mobile phone sampling '3310'; Kadu's 'Zigue Za [Remix]'). Of these, Znobia's pared-down style is closest to that found on the contemporaneous *DJDG* compilation, though several of the Lisbon batida DJs would hone this style even further, removing any gaps that might be used in an Angolan context for singers or MCs to add vocals. This is something Marfox has noted as a difference between the style he developed and what he was hearing in Znobia's music; for Marfox and many of his fellow DJs, the focus was on the beat and dancing, with lyrics mostly excised save for brief, repeated vocal fragments (often indecipherable in terms of semantics).[11]

On *Kuduro Style*, a French compilation from 2008 that collected forty tracks from Angola, Portugal and France over two CDs, there is a distinct split between the tracks produced in Africa and those from Europe, with the latter exhibiting a stronger tendency to raw beats at the expense of instruments and vocals. There is one track by Marfox on this compilation and the pared-down style is not so surprising in his case, but it is interesting to hear that the tracks with the strongest resemblance to those of *DJDG* are the ones produced by DJs seemingly based in France (Puto X, Vielo, Nilcaps). Whether this is from exposure to work by the *DJDG* and subsequent tracks by Marfox (whose work was known in France by this time) or an influence from Znobia is unclear. Still, it is interesting to play Puto X's 'De l'Angola au Brésil' next to Marfox's 'Viva Ao Brasil' and DJ Nervoso's 'Tipo Samba' (both tracks from *DJDG*) and consider them as analogous responses to the diasporic connections and uproutes linking Lusophone Africa, France, Portugal and Brazil.[12] Some similar connections had been made two years earlier when French producer Frederic Galliano released the CD *Frederic Galliano Presents Kuduro Sound System*, collecting music he had produced in Luanda

[11]Various Artists, *African Dance Music: New Beat of Angola 2006* (CD, Som Livre SL894-2, 2006). Marfox's comments about the difference between his and Znobia's styles were made in conversation with Znobia during the previously cited 'Terra Irada/Kuduro Axis' event.
[12]Various Artists, *Kuduro Style* (CD, EMI France 5099926738123, 2008).

with local DJ Kito da Machina and featuring vocals from a range of established kuduristas, including Tony Amado, Dog Murras, Gata Aggressiva and Pai Diesel.[13] In interviews at the time, Galliano made some confusing claims about the possibility (or impossibility) of making kuduro outside Angola while still claiming authenticity for his own project. Likewise, he projected an arguably romanticized idea of unchanging tradition onto the genre (in relation to its non-imitability) while also celebrating it as the first purely electronic music genre to emerge from Africa and highlighting the influences it was drawing from Caribbean and Brazilian musical forms.[14]

Most accounts of the development of kuduro in Lisbon agree that it was the popularity of Buraka Som Sistema – a group made up of first-generation immigrants from Angola with Portuguese-born members who had grown up in or near neighbourhoods with a strong Luso-African presence – that really helped position kuduro within Portuguese popular music, as well as export a sound that would become popular in nightclubs around the world. At the same time, many of these same accounts seek to qualify the sound that the group produced as adjacent to, rather than fully within, the kuduro genre. Sheridan describes the music being made by Buraka Som Sistema and the Angolan-born, Lisbon-raised artist Pedro Coquenão (who would go on to form the band/persona Batida in homage to Luandan beat culture) as 'a distinctly syncretic interpretation of electronic dance music.

[13]Frederic Galliano, *Frederic Galliano Presents Kuduro Sound System* (CD, Frikyiwa FKW 038, 2006).
[14]See interviews archived at http://riobailefunk.blogspot.com/2007/11/kuduro-vs-baile-funk-interview-of.html, accessed 2 August 2021, and https://www.mixcloud.com/stuartbuchanan/fat-planet-frederic-galliano-kuduro-sound-system-interview/, accessed 2 August 2021.

Kuduro was one of the guiding genres, but the form had been further mixed, with the incorporation of UK-derived bass music sounds such as dubstep, breakbeat and grime'.[15] Sheridan also notes how the distorted sound common to the FruityLoops-using second generation of kuduro DJs was largely removed from Buraka tracks to suit the expectations of European club music. Looking back in 2018 to the time when Buraka were gaining attention at the same time Marfox was working on his post-*DJDG* beats, Marfox recalled that he had thought the Buraka sound was 'too processed', going on to note a subsequent change of attitude: 'I was young. Nowadays, after having grown up in this musical environment, I realise that it wasn't processed. Buraka gave some regulation to the music and also managed to implement a "groove" that worked with all the electronic influences cohabiting in Europe at the time'.[16]

***

From the perspective of this book, it is necessary to recognize the evolution of kuduro as something that feeds into and runs alongside the creation of *DJDG*. It is important to know that other music being made in Angola, Portugal and beyond (e.g., the 'international wave' of kuduro charted by Boima

---

[15]Sheridan, 'Hard Ass', 50.

[16]DJ Marfox quoted in Fábio Nunes, 'Em Portugal Parece que Estão a Ver Até Quando Duram as Nossas Pilhas', *Notícias ao Minuto* (6 February 2018), https://www.noticiasaominuto.com/vozes-ao-minuto/940172/em-portugal-parece-que-estao-a-ver-ate-quando-duram-as-nossas-pilhas, accessed 2 August 2021. For discussions of Buraka Som Sistema which discuss the group's work in relation to aspects of Portuguese multiculturalism, *lusofonia* and claims of cultural appropriation, see Sheridan, 'Hard Ass' 50–2; Jorge de La Barre, 'Sampling Lisbon: Kuduro and the Lusophone Imagination', *Journal of Popular Music Studies* 31, no. 1 (2019): 109–30.

Tucker in 2012[17]) was happening independently of, and contemporaneously with, what the young DJs of Lisbon's ghettos were working on. As Sheridan puts it, the sound of the DJs do Guetto crew focussed on

> stripped back compositions that used vocal samples sparingly and focused on heavy, distorted beats with very prominent four to the floor kick drums and frequent hard tom rolls. Melodically, the work of this period features short riffs with frequent use of filters to modulate the lines rhythmically and tonally. These producers favoured sounds similar to early kuduro, using square and sawtooth waves in Fruity Loops' native synthesisers to create sounds similar to the Roland Juno-106 synthesiser.[18]

The stripped-back sounds of *DJDG* were, in their way, as syncretic as those being produced by Buraka Som Sistema, Coquenão and others, but with sights set more on techno than house music sounds, more DJ Znobia than DJ Amorim. That being said, the differences between the Znobia-influenced batida DJs and Buraka should not be drawn too starkly: the latter featured Znobia's distinctive harsh beats on the first two tracks of their debut album, one of which was their 2008 hit song 'Sound of Kuduro'.[19] The importance of techno was reaffirmed by both Znobia and Marfox during an online event called 'Kuduro-Áxis: Luanda, Lisbon & Beyond' in December

[17]Boima Tucker, 'Kuduro's International Wave', *Africa Is a Country* (24 December 2012), https://africasacountry.com/2012/12/kuduros-international-wave, accessed 2 August 2021.
[18]Sheridan, 'Hard Ass', 71.
[19]Znobia features on the first two tracks of Buraka Som Sistema, *Black Diamond* (Enchufada/Sony BMG Portugal 88697398072, 2008).

2020, which also featured the artist Nazar. Asked by the event's curator Pedro Gomes to sum up the 'matrix of kuduro' – its rhythms, cadences, breaks and set-ups – Znobia gave a simple reply, to which Marfox signalled approval: 'it's techno.'

DJDG engages with the uproutings that emerge from historically connected countries (connected through the historically, geopolitically and linguistically maintained Lusophone Black Atlantic) and a more recent digital remapping of vernacular culture that partly follows historical routes while also accelerating beyond them. So, as well as the clearly kuduro-inspired tracks, we find DJ Jesse's 'Tecnho' [*sic*], which channels minimal Detroit techno and the kind of 'bleep techno' associated with the British label Warp.[20] Besides DJ N.K.'s 'Do You Think You're Better' – a kuduro-inspired remix of the 1998 trance/Eurodance hit 'Better Off Alone' by Alice Deejay – we find examples of tarracho, the amelodic, beat-focussed form of tarraxinha (Pausas and Fofuxo's 'Tarracho Exxelentt'; Fofuxo's 'Tarracho do Guetto'; Nervoso's unexpectedly mellow 'Tarracho Nervoso'). In N.K.'s 'Keep Your Hands in the Air', there are elements of big beat with rapid percussion breaks rolling through the loops. Jesse's 'Tukiza', perhaps the most atypical track on *DJDG*, is a ten-minute tour through the softer sounds of kizomba, featuring vocals in English, Portuguese and French. This calling card or show reel for a possible future career as a DJ in the kind of clubs that wouldn't allow kuduro could hardly be further in sound and style from the track that follows it on the compilation, 'Estrago Terrivel', on which Jesse collaborates with Nervoso in a tour de force of brutal Lisbon-style kuduro minimalism.

[20]See Matt Anniss, *Join the Future: Bleep Techno and the Birth of British Bass Music* (London: Velocity Press, 2019).

These and other tracks showcase the DJs do Guetto crew as adept in many styles while also being able to develop their own playful, syncretic take on Luso-African music.

***

The extent to which kuduro can be considered a genre depends to a great extent on whether one wishes to include all the international variants that now exist globally. Certainly, battles about what constitutes kuduro and whether kuduro can or cannot be made outside of its country of origin are still regularly pitched in the comments sections of popular online platforms. This is even more the case with Lisbon batida, drawing as it does from so many sources. In an astute analysis of batida, Príncipe and 'the ghetto sound of Lisbon' in 2014, Ryan Keeling wrote,

> With the exception of [DJ] Lilocox, who said he blends house
> with kuduro, none of the artists I spoke to would describe
> their music. They discussed it in vague terms, avoided
> the question, or said it wasn't up to them to describe it.
> They weren't being difficult, though – the scene is merely
> unconcerned with genre. Instead, individuality is the currency.
> 'People will stop talking to someone just because a song he
> did is imitating too much someone else's style,' says Lilocox.[21]

Another way to understand batida as beat, then, is perhaps to think of moving to your own beat. As Marfox explained to Max Mertens, 'On the same street, you may have two or three different producers and each one has their own identity …

[21] Ryan Keeling, 'The Ghetto Sound of Lisbon', *Resident Advisor* (10 March 2014), https://www.residentadvisor.net/features/2021, accessed 2 August 2021.

They take pleasure from being different from one another.'[22] While it is quite easy to find musicians the world over making analogous points, it's worth noting that the Lisbon DJs are likely to be all too aware of the potential for their music to be collectivised and then dismissed as a result. Highlighting a scene helps the music and its makers to get attention but also hastens the moment when scene watchers are likely to move on to the next hot thing. This has often been an issue for EDM scenes, as noted by commentators on 'global ghettotech' such as Wayne Marshall and Jace Clayton, as well as by Dan Sicko in his study of techno. Sicko argues that the relatively slow development of Detroit techno was due to the city not being an epicentre of cultural production and this helped to prevent the genre 'being burned under critics' magnifying lenses', a tendency that, in Sicko's rather anti-media narrative, has been to the detriment of other EDM scenes.[23]

If it remains important to think of Lisbon batida in relation to historical roots in Angolan kuduro, tarraxinha and kizomba, it is also necessary to recognize that, for many listeners, such contextual labour may be unnecessary or undesirable. In such accounts the viral nature of the beat may be far more relevant. We might be reminded here, too, of the possibilities entailed by considering batida as sonic fiction rather than a historical moment: how does it allow bodies and minds to escape

[22]Max Mertens, 'DJ Marfox Levels Up', *Thump/Vice*, later incorporated into *Noisey/Vice* (5 April 2016), https://www.vice.com/en/article/78j4dz/dj-marfox-spotlight-interview-chapa-quente, accessed 19 April 2021.
[23]Dan Sicko, *Techno Rebels: The Renegades of Electronic Funk*, rev. edition (Detroit, MI: Wayne State University Press, 2010), 11. For Wayne Marshall's comments on global ghettotech, see Camilo Rocha, 'Global Ghettotech', *Norient* (13 June 2009), https://norient.com/stories/rochaglobalghettotech/, accessed 2 August 2021. See also Jace Clayton, *Uproot: Travels in Twenty-First-Century Music and Digital Culture* (New York: Farrar, Straus and Giroux, 2016).

particular historical configurations? What potentials does it unlock? A sonic delinking process might be just as imperative, one that seeks not to root the sounds of Lisbon's twenty-first-century ghettos in a partially evoked 'African' past, not even one that seeks to route them through the pathways of migration, but rather one that listens for what is being sounded in *this* place at *this* time, in *these* contexts and not those. During the 'Kuduro Axis' event, Marfox was keen to highlight what kuduro allowed Black Portuguese partygoers to be, especially when it came time to compete in the dance circle:

> People were always waiting for that moment at the party. We played kizomba, semba, puita, plena, but when kuduro came up, it seems people forgot the conditions in which they lived, the things they were dealing with at the moment, because we lived in slums. Life was happier. They lived. It seemed that for those thirty or forty minutes they were in paradise.[24]

Perhaps it is more accurate to say that this is a temporary forgetting of, rather than a full-blown escape from, historical conditions. Even so, Marfox's highlighting of what the kuduro beat allowed – the potentials it could unlock in the present moment – seems as significant as any attempt to trace precise historical lineages.

The issue of whether genres can even be asserted, let alone historicised and contextualised, is one that many commentators of twenty-first-century music culture are noting, whether in celebratory assertion, resignation, anxiety or a mixture of all of these and other feelings. In a Red Bull Hashtags documentary on the South African style gqom, producer OKZharp says of

[24]DJ Marfox speaking at the previously cited 'Kuduro Axis' event.

music genres, 'They don't really start, do they? They just sort of evolve out of other things. It's fun to think of it like a little petri dish and there's this … weird little toxin, this little virus, that just suddenly grows in this little petri dish of all the Durban nightclubs and all the Durban community centres and all the taxis.'[25] Writing about the Mexican EDM scene, known as *tribal guarachero*, Clayton notes the joy with which the music's young producers 'can playfully experiment with how local roots … tangle with random Internet click-trails'. In the words of one of his informants,

> The same person will be listening to psycho [Israeli
> psychedelic trance techno], Tiësto, Paul van Dyk, and Los
> Tucanes de Tijuana. That person will also be listening to pre-
> Hispanic drums and percussion from who knows where,
> saying 'I don't know where these drums come from. I fucking
> love Santería and I don't understand it, but I'll use it. Plus I'm
> gonna put on some berimbau, though I don't know if it's from
> Brazil or what'. *Tribal guarachero* is catharsis, sonic catharsis.[26]

This notion of sonic catharsis, it seems to me, is a crucial way of framing a response to the information overload that is part and parcel of online and digital culture, especially against those commentaries that would see the seeming randomness in the above list of artists, genres, styles and instruments as a cause for concern, an inability to place sounds in their 'appropriate' cultural contexts. The framework of sonic catharsis suggests that this deliberate mixing of styles is not only an inevitable

---

[25]OKZharp quoted in '#GQOM - HΔSHTAG$ Season II | Red Bull Music Academy', uploaded to YouTube by Red Bull Music Academy, 21 February 2017, https://www.youtube.com/watch?739=&v=ZUZIcIf_mQ0, accessed 2 August 2021.
[26]Toy Selectah, quoted in Clayton, *Uproot*, 209.

result of the ever-increasing velocity with which music travels, but it could actually be a way of dealing with the potentially anxiety-inducing proliferation of stimuli. While previous accounts of the emergence of 'world music' as a marketing category in the 1980s and 1990s have usefully categorised responses to its recorded artefacts into 'celebratory' or 'anxious' takes, it is necessary to question the extent to which such accounts have continued to posit musicians and the music industry more generally as agents responsible for the blurring of generic boundaries.[27] Instead, we should perhaps see music producers as also receivers of a bewildering amount of sonic and other information that can only be made sense of through adapting as much of it as possible to one's own articulations. In such a perspective, beat-making becomes a form of recontextualization as a defence mechanism in the face of an inability or an unwillingness to accurately demarcate generic difference. As Clayton observes,

> most of the social, geographical, and historical forces that shaped ideas of genre [in the twentieth century] cannot be transferred across the narrow bandwidth of cloud-stored musical conversations in the twenty-first century, when clicking a slightly different snare-drum pattern on a screen is sufficient to transform a song from one style to another … Genre enters the game as one more formal structure to be played with.[28]

***

Music escapes attempts to pin it down and, while this is categorically not a reason not to write about it, you do need to

[27]On celebratory and anxious responses to world music, see Steven Feld, 'A Sweet Lullaby for World Music', *Public Culture* 12, no. 1 (2000): 145–71.
[28]Clayton, *Uproot*, 214–15.

consider how much time you wish to devote to tracing origins and fencing off differences. There's little point in defining batida as music having a certain bpm (beats per minute) or a set of instrumental sounds because no sooner have you done so than some innovative DJ is going to produce a bunch of tracks that defy those principles. 'Family' might be a better way of thinking about this music, in that it brings in the idea of personal relationships between actors while also allowing us to think of a family of genres, tied by shared roots, routes and patterns of adoption. Of the tracks on *DJDG* and other Lisbon batida releases, it is possible to say, as Kodwo Eshun does of hip-hop, that batida is 'not a genre so much as an omnigenre, a conceptual approach towards sonic organisation rather than a particular sound in itself'.[29]

We can zoom into the details of the sounds and try to get closer to the music – I try this in the next chapter – then zoom out again to think about the broader family connections. A similar process can be followed when thinking of *DJDG* as an object. On one hand, it's a fairly ephemeral thing from which most people involved have moved on. On the other, it acted as both a marker of past achievements (at the time of its release and since) and a calling card for future projects. It not only helped to open doors but also to define the building and establish its architecture.

---

[29]Kodwo Eshun, *More Brilliant than the Sun: Adventures in Sonic Fiction* (London: Quartet Books, 1998), 014.

3   Close encounters

The first CD of the *DJs do Guetto* (*DJDG*) compilation begins with 'Intro Di Guetto' by DJs N.K. and Pausas. The track opens with a trilling bell: an alarm clock summoning listeners to wake up, perhaps, or a school bell announcing a changeover. A voice enters, pitch-shifted to sound childish, overexcited, doubled by an echo in the time-honoured fashion of dub and sound system culture. The project and the name of the DJ crew are announced, before further sonic effects emerge: the take-off sound of a plane or a spaceship that works as an initial build; a couple of bars of lonely, mid-register beats struggling to find purchase; a tape rewind effect; a more definite kick drum beat, providing a bass to ground the higher, ephemeral sounds; more rewind; then, to get things moving, an accelerating beat leading to a drop that announces the real start of the track. From here the kick drum dominates, mostly staying around 140 beats per minute (bpm), but also stuttering to a halt at regular intervals to highlight some rapid fills or squelching bass synth. As the regular rhythm renews after each turnaround, something is added: sampled vocals on the final beats of the bar, echoey mid-bar vocal and instrumental sounds and, from shortly after the two-and-a-half-minute mark, a staccato bleeping figure that makes the already infectious drum beat even more so. This is the bleeping sound of house and techno as they work their way into turn-of-the-millennium kuduro, leaving little doubt that this is music for the dance floor. Yet, as the track approaches four minutes, the now-expected breakdown leads to a new vocal sample that takes over the narrative logic, accompanied by a booming bass drum that seems to lift the listener momentarily from the real or imagined dance floor to another kind of ritual space, another temporary disorientation. The bleeping figure returns and the pitch-shifted voice of the intro, which has been reappearing throughout to announce the names of the DJs do Guetto crew, now takes over from the beat to give a spoken outro to this five-and-a-half-minute track ('spoken', here, as for most batida tracks, generally refers to digital audio workstation (DAW)-distorted speech, a human presence perhaps, but always a compromised humanity: distorted, distracted, ghostly, machinic, ironic). A final, much deeper, voice also announces the DJs, and 'Intro Di Guetto' is over. The crew has been introduced, the signature style and playful mood established.

DJ N.K.'s 'Estão a Dar Medo', *DJDG*'s second track, appears to start in a similarly playful mood, with pitch-shifted sonic ID tags ('N Kappa', 'DJs do Guetto') alternating between high/sped-up and low/slowed-down registers. But the mood shifts as sound effects enter: whiplashes, heavy breathing, thudding and gargling. This ominous set of sound effects morphs into a beat, the lashes alternating with a metallic twang like a loosened string instrument. It's scarily catchy, an appropriately strange combination for a track whose title translates as 'they are scaring' (literally, 'they are giving fear'). A dark synth tone enters and then starts oscillating with a higher discordant tone, the push-and-pull tension soon joined by a looped vocal sample screaming what sounds to an Anglophone ear like 'open the door'. Is this the source of the beating and the scaring? Violent forces battering down the door in search of victims? This new mixture brings an element of chaos as the beat drops away, leaving the track in a scary limbo before turning these new elements into another rhythmic motif to bring the momentum back and encourage movement; given the violent nature of the source materials, it's ambiguous whether this would be dancing or fleeing. At the midway point, everything stops once again except for some punching sounds, heavy breathing and a thud, like a body hitting the ground. Something begins to dawn about the possible origins of these sounds. The contact noises and punching air are sound effects like those from video games involving hand-to-hand fighting or kickboxing. Does this lessen the ominous timbre of the piece, realizing that we might only be fighting or dancing our way out of a video game? There's little time to dwell on this as the beat picks up again for the second half of the track: relentless, pummelling, exhausting, but also exhilarating.

Despite its title, DJ Jesse's 'Pimp My Ragga', the third track on *DJDG*, does not come across as an obviously ragga-inspired track, operating instead around two initial call-and-response synth notes that are joined for much of the track by a straight four-to-the-floor kick beat. When following the kick, the tempo here is slower than the previous two tracks, closer to the 100–110 bpm typical of tarraxinha and eschewing the offbeats often found in kuduro. Yet, the accumulation of synth tones falling between and around these beats gives the impression of a faster track; here again, the synth pads do as much as the drum sounds to create polyrhythms that seem to exceed the rigid four-beat grid and the track studiously avoids any move towards melody, an example of what the Príncipe liner notes describe as 'pure percussive and amelodical austerity'. But if this sound world is austere, it's also generative and developmental: new sounds bud and bloom across the track's five minutes. Perhaps more clearly than the preceding tracks, we can follow the emergence and growth of a textural rhythm. In this sense, the 'ragga' title can be understood as the building of a digital 'riddim', an aspect that became central to dancehall reggae in the 1990s; this, along with a few well-placed dubby echoes, shows the track's potential affinity to Caribbean precursors.

The sixth track on CD1 of *DJDG* is 'Sirene' by DJs Marfox and N.K. The main elements are a staccato vocal sample, a stabbing siren sound that provides a monotonous rhythm, occasionally rising in pitch to give the briefest sense of melody, and the now-familiar percussive matrix of kick and snare drums, sometimes joined by toms and hats. The track draws the listener in and teases, the elements sometimes locking together to give a sense of forward momentum, sometimes tangling and tensing in agonistic play. (Later in the compilation, similar elements will drive N.K.'s 'Alarme Noturno': droning annoyance mixed with pitch-shifting play mutates into an infectious beat.) There's a sense for the listener–dancer of expectation or desire for the elements to lock together again and to settle the brain and the body further into the groove. And for the DJ? Is this also enjoyable, this adding, withdrawing, intermeshing, fighting of components? Is there communication here or just abstract play? It's surreal at times. You find yourself wondering, why these samples? What is that voice saying?

There's playful surrealism of a different kind in DJ Fofuxo's 'Noddy di Ghetto', which bolts the Portuguese version of the theme from the children's TV programme *Noddy* to a brutal 140 bpm combination of kick drums and claps. The relentless beat and the looping theme work a hallucinatory logic, the kind of distorted merry-go-round effect beloved of psychological horror film soundtracks: out of (over)familiarity, madness looms (see also: murderous clowns). The track could be heard as childhood nostalgia from a DJ still in his teens but far enough from that kind of infantile material to stage ironic distance. Or it could be placed in the subgenre of 'toytown techno', those novelty tracks of the 1990s such as Mark Summers''Summers Magic' (which sampled *The Magic Roundabout*), Shaft's 'Roobarb and Custard', Smart E's 'Sesame's Treet', The Prodigy's 'Charly' (which drew on the British public information film *Charley Says*) and Urban Hype's 'A Trip to Trumpton'.[1]

***

The ingenious way in which sound effects associated with films, TV and video games become elements of intricate, catchy rhythms in 'Estão a Dar Medo' and, in a more overdetermined manner, 'Noddy di Ghetto', is typical of batida tracks, reliant as they often are on unusual sound sources that are both harmonic layers and constitutive of the beats themselves. It also exemplifies the cross-feeding (and cross-fading) polyrhythms common to the style, as well as the use of very heavy beats; in 'Estão a Dar Medo', the kick drum makes itself known as the literal beating of one body against another. Each of the tracks on *DJDG* establishes its own rhythmic world, while also being identifiably related to others in the collection and making references to the broader streams of popular culture.

Listening to *DJDG*, I get a strong sense of play, a lightness of touch that's also reminiscent of meme culture, YouTube

---

[1]Such tracks are often viewed by techno fans as aberrant: see Matt Anniss, *Join the Future: Bleep Techno and the Birth of British Bass Music* (London: Velocity Press, 2019), 223. For a more positive recollection, see Ben Cardew, '"We Were Just Clowning About": How Cartoon Rave Changed Pop', *The Guardian* (11 September 2017), https://www.theguardian.com/music/musicblog/2017/sep/11/cartoon-rave-feature, accessed 2 August 2021.

participation and (more recently) TikTok. There is a feeling, as in the phenomenon known as YouTube Poop Music Videos, of being caught in a helplessly glitching computer game. At around the same time that the early Lisbon batida producers were getting to grips with DAWs loaded onto the same machines that gave access to video games, similar practices were taking place in London that would feed into the sounds of grime. As Dan Hancox noted, many early grime instrumentals were made on PlayStation software and, even with the move to FruityLoops, some producers treated the DAW like a game, playing around with sounds and not taking them seriously until they became another sound of the future.[2] Indeed, as an informative 2020 article about FruityLoops in *DJ Mag* highlights, much of the programme's appeal lay in the gamification of a previously arcane set of skills and knowledge. The bedroom, as a space of gaming, music-making and homework, became a site where labour and leisure were linked in ways that might only be disentangled some years later; only retrospective accounts of grime, batida and other informal and DIY scenes really allow the protagonists to sift the lasting from the ephemeral.[3]

***

[2]Dan Hancox, *Inner City Pressure: The Story of Grime* (London: William Collins, 2018), 61, 72; see also Dan Hancox, 'A History of Grime, by the People Who Created It', *The Guardian* (6 December 2012), https://www.theguardian.com/music/2012/dec/06/a-history-of-grime, accessed 2 August 2021.

[3]On FruityLoops/FL Studio and the gamification of music-making, see Declan McGlynn, 'How FL Studio Changed Electronic Music Forever', *DJ Mag* (20 April 2020), https://djmag.com/longreads/how-fl-studio-changed-electronic-music-forever, accessed 2 August 2021. On the cultural significance of the bedroom for music producers, see Laurent Fintoni, *Bedroom Beats & B-Sides: Instrumental Hip Hop & Electronic Music at the Turn of the Century* (London: Velocity Press, 2020).

We can contextualize and we can decontextualize. Or rather, we can contextualize in different ways, alert to different perceptual possibilities as listeners recording close and not-so-close encounters with music. I have tried to capture some of that here by including some 'naive' observations about the sounds of *DJDG*, including guesswork and speculation where it felt appropriate to do so. The scare quotes in the previous sentence indicate that we are never completely naive about the music we hear. We are situated listeners with listening biographies and, while we may indeed be naive to the histories, social contexts and aesthetics of musical forms that are new or strange to us, we are also translators who negotiate that strangeness into some sort of relationship to what we're more familiar with. There are different dynamics and logics at work here, occasionally competing with, sometimes complementing each other. Working out the logic of a beat, hearing it grow from its source materials, sensing it starting to breathe, break down, stutter and mutate: these are some of the processes of making sense of the sonic worlds we encounter and dwell in, however briefly. We can work though this logic by dancing, thinking, writing, by writing through dancing, by getting up close for a while before stepping back.

Encounters with sonic strangeness and the quest for sense may lead us to new vocabularies, such as when Kodwo Eshun, writing in 1998 about music made three decades before by George Russell, introduces the term 'mixillogical' into his reflections. In doing so, he captures something of the way the various stylistic and sonic worlds that Russell brings into encounter in his music disorients the listener and enables a kind of liberation from wondering who or what is making which sound. The sounds themselves take over, as if they have a life and agency of their own, and the work becomes a 'mixillogical machine', producing 'the fleeting friction of timbral incongruities, incompatible sound blocks rubbing against each other'.[4] This seems to me an apt language pack to bring to translate the sounds of batida; the loops of *DJDG* and other releases by Príncipe-affiliated artists are saturated with such frictions and timbral incongruities. To take a description by Adam Bychawski, written in 2015 at the height of the international press response to the Príncipe sound, 'The most instantly recognizable element of batida is its writhing polyrhythmic percussion fashioned from off-kilter hand drums and whiplashing snares that can mutate several times in the course of a single track. Another distinguishing feature is its punch-drunk melodies: at once hypnotic and unsettling as a result of their harmonic mismatches'.[5]

Another arguably strange aspect of my initial attempt to grapple with the sounds of *DJDG* here is that, even as I have started to gather some family resemblances, I have treated them as isolated tracks. This reflects the way that I have listened (or relistened) to the tracks when writing this book. In most cases, I have visited the folders on my laptop where I store the two 'CDs' that comprise *DJDG*, each one of which consists of a list of MP3s which I then play individually with one of the media players I have installed. Sometimes I listen though my computer's built-in speakers; sometimes I wear headphones; sometimes I connect the machine to a Bluetooth speaker for a different kind of amplification again. None of these ways of

[4]Kodwo Eshun, *More Brilliant than the Sun: Adventures in Sonic Fiction* (London: Quartet Books, 1998), 003.
[5]Adam Bychawski, 'Príncipe Discos: The New Club Sensation from the Portuguese Projects', *The Guardian* (27 October 2015), https://www. theguardian.com/music/2015/oct/27/principe-discos-batida-marfox-firmeza, accessed 2 August 2021.

listening approximates the experience of hearing the tracks in a nightclub or even a decent loudspeaker as might be installed for a house or street party in one of the neighbourhoods where this music was created and first performed. That's fine, of course, because dance music tracks can be listened to in many different spaces. As the liner notes accompanying the reissued *DJDG* put it, the music has been 'millimetrically controlled in order to maximize the brutality of rhythm in any set of speakers'. I only mention how I have been accessing the music as a reminder of the slight oddness of thinking of *DJDG* as an 'album'. I haven't burned the MP3s to CDs as their division into two discs' worth of material afforded, a practice that was more viable when the music was originally released in 2006 than in an era in which CD drives are disappearing from home computers.

At the time of writing, *DJDG* has not been published on the currently popular platforms Spotify or Bandcamp, even though the Príncipe label uses these for their other releases. Outside of the downloadable folders of MP3s, the nearest configuration of the compilation as an album can be found on Príncipe's SoundCloud pages, where each 'CD' is presented as a playlist. The affordances of SoundCloud as a platform mean that it is just as likely the tracks will be encountered outside of these playlists, as they take their place in other users' playlists or are algorithmically recommended as 'related' tracks to others on the platform. Listening – and, we should add, viewing – the tracks on SoundCloud also allow the possibility to add comments at particular points in the track and to see the comments that other listeners have left. To experience Marfox and N.K.'s 'Sirene' here is to listen in conversation, as it were, with others, to note one user's 'OHHHHH' at 0:26 and another's 'Toma!' at 1:17. Does listening alone become a little less lonely at such points?

4   Quinta do Mocho

Walk through the high-rise projects of Portela, Prior Velho or Sacavém, on the northern outskirts of Lisbon, and you'll find yourself in a city very different to the one that has been developing ever faster as a tourist destination in recent years. While the tourist industry sells the charm of downtown Lisbon via an emphasis on the famous yellow trams, the cobbled streets, old tiled buildings, maritime memories, fado houses and sardine stalls, the modernist grids at the outskirts remain largely unpromoted and relatively unvisited. Not surprisingly for areas developed to accommodate rapid urban migration from rural Portugal and from the country's former overseas colonies, these suburbs have a more functional feel than the patinated historical centre. At the same time, these are also some of the first areas of Lisbon that many tourists encounter, albeit fleetingly, given their proximity to the city's airport. Connections from the airport to the downtown areas of Lisbon are well developed (especially since the extension of the city's metro network), quickly whisking away the arrivals from this part of the city. For those living, working or exploring the areas surrounding the airport, negotiating the tangle of motorways, bridges, flyovers, factories and industrial parks can prove trickier and more time consuming. Bus routes exist to carry people through this thicket of concrete but they can be slow and unreliable in the traffic-choked streets and they do little to dispel the sense that these parts of the city are effectively cut off from the infrastructure that supports central and southern Lisbon.

The neighbourhood that is at the heart of this story – the one that is still standing to bear witness to the creativity of the DJs do Guetto – is Quinta do Mocho, a triangular formation of modern apartment blocks located near the end of one of the airport's runways and bounded by Avenida das Communidades, Avenida Amilcar Cabral and Rua Quinta de São João das Areias. At one vertex sits the Casa de Cultura de Sacavém and beyond this is another very different group of apartment blocks known as Terraços da Ponte, built on the site of the old Quinta do Mocho. That earlier settlement, established in the 1970s to house the rising number of immigrants from the former Portuguese colonies in Africa (particularly Angola, Cabo Verde, Guinea-Bissau and São Tomé and Príncipe), was never completed and the inhabitants of the old Quinta do Mocho ended up living in half-built properties or ramshackle buildings of their own construction. In the 1990s, these residents were given the option to relocate to the newly built projects on the neighbouring land and this became the new Quinta do Mocho. As is often the case with social housing, the blocks were built hastily from cheap materials and many started showing signs of dilapidation over the next two decades. In contrast, the newer apartments of Terraços da Ponte are built according to higher specifications and are marketed as desirable residences for well-to-do residents who wish to have quick access to the airport and, in some cases, views of the Tejo river and the impressive Vasco da Gama Bridge. While the residents of Quinta do Mocho live, for the most part, close to the poverty line and with high unemployment rates (estimated between 70 and 80 per cent), the sleek apartments of Terraços da Ponte are designed for those willing and able to spend, on average, 400,000 euros for a home (and closer to a million for a penthouse). The marketing websites for these complexes invariably show white couples and families projected into the idealized residential area, another contrast to the neighbouring social housing project in which 90 per cent of the population is Black.

'Welcome to the last ghetto', says Kally Meru, a tourist guide who lives and works in Quinta do Mocho. He delivers the line with the confidence of a well-practised orator; this is his way of initiating the street tour that he leads. The line also acts as a sonic bridge that reaches from 'outside' the neighbourhood (the pavement next to the Sacavém Cultural Centre, where the tours begin) to the 'inside', the triangle of streets and buildings standing on the other side of the roundabout. I had contacted Kally after seeing an advert on Facebook for the tours that he and some other residents offered to those wishing to visit the 'bairro de arte pública' (public art neighbourhood). While I had come to know a little about Quinta do Mocho through my encounter with the music of DJ Marfox and through reading articles about batida, the neighbourhood was in fact being promoted to tourists through another feature: the more than one hundred massive artworks adorning the outsides of its buildings. I had not really thought of myself as a tourist in Lisbon for a while, having lived in the city for three years in the early 2000s and having also been a regular visitor since moving back to the UK; subsequently, I rarely looked out for tourist activities such as these guided tours. However, by the time of my first visit to Quinta do Mocho in September 2019, I had spent enough time in the newly touristified Lisbon to realize that I was, once again, a stranger to the city (or, as many critical

Figure 4.1 *Mural by António Alves depicting Amílcar Cabral, Quinta do Mocho, 2014. Photograph by Richard Elliott.*

voices have put it in recent years, perhaps the city has become a stranger to those who knew it before its post-recession tourist boom).[1] If that were true even in the once-familiar

[1] For research which examines the recent gentrification of Lisbon with reference to music and sound, see Iñigo Sánchez Fuarros, '"Ai, Mouraria!": Music, Tourism, and Urban Renewal in a Historic Lisbon Neighbourhood', *MUSICultures* 43, no. 2 (2016): 66–88; Lila Ellen Gray, 'Listening Low-Cost: Ethnography, the City, and

central and downtown areas, it was even more so in the areas I had neglected to visit before. So I placed myself as a tourist in the hands of Kally as he introduced me to the murals that have individualized each, otherwise identical, block in Quinta do Mocho (see Figure 4.1). At the same time, I let him know that my initial interest in the area had been its music rather than its visual art, and Kally gladly provided a tour of the area's sounds as well as its sights, pointing out where certain rappers, dancers and DJs lived and showing the places where street parties most frequently occurred.[2]

On a later visit to the neighbourhood, I asked Kally about his opening line referring to 'the last ghetto', and he elaborated: 'This was the last ghetto to become a good place. My neighbourhood and Quinta da Fonte were considered ghettos. They were closed neighbourhoods, no one answering, no one going out. Quinta da Fonte started to get the art before Quinta do Mocho but they didn't change to a good thing.' This reference to 'getting the art' relates to the public art projects that have been used in an attempt to improve the status of these neighbourhoods, for both residents and outsiders.

the Tourist Ear', in *The Routledge Companion to the Study of Local Musicking*, ed. Suzel A. Reily and Katherine Brucher(New York: Routledge, 2018), 417–28. For work that connects the branding of Lisbon with Luso-African music, see Jorge de La Barre, 'Sampling Lisbon: Kuduro and the Lusophone Imagination', *Journal of Popular Music Studies* 31, no. 1 (2019): 109–30.

[2]All speech attributed to Kally Meru, unless otherwise noted, comes from two of the three conversations I had with him in Lisbon. The first was during a tour of Quinta do Mocho on 19 September 2019, which was not recorded. The second was a recorded interview that took place at the Casa de Cultura de Sacavém on 9 January 2020. Kally (whose birth name is José Carlos de Andrade Ribeiro) also helped with translation during my meeting with DJ Marfox in Quinta do Mocho on 19 September 2019. Kally's words can also be found in features on Quinta do Mocho in *The Independent* and *Atlas Lisboa* (cited in note 3).

The example that Kally refers to is a street art festival called 'O Bairro i o Mundo' (The neighbourhood and the world), which was an initiative of Loures Municipal Council and Teatro IBISCO (an acronym for Inter-Bairros para a Inclusão Social e Cultura do Optimismo). The project was launched in 2013 in the neighbourhood of Quinta da Fonte but failed to gain momentum; according to Kally, this was due to a lack of awareness in that neighbourhood of the potential for change that such public projects could create. The murals created during that first festival were later erased. When the festival was held the following year in Quinta do Mocho, it was far more successful, gaining national television coverage and initiating a desire among a group of local organizers (including Kally) to build on the potential offered by such a public-facing project. As more and more international artists arrived to paint their visions on the invitingly blank sides of its buildings, Quinta do Mocho became a spectacular open-air art gallery, providing an opportunity for the local guides to promote their neighbourhood to the outside world. This in turn led to a reappraisal of the area, as Kally relates:

> The first thing we sensed was our self-esteem. We noticed that we were being noticed by people not because of the bad things. Many people thought that this was a ghetto of drugs and many worse things but when they enter it's the opposite: the population say good day, give a smile, no one is robbed. So, what's happening here? We started to show what is happening here, this transformation – one part is us, but the other part is those who came to visit us. Until 2014 it was possible for you to enter the neighbourhood and someone would rob you. For real. But with the tours and people coming to the neighbourhood the population didn't sense

you were looking at us in a different way, they felt that you were looking at us in the normal way, treating us as normal. So they stopped by themselves. There was no union, no neighbourhood meeting, nothing. But things became good by themselves. Like I always say, this is not a physical project, this is a sensorial project. Many things that have changed are not physical. And this was the success.

The success of this sensorial project has been recognized by features in the Portuguese and international press, as well as in some academic research.[3] A recurring feature of these reports is the frequency with which Quinta do Mocho, like other neighbourhoods developed to house immigrant families and their descendants, has been associated in the media predominantly with stories of crime and gang violence. Rather than exploring the sociocultural conditions in which these communities have been forced to live and the lack of infrastructural support for the peripheral neighbourhoods, the populist line has historically been to write these areas off as no-go zones. The extent to which the public art projects have been seen to change this perception varies from writer to writer; my own experience of talking to people who know Lisbon but have never visited Quinta do Mocho is that there is still a long way to go to overcome the common image of such

[3] Jessica Bateman, 'Quinta Do Mocho: How This Crime-Plagued Lisbon Estate Became the City's Coolest Open Air Gallery', *The Independent*, 9 August 2018, https://www.independent.co.uk/travel/europe/quinta-do-mocho-lisbon-estate-street-art-festival-gallery-portugal-immigration-crime-a8484161.html, accessed 2 August 2021; Eden Flaherty, 'A Decade of Change Part Two: Quinta Do Mocho', *Atlas Lisboa* (blog), 15 May 2018, https://www.atlaslisboa.com/quinta-do-mocho/, accessed 2 August 2021; Henrique Chaves, 'Clickbaits, Violência e Arte Pública Na Quinta Do Mocho, Loures', *Trabalhos de Antropologia e Etnologia* 57 (2017): 197–210.

neighbourhoods. At the same time, the growing popularity of the tours offered by Kally and his fellow residents shows that minds can be reached, and changed.

We find a similar narrative of how the perception of Quinta do Mocho has changed, for both outsiders and residents, in the numerous features that have appeared in recent years about the EDM (electronic dance music) producers who live or work there. The first of these to come to widespread attention in Portugal and abroad was DJ Marfox, who moved to the neighbourhood in 2013, after the nearby neighbourhood in which he'd grown up (Quinta da Vitória) was demolished. Marfox is keen to promote Quinta do Mocho and often insists on holding meetings there when journalists, film-makers or researchers wish to interview him. He has become adept at flagging the neighbourhood in interviews and is aware of the importance of having the space be an immediate point of reference for his interlocutors. A typical example can be found in an interview Marfox gave to the journalist Vítor Belanciano in 2013, subsequently included in the latter's 2020 book on Afro-Portuguese music:

> Those from outside the neighbourhoods think that we are all criminals here and those from here think that all outsiders are hostile … It's important to show people from here that there's also another side of Lisbon in which not everyone has preconceptions. Local people don't leave the neighbourhood much, they don't go into Lisbon often. So it's necessary to get people who make incredible music out of here to serve as examples to the youngest. The kids who are watching us from the windows at the moment are going to understand that a journalist was here not because of crime, as happens sometimes. It was because of art. And that's important, because tomorrow they will see a drug trafficker arrested and

they will also see [local DJ] Firmeza go to the Alive festival to perform and they will want to be like Firmeza.[4]

Such narratives often form the basis of Portuguese hip-hop lyrics, as they do in other global hip-hop cultures. And while the music that Marfox and his fellow batida DJs produce is mostly without lyrics, the emphasis they place on location in interviews is as evocative a reminder as any hip-hop or grime lyric of the importance of witnessing locality and community. This sense of not only witnessing, but also of being witnessed – being seen and heard – came through strongly in my own encounter with Marfox on one of my visits to Quinta do Mocho. When arranging an interview, it was clear that the locations we chose were as important as what was being said: the bedroom-cum-studio in the flat Marfox shares with his mother and one of his brothers, in a block in which his sister also has an apartment; the walk from there to one of the local cafes, passing through the painted apartment blocks where many other DJs involved in the batida scene live; and the cafe itself, one of a handful in the area specializing in Luso-African food. To be invited there and shown hospitality is to be called as a witness to the presence of this neighbourhood, its people and its everyday life. In such encounters, there is an insistence on presence, and it is the Black presence in Lisbon and the culture produced by that presence that informs accounts such as Belanciano's.

We can find this insistence, too, in the work of Derek Pardue, whose research on Cape Verdean Kriolu (Creole) music scenes in Lisbon draws on notions of witnessing and presence. In his essay 'Lisbon Is Black: An Argument of Presence', Pardue writes

[4]DJ Marfox, quoted in Vítor Belanciano, *Não Dá Para Ficar Parado: Música Afro-Portuguesa: Celebração, Conflito e Esperança* (Porto, Portugal: Edições Afrontamento, 2020), 106. My translation from Portuguese.

If presence is a fundamental, albeit contested, dimension of urbanism, then art and music are important expressive forms through which sociocultural groups incite presence. Such forms facilitate the connections between identification and materiality and thus constitute nominal places like cities … Lisbon is a black city, because not only are there significant black activities *in* the city but also such expressions provoke us to think about blackness and Africanity *as* the city.[5]

Pardue's use of the term 'black Portuguese' in this essay and other works serve as a reminder that Portugueseness is an essential aspect of identity for many, something which the term 'Luso-African' (which Pardue also uses, and which I have used frequently in this book) does not convey. Batida artists such as Marfox and Nídia have frequently mentioned in interviews that they wish to be seen and heard as Portuguese musicians even as they celebrate their African heritage; they have expressed frustration, especially when travelling abroad, at the tendency for people they meet to ignore their identity as Portuguese citizens in favour of evoking an 'Africanity' only rooted in the continent of Africa. Accounts such as Belanciano's and Pardue's offer reminders of Lisbon's own Africanity and of the ways in which – to adapt the subtitle of Caspar Melville's account of Black music in London – sounds can 'remap the city'.[6]

It was on visits to Quinta do Mocho around 2004 that Marfox, then in his mid-teens, met DJ Nervoso, whose local reputation as a producer of new sounds was well established

---

[5]Derek Pardue, 'Lisbon Is Black: An Argument of Presence', in *The Routledge Handbook of Anthropology and the City*, ed. Setha Low (London: Routledge, 2019), 476–7 (emphases in original).
[6]Caspar Melville, *It's a London Thing: How Rare Groove, Acid House and Jungle Remapped the City* (Manchester, UK: Manchester University Press, 2020).

by then. Nervoso would become an important mentor to – as well as a member of – the DJs do Guetto crew. Given his role and the importance of highlighting local presence, it is fitting that this foundational DJ should be recognized in signature Quinta do Mocho style by having his portrait covering the wall of an apartment block on Rua Pêro Escobar, one of the streets traversing the neighbourhood. The massive likeness, rendered into the side of the building by the renowned Portuguese artist Vhils, depicts Nervoso looking to the side and staring over the boundary of Quinta do Mocho to the land beyond (see Figure 4.2), a dominating presence in the neighbourhood but also a figure whose work has travelled much further.

Quinta do Mocho has become an important feature in many of the stories published on the Lisbon batida scene, some of which I cover later in this book. As a visual presence, it features in photos accompanying magazine features and has a starring role in videos that have been made about local DJs, dancers and street artists. One video, made by the Portuguese hip-hop and electronic music magazine *Rimas e Batidas*, opens with DJ Marfox pointing out Nervoso's block, an assertive linking of place to sonic history as well as a reminder that the musicians who made the scene-defining *DJs do Guetto* compilation are still very much connected to the spaces in which the music was conceived and worked on. As well as functioning as an assertion of its own presence, the neighbourhood also stands in for places which have been destroyed, such as the old Quinta do Mocho and Marfox's childhood home of Quinta da Vitória.

To pick up the Postsoul/sonic fiction narrative applied by Kodwo Eshun to techno, it is possible and sometimes tempting to remove the music from the streets of neighbourhoods like Quinta do Mocho, to attend to the sounds without having to place them. As Eshun writes in a section of his book titled

Figure 4.2 *Mural by Vhils (Alexandre Farto) depicting DJ Nervoso, Quinta do Mocho, 2015. Photograph by Richard Elliott.*

'Electronic Secession', 'By opting out of [hip-hop's] logic of representation, Techno disappears itself from the street, the ghetto and the hood. Drexciya doesn't represent Detroit the way Mobb Deep insist they represent Staten Island'.[7] But to take

[7]Kodwo Eshun, *More Brilliant than the Sun: Adventures in Sonic Fiction* (London: Quartet Books, 1998), 102.

this approach is also to fight something of a losing battle. It's not just journalists and academics who want to connect batida to the streets of Lisbon's housing projects; musicians also wish to. Can we have it both ways? Can we hear these sounds as somehow anchored to these streets and also escaping them, finding new homes on dance floors, record players, computers and phones? Dan Hancox has given us a sense of how this might work in his account of UK grime, where he detects 'an alien futurism to a lot of the computer-generated aesthetics' and reflects on 'the sheer alien newness of the sonics' even as he recognizes the sounds of everyday 'inner city pressure' marking the music as reflective of a specific time and place.[8] So too in the music that emanates from Quinta do Mocho, a set of sounds at once heavy with the history of place, eager to insist on the presence of this community and its creativity ('Quinta dos Talentos', as Marfox likes to say) even as it broadcasts alien comms to whoever wishes to tune in.

[8]Dan Hancox, *Inner City Pressure: The Story of Grime* (London: William Collins, 2018), 61–70.

5 Looped encounters

Earlier I attempted a close but semi-naive approach to five of the tracks on *DJs do Guetto* (*DJDG*), a way of meeting them as if I hadn't heard them before, as if I didn't possess the right language to translate them properly into narrative. But narrative was still present: my accounts are saturated with the logic of 'and then this happens', saturated too with metaphors that assume a shared experience and context even as, in other ways, I decontextualize the music from any 'natural' space it might be expected to occupy. I also showed a certain fidelity to the ways that others have emphasized its newness, strangeness and sense of futurity, even as any attempts to write about such things emanate from a position where the writer is forced to refer to familiar contexts. As we will hear later, this contextual challenge is there when DJ Marfox hears in the sounds of DJ Nervoso something that he has never heard before, or when journalists with expertise in writing about electronic dance music (EDM) profess a bewilderment at hearing and trying to explain batida.

It seems that we struggle to escape the tendency towards teleology that narrative demands of us: the sense of beginnings, middles, endings, departure points and destinations. Even so, there are moments when we either feel the strangeness of music newly experienced or, as a supplementary process, when we wish to *enstrange* music as a strategy for putting it in focus (whether for analysis, wonder or some other reason). 'Enstrangement', with its deliberately attention-seeking first 'n', is a word coined by translators of the Russian formalist theorist Viktor Shklovsky, whose concept of *ostranenie* related to an artistic device that 'consists in not calling a thing or event by its name but describing it as if seen for the first time'.[1] It's a device which I believe we can usefully put alongside Johannes Ismaiel-Wendt's sonic delinking and Kodwo Eshun's sonic fiction as a way of staying within sight and sound of the strangeness that many commentators have found in batida. Furthermore, as an authorial device used by DJ producers, it can refer not only to ways in which the seemingly familiar matrices of FruityLoops (FL Studio) and other digital audio workstations (DAWs) are used to make the familiar seem unfamiliar, but also to the titling of tracks using creole and slang terms. These may not be unfamiliar to scene insiders (who, whether they have grown up with creolized terms or not, will have become used to them through the codes that every scene establishes), but we must remember that *DJDG* is one of the vehicles by which these sounds, and the terms attached to them, started to move into wider circles. In such circles, the dominant Portuguese language becomes enstranged by the terminology used to describe beats. Something analogous happens early in Jeffrey Boakye's book about UK grime, when he describes

[1]Viktor Shklovsky, 'Art as Device', in *Viktor Shklovsky: A Reader*, ed. Alexandra Berlina (New York: Bloomsbury Academic, 2017). Berlina describes the concept in detail in her translator's introduction to this work. For an application of the concept to the DJ-relevant record turntable, see Charles Mudede, 'The Turntable', *CTheory* (24 April 2003), https://journals.uvic.ca/index.php/ctheory/article/view/14561, accessed 20 February 2020.

the ubiquitous 'Amen Break' and its creator Gregory Coleman, initially unnamed in Boakye's account:

> During his life the man did many things. including drumming in various bands. In the year 1969 he drummed on a song with a band called The Winstons. The man spent one hundred and fifty-three seconds drumming throughout this song. For six of these seconds, he was drumming unaccompanied by any other instruments. This is known as a drum break.[2]

By writing about the 'Amen Break' in this manner, Boakye enstranges a sonic texture that, as he goes on to point out, every reader of his book probably knows, even if they don't know that they know it.

We may not be able to escape narrative logics, but we can be aware of how emphasis on repetition and looping can challenge certain narrative tendencies, especially end-driven ones. This is a process explored by Susan McClary in a 1999 lecture entitled 'Rap, Minimalism, and Structures of Time in Late-Twentieth Century Culture', where she uses the deliberately enstranging device of the time traveller (in her case, a visitor from the late nineteenth to the late twentieth century) to highlight a move from melodic and harmonic narrative (she is thinking mainly of musical language as developed and understood in the West) to a focus on repetitive elements. McClary asks her audience to consider the importance of repetition in a range of late twentieth-century musics, encompassing art music (minimalism) and pop music

---

[2]Jeffrey Boakye, *Hold Tight: Black Masculinity, Millennials and the Meaning of Grime* (London: Influx Press, 2017), 17.

(rock, hip-hop, EDM). To do this seems counterintuitive in some ways, as McClary acknowledges:

> Left to our own devices, we probably would not ask these questions of ourselves: to those of us invested in any of the genres to which I refer, distinctions count for far more than resemblance. Only listeners not familiar with Tupac Shakur or Philip Glass would privilege the repetitive procedures within which each operates: indeed, a knowledgeable fan or connoisseur might scoff at the idea of dwelling on that most elementary level of activity … To a large extent, the structures of repetition used by these artists have ceased to register as significant: they constitute merely the neutral ground of basic assumptions up against which the actual music occurs.[3]

As McClary notes, there is an extensive history of attending to repetition in popular music, especially in African American genres. There is also, as people like myself working in the academic discipline of popular music studies know all too well, the felt need to respond to dated but still prevalent critiques of the 'standardization' of popular music.[4] Rather than engaging with that literature here, I want to dwell briefly on the importance of the loop and what we might think of as the

---

[3]Susan McClary, 'Rap, Minimalism, and Structures of Time in Late Twentieth-Century Culture', in *Audio Culture: Readings in Modern Music*, ed. Christoph Cox and Daniel Warner, revised edition (New York: Bloomsbury Academic, 2017), 456.

[4]The obvious figure is Theodor Adorno. For a clear account of Adorno's views on popular music, as well as an elegant refutation of them that draws on doo-wop music and emphasizes the importance of timbre and other factors over melodic and harmonic language, see Bernard Gendron, 'Theodor Adorno Meets the Cadillacs', in *Studies in Entertainment: Critical Approaches to Mass Culture*, ed. Tania Modleski (Bloomington: Indiana University Press, 1986), 18–36.

looped encounter. Here. I'm thinking not only of how batida employs loops in a tradition that could be traced back through many styles of music, but also how it actively promotes the use of loop-based software, most notably FruityLoops/FL Studio. The name of this programme features in the titles of batida tracks, and the programme is often mentioned by producers in interviews. In the discourse around batida, there is a celebration of the loop and what can be done with it. Batida is hardly alone in this, as similar production methods are used by DIY producers around the world. The move towards minimal loop-based material is, in many ways, typical of much contemporary EDM, the evolution of which, as Philip Sherburne relates, 'has entailed parallel processes of reduction and extension: stripping away extraneous ornament, paring down to only the most salient rhythmic and tonal components, and extending those few elements as far as they can be stretched'.[5] Like McClary, Sherburne notes how EDM shares many of the distinguishing features of minimalism as it was applied to art music; like her, he also notes how the embeddedness of such features makes them seem unremarkable: 'They are simply part of the background, as invisible as water to fish.'[6]

Loops are what allow producers to make the music they wish to make for dancers who wish to work though dialectics of familiarity and unfamiliarity. This may lead to what Sherburne describes as the 'heavily repetitive, almost trance-inducing churn' of jungle and drum 'n' bass' or to a process that seems to demand a non-trance–like awareness and even

[5]Philip Sherburne, 'Draw a Straight Line and Follow It: Minimalism in Contemporary Electronic Dance Music', in *Audio Culture: Readings in Modern Music*, ed. Christoph Cox and Daniel Warner, revised edition (New York: Bloomsbury Academic, 2017), 465.
[6]Ibid., 466.

a kind of hypertension created by 'waiting for a change that never comes'.[7] In the latter case – quite common in batida – the loop provides inherent drama and a narrative that exists in tension with the teleological narratives connected to melodic or harmonic development. One of the features associated with minimalism is static harmony, and this sense of stasis can lead to both a trance-like locking into the groove or a stop–start dynamic that puts the human into hyperactive community with the machine. Listening and dancing become looped endeavours. Looped encounters are also experiences of different levels of repetition: the beat, the melodic loop, the track itself when one revisits it, to match one's responses to the demands of a beat which may or may not change. The more material is removed from the loop, the more intense the situation may become, as in a description of DJ Nervoso's live DJing by Ryan Keeling as 'high-intensity loops, which often felt like a two-beat phrase on repeat'.[8] In such a process – also evident in Nervoso's recorded music – the loop is reduced to such an extent that what appears to be almost static paradoxically creates ecstatic responses. Nervoso's ability to drive dancers to ecstatic heights is much commented on in the batida community.

Though songs and instrumental pieces have long been multitracked, there is something about minimal EDM that seems to take the listener right into the tracks (or channels) of the track, especially with heavily loop-based material like batida. Instead of the illusion of wholeness that attends other multitracked songs (or tracks) as the layers blend and

[7]Ibid., 465, 467.
[8]Ryan Keeling, 'The Ghetto Sound of Lisbon', *Resident Advisor* (10 March 2014), https://www.residentadvisor.net/features/2021, accessed 2 August 2021.

disappear, here there remains an overt awareness of the various elements. Listening to some of these recordings is like playing one of those stereo demonstration records from the 1960s: the focus is on sound per se, its location, what it does to perception. Batida tracks are as much about what happens to your head as to the rest of your body. There is an invitation to enter the loop, which exists as both an ever-present insistence and also as a kind of void, the kind that opens up in trance-based music to allow the trancing body–mind to reach the desired level of engagement. Looping, while seeming like perpetual motion, can also become a kind of stasis, while occasional glitches serve as reminders of the imperfections of loops, of how repetition messes with the mind to create new patterns.

Glitch offers interference and friction. Perhaps it is glitch's imperfections that encourage human interaction with the machine, a recognition that the machine is as imperfect as the human. Entering the glitching machine, the mind travels and the body twitches. Angolan kuduro, to which so much Lisbon batida is related, is a glitch form, a dance of breaking or broken bodies that also says something of the broken social bond: it is a dance for individuals, even when it is a group of synced dance crews.[9] It offers the opportunity for the individual to become inhuman, to become one with the machine.

Jace Clayton connects the ubiquity of loop-based music-making to the seemingly random ways in which producers get their music out into the world, through a variety of online platforms. SoundCloud and similar platforms challenge

---

[9]In addition to the kuduro articles cited in Chapter 2, see Ananya Jahanara Kabir, 'Oceans, Cities, Islands: Sites and Routes of Afro-Diasporic Rhythm Cultures', *Atlantic Studies* 11, no. 1 (2014): 106–24.

longstanding release schedules for artists. For Clayton, writing about the Mexican DJ Javier Estrada, the connection between loop-based DAWs and release schedules reflects a broader way of being in the world:

> The orderly timelines of release schedules and clearly defined back catalogs help make artists legible to us. This is particularly true for music journalism, which still treats the artist album as the primary unit of contemplation and coverage. The superabundance of Estrada's FruityLoops compositions helped me to understand that the program's acolytes promote cyclical time as a worldview: engaging the world not as a start-to-finish symphony but as a proliferation of interlocking, interchangeable loops.[10]

However, Clayton is also critical of FruityLoops, noting its rigidity of form and observing that 'the ability to work with decent, commercial-quality sounds from the get-go can make musicians less inclined to creatively mess it up … The software gives access, but it also exacerbates sameness.'[11] He goes on to describe the challenges faced when trying to reflect more complex, polyrhythmic musical styles within the digital realm and highlights some problematic issues that arise from being able to sample so many sounds from around the world:

> Say you're making a song and want to incorporate an Indian tabla drum. Either you can look for someone who plays the instrument, explain the project, and negotiate a price (if

---

[10] Jace Clayton, *Uproot: Travels in Twenty-First-Century Music and Digital Culture*, 1st edition (New York: Farrar, Straus and Giroux, 2016), 215.
[11] Ibid., 179–80.

any – at least you have the talk). Or you can nick tabla sounds from the Web. The first route is long, but it involves two-way communication and an opportunity to learn. The second approach is easy: there's no accountability to slow things down, nothing to coax you outside your comfort zone. More and more I saw sampling used to maintain cultural distance. Naive at best, creepily segregationist at worst.[12]

The humanism that runs through Clayton's *Uproot* is evident here and accords with what other critical thinkers on 'World Music 2.0' have noted: a tendency in global beat cultures to erase the subtle differences that exist in diverse human cultures. To balance such narratives, it is worth recalling the post-humanist accounts of electronic music, such as Eshun's sonic fiction approach. For Eshun, it is more interesting to attend to what we might think of as the agency of machines, where the use of new technology leads to accidental discoveries. Early in *More Brilliant than the Sun*, Eshun introduces the idea of 'AutoCatalysis', described as 'when sound emerges by itself, when the machine generates a new sound autonomously'. Of the musics he is describing, he claims: 'All these soundworlds begin as accidents discovered by machines.'[13] Where Clayton worries about conformity – the overly rigid grids of DAWs, the too-ready-at-hand sample libraries – Eshun sees liberation via the machine.

While it is certainly useful to be reminded of the way musical decisions map onto social relations and ways of being in the world, I am not so sure this should be done by singling out

[12]Ibid., 184–5.
[13]Kodwo Eshun, *More Brilliant than the Sun: Adventures in Sonic Fiction* (London: Quartet Books, 1998), 019.

a tool like FruityLoops. It is, after all, just another instrument, albeit perhaps something of a meta-instrument given the sounds it gives access to. Any instrument has its affordances and its restrictions; it enables and inevitably homogenizes or stylizes. Musical instruments, like musical styles and genres, show a tendency to evolve through templates that are imitable and, to an extent, coercive, even as they offer opportunities to work against the grain. We might feel the anxious possibility of that situation evoked by Jorge Luis Borges, and used by Jean Baudrillard to open his book *Simulacra and Simulation*, wherein the map of the territory becomes more detailed than the territory itself, eventually becoming the reality in which people dwell.[14] But as long as there is the possibility of a technological glitch and as long as we feel that technology, in its (perhaps deluded) quest for improvement ('perfecting sound forever'), is a process rather than an end point, there can still be hope for the kind of creative messing up that Clayton elsewhere praises.

***

One way to think of *DJDG* is as a series of looped encounters. In doing so, we may need to listen beyond the obvious because it's obvious that this is music made on loop-based DAWs and it's obvious that it's going to be repetitive, that we're going to be asked to lock into the grooves of these tracks with our minds and bodies, to give ourselves over to the ecstatics of the static. We can loop back and listen again, as if from a strange distance or a weird proximity, learning what it feels like to live in each loop. Remembering the oddness that attends the constant repetition of a single phrase (a strategy used by

[14]Jean Baudrillard, *Simulacra and Simulation*, trans. Sheila Faria Glaser (Ann Arbor: University of Michigan Press, 1994), 1.

many sound artists keen to mash up their auditors' distinctions between sound and sense[15]), we can listen in and out for that nonsense moment when an everyday sound morphs into a block-rocking beat. DJ N.K.'s 'Alarme Noturno' works well for this, scooping out of the everyday annoyance of the neighbourhood alarm an undeniably brutal but catchy loop that pitch-shifts its way into acid rave trance by way of bleep techno. Other brutally effective loops – loops to get lost in – can be found in Pausas's 'Horáá' and 'Me Respeitam', where a single vocal fragment is repeated nearly a hundred times in the first minute and then continues to repeat for the rest of the track. Here, vocals become percussive texture, an aspect often felt in MC-fronted Angolan kuduro but now shorn of any semantic content, any sense that one should listen for a narrative in something as conventional as words. Then there's Fofuxo's 'É Africa', in which a repeated vocal sample moves into an echoey dubby break each time the beat pauses, while a minimal melodic bleep pans left and right to evoke an acid daze. Fofuxo constantly teases the beat towards something more developed, something like an ecstatic soul-based house track, only to draw back to the beat and the repeated 'é Africa' vocal sample. The track's title, meanwhile, like many from Lisbon batida, evokes the Black Atlantic and its looped movements and histories, a reminder of the loops within loops that uprouted musics reflect and create.

[15]See Richard Elliott, *The Sound of Nonsense* (New York: Bloomsbury Academic, 2018).

6 The making and unmaking of a DJ crew

Marlon Silva was born in June 1988. His parents, originally from São Tomé and Príncipe, had moved to Lisbon before Marlon was born and he grew up in the Quinta da Vitória area of Portela, not far from Quinta do Mocho. Quinta da Vitória was one of many *bairros de lata* ('tin towns', or shanty towns) created to house the increased migration to Lisbon in the 1970s, initially from the north of Portugal and then increasingly from the former Portuguese colonies in Africa and India. As well as the corrugated metal sheets that formed roofs and occasional walls, there were wooden and brick buildings, known as *barracas*. In early 2014, after Marlon had become established at home and abroad as DJ Marfox, he was interviewed for a Portuguese television show celebrating his work and that of the Príncipe label. He was shown walking through the now demolished buildings of Quinta da Vitória, carrying a brick from the house in which he had grown up:

> I'd say this brick is roughly nineteen, eighteen years old, when magic markers appeared here. I decided to write my name, my so-called artistic name, what I dreamed I could be today, and what I actually am now. It was a childhood dream come true and I first wrote it in this brick. This brick kept my hopes alive.

Every time I came home, I opened the door and there it was. I always looked at it, it kept reminding me 'I wrote that for a reason, so I've got to keep going, keep fighting I've got to get ahead, I've got to become Marfox, a real DJ and producer'.[1]

In this feature, we see again the importance of place in the batida narrative, as well as the importance of marking one's presence on place and space, establishing an identity that marks the present while projecting into future hopes and becoming a memory of the past. For the mark to remain, it must become mobile. The destroyed neighbourhood where Marfox was filmed in 2014 has been further erased and a Continente hypermarket now stands on the site. The Quinta da Vitória brick remains, its image also adorning the disc of one of Marfox's CD releases.

Marfox has frequently described how his fascination with DJing goes back to his early childhood. In a 2018 interview, he spoke about a cousin who was performing as a DJ in well-known Lisbon clubs such as Coconuts and Mussulo in the 1990s:

I was four years old and I watched him there, with those big speaker columns, everyone admiring him. When there were parties in the neighbourhood, more people would always gather, sometimes hundreds of people. And he was the DJ, the central figure. I started to realize that he had people's attention. He managed the times, he managed emotions, wants, desires, ambitions. I thought it was funny because when he put on slower music, people danced more slowly.

[1] DJ Marfox, interviewed for *Agora*, RTP2 (16 February 2014), uploaded to YouTube by Príncipe Discos as 'RTP2: Agora/Marfox/BNM/Príncipe' on 19 February 2014, https://www.youtube.com/watch?v=gfElOKA71uo, accessed 2 August 2021. Quoted from English subtitles accompanying the excerpt.

When he put it on faster, people danced faster. When a
kizomba came on, people danced in a more romantic way.
When kuduro or hip hop went on, people danced differently.
That awakened my DJ side.[2]

Later, it was through his cousin that Marfox became aware of
kuduro, which he describes as unlike anything he had ever
heard before. Growing up in a Luso-African environment, he was
familiar with styles such as funaná, semba, kizomba, puíta and
bulauê:

> Kuduro was something new, happy. I heard my parents
> lamenting with friends about the way they had come to
> Portugal and left everything behind, how they had come with
> one hand in front and the other behind. And I thought, 'How
> does a country that is at war make music that is so happy?'.
> When my cousin played music and came to the kuduro part,
> the party changed, it was totally different. Everyone, from kids
> to older people, wanted to dance kuduro. And it made me
> think even more that I wanted to be a DJ.[3]

That ambition started to materialize at some point in his
fourteenth year, when Marfox began to make his own beats.[4]

---

[2]DJ Marfox, quoted in Fábio Nunes, 'Em Portugal Parece que Estão a Ver até
Quando Duram as Nossas Pilhas', *Notícias ao Minuto* (6 February 2018), https://
www.noticiasaominuto.com/vozes-ao-minuto/940172/em-portugal-parece-
que-estao-a-ver-ate-quando-duram-as-nossas-pilhas, accessed 2 August
2021. My translation from Portuguese.
[3]Ibid. As noted in Chapter 2, semba and kizomba are styles of Angolan music.
Funaná is a fast-paced dance music from Cabo Verde which historically
employs an accordion and a scraped metal bar known as a *ferro* or *ferrinho*.
Puíta and bulauê are dances from São Tomé & Príncipe.
[4]From this point, the majority of the information about Marfox and the
formation of the DJs do Guetto crew is taken from an interview I conducted

It was at this point that he came up with his DJ name, which combines the first syllable of his first name with the title of the 1993 Super Nintendo video game *Star Fox*. The importance of self-branding recurs often in Marfox's narrative, as it does with other DJs. Just as writing his DJ name on a house brick was important as a motivator so too was getting his name associated with the DJ software he was starting to learn. When he first started using FruityLoops (now FL Studio), the beat-making programme that would be central to the batida DJs' story as it was to contemporaneous producers from London to Luanda, the first – and, for a while, only – thing he did was to enter the Marfox tag into the speech generator's text box. Such audio tagging, or watermarking, acts as a way of promoting a DJ's ID and asserting ownership over beats. As well as FL, Marfox's early experiments were with Atomix, a DJing programme which later became a part of the Virtual DJ package. Early versions of Atomix were given away in various promotions; Marfox got his CD with a box of Chocapic cereal.

Not having a computer at home, he installed the software on the library computers at school, saving any work he did to his own account. His early attempts at beat-making and creating DJ sets involved cutting and pasting existing songs, putting them together like a jigsaw, trying to make something new from other people's music. He attended lots of parties and *noites africanas*, where Luso-African styles would be mixed together. In the early 2000s, kuduro was especially popular having travelled rapidly from its origins in 1990s Angola. Kuduro first began as a dance, then became an instrumental

with Marfox at his home in Quinta do Mocho on 19 September 2019. Any unattributed quotations from Marfox in this chapter are taken from the interview.

style before successive waves of kuduro musicians added Jamaican-style toasting and hip-hop–style rapping to the mixture. This meant that, for young people getting into the music and perhaps wanting to try out their own skills, there were options available for dancers, rappers, DJs and producers. Marfox identified as a DJ but it was inevitable that any music-making he might do would likely involve the participation of these other actors.

***

'Behind a great movement there is always a love story,' Marfox jokes, recalling the formation of the group that would become the DJs do Guetto.

> I had a girlfriend who lived in Massamá and at that time I was studying in Chelas. I would go every day to Massamá to see my girlfriend. I would wear a T-shirt that had the name 'DJ Marfox' on it. I thought 'I don't care about the world, I just like my music and I will make publicity for myself and, if someone wants to know more, they can come to me or search for me online'. This is how it started.

One of the two main train routes connecting Lisbon to the town of Sintra to the west runs from the Oriente station, near the Tejo river, through the suburbs of Benfica, Cova da Moura, Amadora and Massamá. On one of his trips to see his girlfriend, Marfox bumped into a young man from Amadora called Armandão, who recognized the name on the T-shirt and told Marfox that he had been dancing to one of his beats. Armandão mentioned that he was part of a group called Máquinas do Kuduro, made up of dancers and DJs. Intrigued, Marfox went with Armandão to meet the group, which included two young

DJs who went by the names Pausas and Fofuxo. Following their common interests, Marfox became part of the group, DJing for the dancers and working alongside Pausas and Fofuxo. He started to spend most of his time at locations along the Sintra line, seeing his girlfriend and making music with his new friends.

When the relationship with his girlfriend broke down, Marfox started to spend more time in Quinta do Mocho. Another leap forward came in 2004, when Marfox witnessed DJ Nervoso driving the participants of a Quinta do Mocho party crazy with a range of unknown tracks. As a frequenter of many African parties, Marfox knew much of the music that would be played and, while you could always expect to hear a few new tracks, Nervoso was playing at least thirty unfamiliar numbers, perhaps as many as fifty. 'This was a massive shock,' Marfox recalls. In those pre-social media days, without the chance to get tracks shared online ahead of a party, it could be a major risk for a DJ to venture too far into the unfamiliar. 'But everyone was dancing, everyone was ecstatic.' After an hour or so, Marfox approached Nervoso and asked him what artists he was playing. 'They're mine,' Nervoso told him. Seeing Marfox's disbelief, Nervoso showed him the FL originals on his laptop and explained what he was doing.

Nervoso opened Marfox's eyes and ears to new ways of making music, using FL to forge the kinds of beats that Marfox had seen the Quinta do Mocho partygoers dance to so ecstatically. With Nervoso as his teacher and mentor, Marfox began to move more towards the style that would allow him to take the international music he was listening to and 'Africanize' it, to fit with what the residents of Quinta do Mocho and other Luso-African neighbourhoods wanted to hear. 'I would hear a R&B track and want to give it a tarraxinha flavour.' At that time it wasn't as easy as now to search Google for the acapella versions of the tracks to remix, but Marfox would take what he could find of American and European musics and alter them to fit with the bpm (beats per minute) of kuduro or tarraxinha.

Marfox felt that Quinta do Mocho represented something of an island among the housing projects. Few visited from outside the neighbourhood, meaning that the music that Nervoso and others were making stayed close to home. Marfox felt a kind of privilege because he got musical information and inspiration from Quinta do Mocho and the rest of the world: learning from Nervoso, pooling ideas from the music he heard around him in Portela and its environs and integrating it all with the dominant forms of popular music entering the neighbourhoods from the outside world.

Marfox, Pausas and Fofuxo continued working on music together, combining what they already knew with what Nervoso could teach them. Although well known as a local DJ, Nervoso was not able to commit to music full time. A construction worker with a young family to support, he would be at work until at least five o'clock each evening. He would offer to help with music in the evenings when he could, but knowing his other commitments, the group tried not to bother him too much. At this point, they started to benefit from the knowledge of another young DJ, Jesse, who was from Massamá but had been out of the scene for a while, having spent some time looking for work in the UK. Now back with a broader musical knowledge, a desire to become a DJ and a mastery of FL that surpassed what the existing group had, Jesse was ideally placed to help them take the next steps. He was introduced to the group by Fofuxo, who went to the same school. Being of similar age helped with the teamwork. Because Nervoso was a few years older than the others (apart from Pausas), and because a few years can be a huge gap for teenagers, they had been timid about asking him too many questions when they didn't understand something. With Jesse, they felt no need to hold back and subsequently their knowledge of the software and techniques accelerated. Much of the summer of 2004 was spent making music at Jesse's house, and the practice continued through the following school year. By this time the initial trio of Marfox, Pausas and Fofuxo had started using the name 'DJs do Guetto'. Marfox doesn't recall any particular member coming up with the tag; it just made sense to them: 'I lived in the Portela *barracas*, Fofuxo was living in Massamá but had been born in Damaia, Pausas was living in Queluz and had been born in Amadora. We came from ghettos and we were moving from ghetto to ghetto. It was like our identity; we even wrote the word in a ghetto style: *guetto*.'

But the crew was not yet complete. In 2005, they became aware of a name that was doing the rounds of those who followed the kind of music they were making. DJ N.K. had been making beats for a few years by this point but it was an online clip of his track 'MSN Kuduro' that got everyone talking. Mixing the then-familiar sounds of the Windows Messenger service with a hard kuduro beat, N.K. captured exactly the kind of playful-catchy aesthetic that was appealing to the DJs do Guetto crew, while also showing fidelity to the computer-generated sounds of Angolan kuduro and an awareness of the kinds of digital *musique concrete* techniques being tested out by FL users around the globe. Marfox remembers thinking, 'Who is this guy? Did this sound come from Angola or from here?' Pursuing the mystery with others at school, Marfox decided that N.K. couldn't be Angolan 'because Angolans didn't make kuduro like this. It had a kind of European feel to it.' N.K.'s music became popular on peer-to-peer file-sharing platforms such as eMule, but there was no accompanying information about the elusive DJ. Eventually, Marfox tracked him down and they became friends. It turned out that N.K. (aka Pedro Cardoso) was born in Lisbon to a Portuguese father and an Angolan mother, which might go some way to explaining the mix of styles Marfox heard in his music; at the same time, it is just as likely that these were the result of the multiple sonic channels available to a curious young man with an interest in digital aesthetics.

N.K. became a correspondent for the young DJ crew, communicating by Microsoft Network (MSN) Messenger as they traded musical ideas. Marfox felt that N.K. should be part of the DJs do Guetto crew and, although this met with some initial disagreement, Marfox arranged for N.K. to be involved and the others soon came around to his way of thinking. They realized that N.K. could bring a new level to what they were doing, not least the fun of combining music with playful sound effects and cultural references. Any still-existing barriers to what kinds of sounds could be repurposed into batida disappeared as they explored this new world. With N.K. now part of the group it made sense to ask Nervoso to join too and the DJs do Guetto became a crew of six. The more established DJs were happy to be part of the group; while it was clear that they could trade on their own names independently, love of the music seemed at this stage to have trumped any sense of needing to work alone or aim for bigger gigs.

The working method for the group was generally for each to produce something and then share it with the others online for further development. School computers were used where necessary, with IT support offered by N.K. at times. The music would be shared in zip files so that each DJ could load it into

FL Studio. The less-experienced DJs would see what changes Nervoso and N.K. would make to the FL projects and learn from them. The production rate ramped up, with new beats added every day. The DJs would try the music out at small parties, learning as they went. Marfox doesn't believe the whole crew ever played at a single event; instead, different combinations took different gigs.

***

Given the productivity with which the DJs do Guetto crew was working, it was not surprising that its members would have enough material to release as an album, playlist or extended set. By the end of 2005, the 'album' was almost complete, but they didn't want to release it at Christmas time. The plan then became to launch the album during the Easter holidays, but this got postponed initially to the summer break, then to the date of Pausas's birthday. For some reason this was passed over too and, in the end, they went for September 2006, the first day of the new school year (the final year for the younger members). As Marfox relates, this was a time when MP3 technology was expanding in Portugal and DECO (Associaçáo Portugesa para a Defesa do Consumidor, the Portuguese Association for Consumer Protection) was giving away small MP3 players for free. 'At the start of the school year, everyone thinks about new clothes, new books, new everything and, because we've also got a new MP3 player, what's missing? New Music!' They released the compilation on 18 September 2006 and promoted it via MSN Messenger under the name *DJs do Guetto Volume 1*, with a direct link to a website where it could be downloaded as a zip file containing two CDs' worth of music. Formatting the music as two volumes was a deliberate move so that, even though most downloaders would play the music on PCs or MP3 players, they could also burn it to discs if they wanted, for example, to play on home or car stereos.

When I asked Marfox whether it felt important to compile the music in this way, to have this collective thing to act as a container for the young crew's experiments, he was quick to respond:

> It was everything. That CD was a radical change within the ghetto and beyond. We started to get feedback from France, from England. Until that CD, we were making music through a shared passion, but also as a diversion, for pure pleasure. It wasn't necessarily the beginning, but the CD got us recognized. Now we weren't just a bunch of kids playing at being DJs; we *were* DJs. It transformed how people looked at us and how they saw and heard the music from the ghetto. I sometimes ask myself what would have happened if we hadn't released that CD, what would have happened to DJ Firmeza, to Nigga Fox, to the many DJs who followed on from that, to the life I've built in this city.

With their newfound fame, the DJs were in demand to perform at school parties and neighbourhood events. There were logistical problems with this as not all of them could be at all the events. Splitting the profits from any paid work became a challenge. Jealousies and in-group arguments started to emerge, especially around money. In addition to this, the various group members had other things going on and couldn't devote as much time as before to making music. Nervoso had his work and family life, as well as a DJ career that had started before the DJs do Guetto; his music would later be released by Príncipe Discos. N.K. also had his own career, which would lead to the release of an album in 2016, entitled *DJ do Ghetto* in tribute to the youthful crew of a decade before and featuring collaborations with Nervoso and Marfox.[5] As a keen footballer, Jesse became more interested in sport. Pausas, who was a similar age to Nervoso, needed something more stable as he had more financial commitments than the younger members. He continued DJing, but moved to the cross-genre styles popular with African nightclubs and away from the harder, more specialized styles of the 2006 album.[6] Fofuxo became a father in 2006 and once again the following year, and then went to work in Spain; when he returned to Portugal in 2009, his music, according to Marfox, had taken on more of a reggaeton sound. Marfox found himself working alone much of the time, wanting to keep the group going but also needing to respect others' priorities. Plans for a second album never came to fruition, even though there was enough material.

The DJs do Guetto never officially ended but, by 2009, it was clear that the group was unlikely to work together or gather around another collection of music. 'It felt like we were divorced,' says Marfox. 'But it was better this way. From summer 2007 to 2009 the group had been in a limbo, an impasse. I felt I needed to pass a test, the test of being DJ Marfox. I'd done *DJs do Guetto* and people came to know my value through that, but now I was alone.' He was still making new beats to try and get followers online, posting tracks for free as a way of advertising for further work. He maintains that his desire to

[5]DJ N.K., *DJ do Ghetto*, digital album (Lit City Trax, 2016), https://litcitytrax. bandcamp.com/album/dj-do-ghetto, accessed 2 August 2021. Nervoso's music appeared under his own name on a self-titled EP (Príncipe Discos P016, 2016) and on various artist compilations released by Príncipe and other labels. [6]DJ Pausas went on to a career as a kizomba DJ, released an album entitled *All Night Long* in 2013 and a second album, *The Evolution*, in 2015. He has been involved in multiple collaborations, including an album called *Order* with DJ Palhas Jr in 2019, https://soundcloud.com/dj-pausas/tracks, accessed 2 August 2021.

make it as a DJ never wavered, and this is another reason he feels he persevered: the determination that this work could bring a living wage. 'The group didn't die because everyone had their own lives. The group died when people didn't believe that it was possible to make a living making that kind of music.'

7 Nobility

'Un Bes Bai', the fifth track on *DJs do Guetto* (*DJDG*), is the first credited to DJ Marfox. It's a furiously paced take on the Cape Verdean funaná style, asserting itself from the off via a synth figure that wouldn't sound out of place in an early 1980s synthpop track, its winding arpeggios exchanging textures across the squelch/bleep spectrum (think the Eurythmics' timeless 'Sweet Dreams' riff sped up for Afro house purposes by way of bleep techno). Percussion is handled by a pounding kick drum operating at 164 bpm (beats per minute) that sometimes alternates with, sometimes accompanies, a three-beat clap that serves to increase the rhythmic pace. Every now and then the interlocking beats seem to wear the synthesizer figure out, to unwind it, only for it to burst back to life and restart the dance. Shouts and echoes of 'Un Bes Bai', 'DJ Marfox' and 'funaná' appear at various points, claiming identity for the track and its maker. The coming and going of the beats, synths and vocals, along with the various treatments applied to the sounds throughout, give a sense of successive waves of sound, the limitlessness of dub mapped to the relentlessness of techno, kuduro and funaná.

Marfox describes 'Un Bes Bai' as a tribute to his old neighbourhood in Portela. By 2006, residents of Quinta da Vitória knew that they were going to be moved to other neighbourhoods, even if it wasn't yet clear how long the process would take (in the end, there were two major reallocation processes, one in 2006–7 and another in 2012–13). Marfox named his technofied funaná as a way of recording the existence of a neighbourhood destined to disappear. In 2007, the track would contribute to moving his career forward in important ways. One short-term opportunity that arose came from the popularity of this and other Marfox tracks among Luso-African communities living in France, leading to trips to the country for Marfox and Nervoso to perform. Another connection would prove to have longer term consequences. Kotalume, a Lisbon-based funaná singer who Marfox occasionally worked with and who had provided vocals to 'Un Bes Bai', was invited to perform in an event called '9 Bairros, Novos Sons' (Nine Neighbourhoods, New Sounds), co-organized by the record label Enchufada and the Calouste Gulbenkian Foundation. It was a launch event for a CD of the same title, which featured Kotalume's song 'Dor Ku Fomi', built on the base of the 'Un Bes Bai' instrumental.[1] Marfox wasn't invited to the event but, when Kotalume contacted him for help with providing the beats to accompany his performance, Marfox insisted on appearing too so that his contribution would be recognized.

The Kotalume/Marfox collaboration caught the ears of Filho Único, a self-described 'cultural association' that had recently been founded by Nelson Gomes and Pedro Gomes to bring a series of unusual and experimental concerts to Lisbon and to raise the profile of longstanding members of the Portuguese underground alongside its international counterpart. They hadn't heard a funaná beat quite like Marfox's before and were

[1] Various Artists, *9 Bairros, Novos Sons* (CD and digital release, Calouste Gulbenkian Foundation / Enchufada, 2007).

keen to know who had created it. Through Kotalume (who Filho Único represented), contact was made with Marfox, leading to an encounter which the DJ has described in several interviews. In a version narrated by Ryan Keeling in his 2014 article on Príncipe Discos and 'the ghetto sound of Lisbon', we hear from both sides of the meeting:

> 'What do these guys want?' says Marfox, remembering Nelson and Pedro approaching him after the show. 'Do they want to take advantage of me? Do they want to get something out of me? I wasn't used to dealing with those kinds of people. It was very confusing for me in the first 24 hours. Do they want to work with me?'
>
> Over the following months, the group slowly got to know one another, gradually building each other's trust. As they began their research, Pedro and Nelson confirmed a shared suspicion that electronic, club-focussed versions of kuduro and funaná were being produced in Lisbon. Pedro started recognising Marfox beats blaring from cars in the city centre. Nelson and Pedro got talking with Márcio [Matos] and José [Moura], and decided that, with Marfox and other local acts like Photonz and Niagara on board, they would start a label that presented Lisbon club music to the world. 'Let's work together and change things,' Nelson says of their proposal to Marfox. 'Let's make your music work in the city, and expose the amazing things you do to everybody.'[2]

Márcio Matos was working at Flur, a record shop run by José Moura. The label that the four men would set up was Príncipe

[2]Ryan Keeling, 'The Ghetto Sound of Lisbon', *Resident Advisor*, 10 March 2014, https://ra.co/features/2021, accessed 2 August 2021.

and in late 2011 it would put out Marfox's 'Eu Sei Quem Sou' as its first release. Between 2007 and the launch of the label, the Filho Único team spent some time getting to know Marfox and working with him on a range of projects, mostly small club nights in Portugal and abroad, along with occasional festivals. By all accounts, this was a period of mutual testing: Marfox needing to overcome his initial suspicions about the motives of those outside of the Luso-African neighbourhoods where his music had mostly been contained; the Filho Único team wanting to know how serious Marfox was about making a career out of his music; everyone in this growing interracial community working to challenge decades of geographical, cultural and racial segregation that had taken root between the centre and peripheries of Lisbon.

During this time, the members of Buraka Som Sistema were becoming the ambassadors of kuduro in Portugal and abroad, taking their music, as the title of their 2006 EP had it, 'from Buraka to the world'.[3] Marfox and others watched this happening, knowing that their own particular take on these sounds had a harder, and harder-to-market, aesthetic, an African electronic dance music (EDM) sound stripped back to 'amelodic austerity', as the liner notes to the *DJDG* reissue would later put it. Marfox admits to having had misgivings about the success of Buraka Som Sistema, seeing a group who had seemed to move too quickly, too easily; later, he would change his mind, seeing that there was space for different approaches to kuduro and related genres. For now, he bided his time, heeding the advice of his new collaborators at Filho Único to build on the legacy of *DJDG* but to stop giving his music away for free, to establish its value more firmly.

[3] Buraka Som Sistema, *From Buraka to the World*, CD (Enchufada ENCD002, 2006).

A good overview of Marfox's work from the *DJDG* era to his Príncipe debut can be found on the album *Revolução*, released as a CD by the Portuguese label Nos Discos in 2015 and also given a vinyl release the following year on an imprint run by the British record store Boomkat.[4] Three of the tracks had appeared on *DJDG*, one of them being 'Un Bes Bai'. 'Drift Furioso', another *DJDG* track created in 2005, can be heard as a blueprint for the kind of Nervoso-inspired, loop-based batida that Marfox and his fellow DJs would collect on their groundbreaking compilation, the furiosity announced in its title arising from the interplay of a tightly clipped percussion loop, an insistent chime melody and staccato vocal snippets. 'Funk em Kuduro' (2006), by contrast, is full-on Afro house with throwbacks to the kind of scratchy, snaking funk lines found in late-1970s Chic, the whole thing jacked to a kuduro pace. Of the non-*DJDG* tracks, 'Revolução' is the earliest, again from 2005. The album contains two collaborations with DJ Nervoso, 'Macongos Graves' (2007) and 'A Própria' (2008), as well as 'Sem Fronteiras'. This Nervoso-inspired minimal loop manages to sound like a live drummer establishing a groove that they subsequently get locked into, start to move on from, then loop back to, the whole hypnotic cycle punctuated by a scraped guiro (or similar instrument) and a clipped vocal sample that evokes great effort being expended then curtailed. Speaking shortly after the release of *Revolução*, Marfox related how 'Sem Fronteiras' (which translates as 'without borders') had been a track that helped him build his independence from Nervoso and the other DJs do Guetto,

[4]DJ Marfox, *Revolução: 2005–2008*, CD (Nos Discos NOS#05, 2015); double 12-inch (Boomkat Editions BKEDIT01, 2016).

even as it still gained the approval of his former mentor and became a future reference point:

> I lived in Portela and I used to come here [to Quinta do Mocho] to play and every time I made a track to play at parties I would first go to Nervoso's house to show him and have his thumbs up to play it. This was the first track I took to a party without Nervoso having a listen so I didn't know if it was OK, but decided to play it, to take the risk. So I played it and suddenly Nervoso comes rushing, asking who's the track from. I told him it was mine and he loved it. Only after his fifteenth time saying it was awesome did I believe his word. So I played the track in this neighbourhood and here we are all today and the first track he plays is 'Sem Fronteiras'. It really is without borders.[5]

***

As noted already, Príncipe Discos was the outcome of a group of people with strong connections to the musical culture of Lisbon. Pedro Gomes and Nelson Gomes brought their experiences of organizing live music events with Filho Único, as well as separate careers as musicians going back several years. Matos, as well as helping to curate Lisbon's recorded sound experience though his work at Flur, is a visual artist whose style would bring an instantly recognizable identity to the recorded works and event flyers of Príncipe artists. Moura, alongside running Flur, worked as a sound artist and DJ and was part of a collective known as Zonk (whose members also described themselves as Escravos de Zonk, or Slaves of

[5] DJ Marfox, 'RBTV apresenta … DJ Marfox', uploaded to YouTube by Rimas e Batidas on 20 April 2015, https://www.youtube.com/watch?v=4SRv2yi6x1c, accessed 2 August 2021.

Zonk) and that also involved Matos and the EDM duo Photonz (Marco Rodrigues and Miguel Evaristo). Both Filho Único and Zonk were involved in events hosted by the Galeria Zé dos Bois (aka ZDB), an art space founded in the mid-1990s in Lisbon's Bairro Alto neighbourhood. It was through their shared endeavours at ZDB that they began to work together on developing what would become the Príncipe record label and club nights. Later, the team would be supplemented by André Ferreira, who brought expertise (via Filho Único) in establishing links with the kind of international establishments (including retailers, venues and media outlets) that could effectively spread the word about Príncipe's activities. In an interview with the *Juno Daily* website shortly after the launch of the label, Moura described the venture as 'a cooperative based on mutual respect and common principles of locality, heritage, expression, realness and a constructive vision of the future not really oblivious of market considerations but keeping them well at bay'. As for the royal connotations of the label's name (which, as well as being part of the name of the country that Marfox's parents had emigrated from, is also the Portuguese word for 'prince'), Moura stated that a core ideal was 'to discover hidden nobility, true nobility to counteract the mostly insipid royalty out there'. This reference to 'insipid royalty' was a way of noting that much of the music being made by big names on the global EDM scene, including DJs who played guest sets at major Lisbon nightclubs like Lux, had become staid. Many of the local and lesser-known artists, according to Moura, were already some way ahead in terms of sonic innovation. As Pedro Gomes put it in the same interview, the time had come for the music of the suburbs of Lisbon to be heard; what was needed was 'a platform, a structure where it could fully blossom and reveal itself in all

Figure 7.1 *Labels for DJ Marfox's Eu Sei Quem Sou, released by Príncipe Discos, 2011. Designed by Márcio Matos.*

its glory – worldwide, for the first time in many, many cases to come'.[6]

The two inaugural releases from Príncipe were announced in a blog post on the Flur website on 18 November 2011. P001 was DJ Marfox's 'Eu Sei Quem Sou' 12-inch (see Figure 7.1), a well-produced four-track expansion of the *DJDG* sound that announced itself clearly with the staccato blasts, bleeps and heavy percussion of the title track before moving through a range of exciting percussion workouts on the remaining tracks, some of which use stereo panning to great effect. The label's second release was 'WEO/Chunk Hiss' by Photonz, the duo who had been part of the original team involved with setting up the label but who had decided to focus on their music instead. Their 12-inch consisted of two long house tracks full of psychedelic samples and sound effects. In the descriptions of the Marfox tracks, the unnamed Flur blogger suggested

[6]Tony Poland, 'Príncipe: Discovering Lisbon's Hidden Nobility', *Juno Daily* (blog), 4 April 2012, https://www.juno.co.uk/junodaily/2012/04/04/principe-discovering-lisbons-hidden-nobility/, accessed 2 August 2021.

that the title of the record (which translates as 'I Know Who I Am') be understood not as a statement of arrogance, but of identity: 'From an African techno [*techno africana*] base, Marfox interprets and amplifies the signs of origin for another notion of hardcore, a certain radicalization that … represents a genuine departure from established trends. Listen to "Pensamentos", the last track, to imagine how the rave tradition is driven by Africa.'[7] The novelty of the sound was also recognized in a January 2012 review by Philip Sherburne for *Resident Advisor*, an early example of the international reach that Príncipe was now bringing to Marfox's music. Noting that 'interesting things are afoot in Lisbon', Sherburne gave some background to the label's formation before focussing on the sounds:

> All four tracks are studies in tension, with fast, elastic loops of hand drums – shambling and shuffling, but wound so tight they could take your head off – and buzzing, staccato synth leads. (The only exception is the percussive workout 'Bit Binary', which replaces the sawtooths with shrieking guiros.) Marfox has a way with weird, modal scales and unsettling harmonies – something that many bass-music producers overly reliant on minor thirds and sevenths could learn a thing or two from.[8]

From the outset, Príncipe established a release model based on limited vinyl releases (typically 300–500) and digital releases

---

[7]'Marfox "Eu Sei Quem Sou EP" + Photonz "WEO/Chunk Hiss" em stock', *blog.FLUR.pt*, 18 November 2011, archived at https://web.archive.org/web/20111211072033/http://blog.flur.pt/2011/11/18/marfox-eu-sei-quem-sou-ep-photonz-weo-chunk-hiss-em-stock/, accessed 2 August 2021.
[8]Philip Sherburne, review of DJ Marfox, *Eu Sei Quem Sou* EP, *Resident Advisor*, 27 January 2012, https://www.residentadvisor.net/reviews/10337, accessed 2 August 2021.

that could be downloaded from various online retailers. Over time the list of digital retailers was replaced by a link to the label's Bandcamp page, where vinyl and digital formats could be purchased, though the label continued to provide links to a variety of record shops and mail-order companies that stocked the vinyl releases; over the years these have included Flur, as well as other record shops and indie-friendly mail-order sites based in Portugal, the UK, Germany, the Netherlands and Japan. The label also established a SoundCloud site at an early stage, giving music streamers an opportunity to add Príncipe tracks to their own playlists and to hear the music within the context of other material available on the platform.

Many things have remained constant with Príncipe in the years since it was established. This includes not only personnel, but also the style and sound of the recordings. Each release has been decorated with artwork by Matos, who has also designed posters for the Príncipe nights at downtown Lisbon club MusicBox that have served as a regular showcase for the batida DJs associated with the label (see Figure 7.2). Matos's visual style is so associated with these DJs that his artwork was also used for a series of Lisbon batida records released by the British label Warp in 2015.[9] The WordPress site that Príncipe have been using since their first release has maintained a consistent look over the years, as has the label's Bandcamp site. Most releases have been accompanied by evocative liner notes published on the Bandcamp and WordPress site that mix biographical and historical information about the DJs with metaphorical

---

[9]Various Artists, *Cargaa 1*, *Cargaa 2*, *Cargaa 3*, 12-inch EPs (Warp Records WAP378, WAP379, WAP380, all 2015). In titling this series, Warp used a term employed by commenters on SoundCloud, and other platforms, in response to batida tracks, translating as 'hot' or 'heavy'.

Figure 7.2 *Poster for Noite Príncipe, June 2013. Designed by Márcio Matos.*

descriptions of the sounds to be found on each release. As for sound, the stability here is not to be found in the broad range of musical styles that the Príncipe artists have worked in, but rather with the mastering of the music. All releases have been mastered by sound engineer Tó (António) Pinheiro da Silva, whose long career includes membership of the prog-folk group Banda do Casaco, in the 1970s and 1980s, and engineering work for many well-known Portuguese pop, rock and fado artists, including Sérgio Godinho, António Variações, Camané, José (Zeca) Afonso, Lena d'Água, Madredeus and Rodrigo Leão.

When Príncipe reissued *DJDG* in 2013, the compilation was accompanied by a new 'cover' designed by Matos and the most extensive liner notes yet produced by the label.[10] The music was also remastered by Pinheiro da Silva, adding another layer of newness to the album. The release was given a Príncipe catalogue number which not only situated the compilation within the newly visible and audible batida scene that the label was promoting but also set it apart as a progenitor of that scene; where Marfox's and the label's debut EP had been P001, with subsequent releases following the same format, *DJDG* was released as PR001. The album thus became a new chapter in the unfolding and interlocking stories of Príncipe and Lisbon batida, while also being singled out as the 'original' document, the thing that made it all possible. This provided a certain amount of mythology around the album, one that was regenerated in press coverage of the batida scene as awareness of it spread. This has helped to further establish *DJDG* as a ghostly presence in the story of batida, a vital document which

[10]Matos's 'cover' for *DJDG* does not exist as a physical item in the way that his covers for Príncipe's vinyl and CD releases do. That is, of course, a common aspect of digital music culture in the twenty-first century, where covers have been 'remediated' as visual accompaniments to sound recordings as a way of retaining something of the identity of physical formats such as records, cassettes and CDs. For remediation (the transformation, incorporation or updating of one media form(at) into another), see Jay David Bolter and Richard Grusin, *Remediation: Understanding New Media* (Cambridge, MA: MIT Press, 2000). The cover of this book uses the original 'cover' created by the DJs do Guetto to accompany the 2006 release.

remains (for now) accessible but which still exists as a more ephemeral and unstable presence in the firmament of batida releases than the more widely disseminated and publicized recordings of Príncipe and other labels. Arguably, the move towards streaming and cloud-based access and 'storage' has made this the common fate for sound recordings, yet some audio objects feel more fragile than others.

8 Strange futurity

If we can think of the development of Príncipe and its roster of artists as something announced by, if not necessarily caused by, *DJs do Guetto (DJDG)*, it is instructive to consider the press coverage that emerges around the label and the Lisbon scene as a way of gauging the kind of critical response that might have accompanied the earlier album had it been more widely known. While this inevitably involves a degree of speculation, I don't believe it is too far-fetched a thing to do given that the making sense, historicizing and contextualizing of such scenes often involve a mixture of retrospective narrative and presentist reaction. From my own listening experience, I can say that the response I had to *DJDG* when I became aware of it around 2014–15 was on par with how I felt about the recordings by Marfox, Nervoso, Nigga Fox, Firmeza, Nídia and other batida artists being released at the time. Yes, there was a gap of several years between the work of Marfox the unsigned bedroom producer and Marfox the Príncipe artist. And yes, it was evident that, as an artist, Marfox was developing and trying out new techniques, playing with new sounds and finessing his approach to music-making. But there was also a clear sense of continuity, affirmed by the subsequent release of the *Revolução* collection. By considering the press response to the later recordings, we can benefit from seeing what kinds of vocabularies could be applied to *DJDG*.

Over the years, the Príncipe WordPress site has become an extensive archive for the recording of live events, record releases and press coverage of the label's artists. It therefore gives a good sense of the growth of international awareness of Lisbon batida over the past decade. While gauging the success of a scene should not necessarily be predicated on how well it is known elsewhere, it has been clear over the years that the international success of the batida DJs has been both a source of pride for all involved and a tool for leveraging new opportunities and keeping the scene vital and sustainable. For the label and its artists, international press coverage has been a way of putting the scene on the map, establishing the presence of this music and its community in Lisbon, claiming a seat at the table of global pop and sets at nightclubs and festivals around the world. This sense of pride and achievement extends to Portuguese language publications on batida, which invariably mention its international popularity, its positive reception in the Anglophone press and the venues that the various DJs have performed. For example, Vítor Belanciano's book *Não Dá Para Ficar Parado*, which draws on features, reviews and interviews published by the author over several years in the Portuguese newspaper *Público*, makes frequent references to the international recognition of Black Portuguese artists. Likewise, an extensive 2015 feature on DJ Marfox and Príncipe Discos by *Rede Angola* makes sure to list the prestigious international venues that Marfox has played and the magazines that he has been featured in, while also asserting that success has not gone to his head and that he is still an authentic representative of his community. For the Angolan publication, this feature also served as a way of expressing pride in African music as it reinvented itself in the Lisbon ghettos.[1]

As noted in the previous chapter, an early and positive response to the newly promoted batida sound came from Philip Sherburne, a journalist who has been focussing on electronic, experimental and underground music since the late 1990s. Sherburne's review of Marfox's debut EP appeared on the *Resident Advisor* site in January 2012 and he also wrote about the DJ in July of that year for *SPIN*. An interview with Marfox appeared (in English) in the German publication *Electronic Beats* that March, in which he spoke about inspirational figures from the Luanda and Lisbon kuduro scenes such as Tony Amado, DJ Znobia, DJ Nervoso and DJ Firmeza. Tony Poland's feature on 'Lisbon's Hidden Nobility' for the British dance music retailer Juno Records was an early longer feature on Príncipe and the Lisbon scene, appearing in April 2012 on Juno's blog. The following year saw some more extensive coverage of the scene as the number of Príncipe releases increased. There was not an extensive coverage of the reissue of the *DJDG* compilation (although Benjamin Lebrave, founder of the Ghana-based Akwaaba Music and a journalist for *Fader* magazine, did write about the release) or the label's third EP (by the 'raw house' group Niagara). A breakthrough moment seems to have come with the label's fourth vinyl release, Nigga Fox's *O Meu Estilo*. Tracks from this EP featured on many critics' and retailers' best-of lists in 2013 and the artist was one of those featured in Robert Barry's article 'This Is Our

[1]Vítor Belanciano, *Não Dá Para Ficar Parado: Música Afro-Portuguesa: Celebração, Conflito e Esperança* (Porto, Portugal: Edições Afrontamento, 2020); Jorge Pinho, 'A Música Africana Reinventa-se nos Guetos de Lisboa', *Rede Angola* (12 February 2015), http://www.redeangola.info/especiais/a-musica-africana-reinventa-se-nos-guetos-de-lisboa/, accessed 2 August 2021.

Grime', published by *Fact* in October 2013. The year 2013 also saw the release of a shared EP by Blacksea Não Maya (aka B.N.M.), a group from the south of Lisbon, and Piquenos DJs Do Guetto (P.D.D.G), a Quinta do Mocho–based group of young DJs who named themselves after the original DJs do Guetto. This shared record received good reviews and featured in end-of-year lists. The realization that there was a group of DJs (P.D.D.G.) who were already claiming allegiance to a tradition initiated by Nervoso, Marfox and other local figures and were presenting themselves as the next generation of 'ghetto DJs' helped to alert many music journalists that this was a scene with an established history that needed articulating to a wider audience.[2]

In the Anglophone press, interest in Príncipe and the Lisbon batida scene peaked in the years 2014–15, with reviews and features appearing in publications such as *Dazed*, *Resident Advisor*, *Thump*, *Rolling Stone*, *Pitchfork*, *Do Androids Dance* (later incorporated into *Complex*), *Rookie*, *i-D/Vice*, *The Wire*,

[2]Philip Sherburne, review of DJ Marfox, *Eu Sei Quem Sou* EP, *Resident Advisor*, 27 January 2012, https://www.residentadvisor.net/reviews/10337, accessed 2 August 2021; unidentified author, '10 x 4 – DJ Marfox', *Electronic Beats*, 27 March 2012, https://www.electronicbeats.net/10-x-4-dj-marfox/, accessed 2 August 2021; Tony Poland, 'Príncipe: Discovering Lisbon's Hidden Nobility', *Juno Daily*, 4 April 2012, https://www.juno.co.uk/junodaily/2012/04/04/principe-discovering-lisbons-hidden-nobility/, accessed 2 August 2021; Philip Sherburne, 'DJ Marfox's Hypnotic, Hard-Assed Dance Mix', *SPIN*, 5 July 2012, https://www.spin.com/2012/07/dj-marfoxs-hypnotic-hard-assed-dance-mix/, accessed 2 August 2021; Benjamin Lebrave, 'DJ's Do Guetto – Free Comp – A Slice of Luso History', *Akwaabamusic.com*, 2 April 2013, archived at https://web.archive.org/web/20130405004832/http://www.akwaabamusic.com/kuduro/djs-do-guetto-free-comp-a-slice-of-luso-history, accessed 2 August 2021; Robert Barry, 'This Is Our Grime: DJ Marfox, DJ Nigga Fox, Principe Records and the Sound of the Lisbon Ghettos', *Fact*, 18 October 2013, https://www.factmag.com/2013/10/18/this-is-our-grime-dj-marfox-dj-nigga-fox-principe-records-and-the-sound-of-the-lisbon-ghettos/, accessed 2 August 2021.

The Guardian and many more outlets.[3] Over a slightly longer period, a series of video features and documentaries started to emerge. Following coverage on Lusophone outlets in early 2014 – including the edition of RTP2's 'Agora' in which Marfox was interviewed on the site of his former home in Portela, a profile of Marfox and Príncipe on RTP África and a video by RBTV, the audiovisual outlet of Portuguese hip-hop and electronic dance music (EDM) magazine *Rimas e Batidas* – came

[3]A representative list: Sian Dolding, 'Introducing DJ Marfox', *Dazed* (27 February 2014), https://www.dazeddigital.com/music/article/19037/1/introducing-dj-marfox; Ryan Keeling, 'The Ghetto Sound of Lisbon', *Resident Advisor*, 10 March 2014; Charlie Robin Jones, 'Meet the Lisbon Ghetto Kids Setting the Bairros on Fire', *Dazed*, 20 May 2014, https://www.dazeddigital.com/music/article/19737/1/the-bairros-are-on-fire; Andy Beta, 'DJ Marfox', in '10 New Artists You Need to Know: June 2014', *Rolling Stone* (19 June 2014), https://www.rollingstone.com/music/music-lists/10-new-artists-you-need-to-know-june-2014-10312/matrimony-256273/; Cedar Pasori, 'DJ Marfox Talks Playing in the US for the First Time, the Spread of Lisbon Kuduro, and Mentoring the Youth', *Complex* (20 June 2014), https://www.complex.com/music/2014/06/dj-marfox-interview, originally published as Young Cedar, 'DJ Marfox Talks', *Do Androids Dance* (20 June 2014), available at https://web.archive.org/web/20140625050743/http://doandroidsdance.com/features/dj-marfox-interview/; Jessica Hopper, 'Nidia Minaj: Estudio de Mana', *Rookie*, 28 July 2014, https://www.rookiemag.com/2014/07/nidia-minaj/; Andy Beta, 'Lisbon's Batida Revolution', *Pitchfork*, 29 August 2014, https://pitchfork.com/features/electric-fling/9490-lisbons-batida-revolution/; Charlotte Sarrola, 'Les Princes du Ghetto: Principe Discos', *I Heart* magazine, Lisbonne issue (Autumn 2014), online version posted by Eliza on 15 October 2014, archived at https://web.archive.org/web/20160709112337/http://www.iheart-magazine.com/9382-en-couv-les-princes-du-ghetto-principe-discos; Robert Barry, 'Review of Various Artists', *Cargaa Vol. 1* and DJ Nigga Fox, *Noite e Dia*, *The Wire* (May 2015), archived at https://principediscos.wordpress.com/tag/robert-barry/; Ian McQuaid, 'Pleasure Principe! The Sound of Lisbon's Bairro's Won't Be Stopped…', *i-D/Vice*, 6 August 2015, https://i-d.vice.com/en_us/article/vbd9mj/pleasure-principe-the-sound-of-lisbons-bairros-wont-be-stopped; Adam Bychawski, 'Príncipe Discos: The New Club Sensation from the Portuguese Projects', *The Guardian* (27 October 2015), https://www.theguardian.com/music/2015/oct/27/principe-discos-batida-marfox-firmeza. (All sources in this note last accessed on 2 August 2021.)

Sons do Gueto, a documentary by Tim & Barry (a film-making duo who had been busy documenting the UK grime scene) which was shown at festivals in Lisbon and London. Another London–Lisbon link came with several batida DJs performing sets for 'Boiler Room Lisbon', an offshoot of the London-based electronic music broadcasting platform Boiler Room. The same company, in corporate partnership with whisky producers Ballantine's, included a feature on Portugal in their 'Stay True' series, part three of which focussed on Príncipe DJs and contained footage of Quinta do Mocho. The neighbourhood was also highlighted in an episode of Portuguese radio station Rádio Renascença's 'Quarto Mágico' (Magic Room), filmed in Marfox's family apartment in 2016, and again in a film about Príncipe by Major Lazer uploaded to YouTube in 2019.[4]

While the audiovisual features generally focussed on allowing the scene participants to tell their own stories, the text-based articles and reviews allowed for a more obvious external reaction. From the start, key tropes started to emerge in the Anglophone response to batida, the most obvious ones being a sense of strangeness and futurity.

[4]Feature on DJ Marfox and Príncipe broadcast on *Agora*, RTP2 (16 February 2014), uploaded to YouTube by Príncipe Discos as 'RTP2: Agora/Marfox/BNM/Príncipe' on 19 February 2014, https://www.youtube.com/watch?v=gfEIOKA71uo; feature on RTP África (20 February 2014), uploaded to YouTube by Príncipe Discos on 21 February 2014, https://www.youtube.com/watch?v=Whj5IPtkSUU; 'RBTV apresenta … DJ Marfox', uploaded to YouTube by Rimas e Batidas on 20 April 2015, https://www.youtube.com/watch?v=4SRv2yi6x1c; *Sons do Gueto*, directed by Tim & Barry (UK, 2016); 'Quarto Mágico, Episódio 9: DJ Marfox', *Rádio Renascença* (3 March 2016), https://rr.sapo.pt/quartomagico/episodio/95290/; 'Stay True Portugal Part Three: Principe & The Lisbon Takeover', uploaded to YouTube by Boiler Room, 25 August 2016, https://www.youtube.com/watch?v=PqO6Fmns_T8; 'Principe Records – Blow Your Head Season 3', uploaded to YouTube by Major Lazer Official (9 April 2019), https://www.youtube.com/watch?v=77GVsZxU7Ac. (All sources in this note last accessed on 2 August 2021.)

Sherburne sounded the keynote in his early review of DJ Marfox: 'You wonder: what the hell is this stuff? How can it sound so familiar to the club music I know, and yet so alien?' Barry described Nigga Fox's *O Meu Estilo* EP as 'one of the strangest, most distinctive dance 12" s of the decade', while the same artist's 'O Badaah' (one of the tracks from *O Meu Estilo*) was singled out for a similar response from Sherburne, this time writing for *SPIN*: 'Jellied and atonal, it's the kind of fourth-world vanguardism both M.I.A. and Ricardo Villalobos have been struggling for years to articulate, from different angles, without ever achieving this degree of deeply intuitive strangeness.' 'Hwwambo', another track from that game-changing EP, reminded the uncredited writer at *Fact* 'of the sheer alterity of first-wave eski [UK grime] – a lo-fi, pressure cooked fusion of impossible rhythms, written for unborn dancers pulling shapes that don't exist yet'.[5]

The futurity aspect was picked up in an interview from early 2014 that Pedro Gomes gave to the London-based online radio station NTS when Príncipe was featured in their 'Spun Out' series:

NTS: Music journalists – notably those of US and UK publications – seem keen to characterize the music particularly music produced by Nigga Fox and other Príncipe artists as of the future. Why do you think this is?

[5]Sherburne, review of *Eu Sei Quem Sou*; Barry, 'This Is Our Grime'; Philip Sherburne on 'O Badaah', 'SPIN's 50 Best Dance Tracks of 2013', https://web.archive.org/web/20200613001736/https://www.spin.com/2013/12/50-best-dance-tracks-of-2013/131218-nigga-fox_by_diogo-simoes/, accessed 2 August 2021; 'The 100 Best Tracks of 2013', *Fact* (16 December 2013), http://www.factmag.com/2013/12/16/the-100-best-tracks-of-2013/5/, accessed 2 August 2021.

PG: I think when you listen to something that sounds very new, or very fresh, it's normal that you hear it as something that's coming from the future, because it seems too far in advance from what you know. This has happened several times throughout history, and every time it does, this feeling gets more and more pristine, more and more refined, more and more potent. Incredibly enough, it has to do with the positive effects of globalization. It's almost post-genre music: it's not strictly kuduro, it's not strictly afro-house, it's not strictly deep house, straight house, techno … producers like Nigga Fox, and all the producers on our newest release – they're not limiting what they do to a sense of genre. They have this intuitive notion of history which is based on their daily lives, on their quotidian habits of music-making and music-listening. I don't think they consider themselves to be part of a [musical] continuum historically, per se. If you look at somebody like Arca, for instance, or the more recent works by DJ Rashad – these are people that are making beats. They're not entrapped (or not too entrapped) by a formal reading of music history, [however] recent that music history may be. They're amalgamating all this musical knowledge that they possess, and producing music in a post-genre, globalist manner … I don't like the word global because it's connected with a world music type of milieu, which is a problematic milieu, but some [young producers] are transforming all the things they know into this unified singular vocabulary. When you do something like that you're not just working quantically through time but pancontinentally, through cultures. If you do that in a way that is not a fetishized, stylized fusion of cultures, but just naturally who you are – this automatic processing of all these cultures and idioms – it sounds futuristic, to whoever is listening to it, because it is a new way of processing a new reality.[6]

Gomes's framing of futurity here as a mixing of genres that is inevitable in a global pop/EDM context, as well as his suspicion of the 'world music' narrative, accord with much of the commentary that has accompanied the concept of 'World Music 2.0' in the second decade of the twenty-first century. The sense of confusion which comes through many of the responses to batida is arguably also a part of the broader set of responses to music being released in a period of hyperconnectivity and overwhelming choice. As Ben Ratliff writes at the start of his book *Every Song Ever*, 'Sounds are running ahead of our vocabularies for describing them … The feelings of disorientation, of not knowing what process makes what sound, of not really understanding what "producers" do, are question marks now built into our hearing.'[7] This passage is also cited in an essay by Noel Lobley on the local, global and networked articulations of genres such as Chicago footwork, Shangaan electro and gqom from Durban. These musics – intimately connected to local spaces and yet flourishing internationally via networked online platforms such as YouTube, SoundCloud and Bandcamp – bear strong similarities to batida's situation, making it perhaps unsurprising

[6]Interview archived at https://principediscos.wordpress.com/2014/01/11/nts-radio-hosts-principe/, accessed 2 August 2021. The music included in the show can be found as a mix at https://www.nts.live/shows/ttb/episodes/spun-out-11th-january-2014 and https://www.mixcloud.com/NTSRadio/spun-out-11th-january-2014/, both accessed 2 August 2021.
[7]Ben Ratliff, *Every Song Ever: Twenty Ways to Listen in an Age of Musical Plenty* (New York: Farrar, Straus and Giroux, 2016), 8–9.

that these and other contemporary global scenes are spoken of together.[8]

We may, of course, harbour suspicions about responses to musics from other countries and cultures that deploy strangeness as a way of othering 'foreign' musics. We may equally see them as invitations to begin the process of translation (into the familiar), to take tentative steps towards cosmopolitan perspectives and to showcase mastery and expertise on the part of journalists, curators and other actor/collaborators. Those employed in writing about fast-moving and often trend-based fluctuations of global pop (and especially EDM) are tasked with the challenge of making sense of new sounds that they may not have vocabularies for, while also needing to articulate the excitement that comes from experiencing new sounds. Unfamiliarity is a necessary part of hearing what the world has to offer.

[8]Noel Lobley, 'Hyperactive Musical Communities On- and Offline: Dancing and Producing Chicago Footwork, Shangaan Electro, and Gqom', in *The Routledge Companion to the Study of Local Musicking*, ed. Suzel A. Reily and Katherine Brucher (New York: Routledge, 2013), 55–66.

9 Translation

Reviewing DJ Marfox's *Artist Unknown* EP in 2013, Philip Sherburne wrote:

> If techno is George Clinton and Kraftwerk stuck in an elevator, as Derrick May put it, then batida must be a samba school and a Belgian rave jammed into a trash compactor. At least, that's how it comes out in the work of Portugal's DJ Marfox … his forthcoming *Artist Unknown* EP is a riot of hand drums and whistles and shrieking guiros; strafing lasers and neon fizz give it a queasy air of high-tech tribalism, like *Blade Runner* if it took its stylistic cues from Africa instead of Japan. 'Zumbidos' plays darkside synth riffs and demonic laughter off of bubbling chants and nimble stick work; 'Dark Emotion' is a fourth-world update of Joey Beltram's 'Mentasm'. 'Artist Unknown' and 'Me Gorda', meanwhile, feature gliding leads reminiscent of DJ Mujava's 'Township Funk' set to some of the most bewilderingly syncopated rhythms you'll hear this year – maybe this century.[1]

The range of comparisons is worth reflecting on not to critique this kind of comparison/translation work (it's a

---

[1] Philip Sherburne, 'Control Voltage's Friday Five: Damaged Beats from Blawan and Theo Parrish', *SPIN* (21 September 2012), https://www.spin.com/2012/09/damaged-beats-from-blawan-and-theo-parrish/, accessed 2 August 2021.

typically evocative and knowledgeable response from Sherburne), but rather to show how such work provides journalistic context for the music under consideration. Far from suggesting that Marfox's work is an imitation of any of the referents, or that it is reducible to this set of coordinates, Sherburne's text gives context to Marfox for those who have yet to hear (or situate) his music, while also asking us to reconsider the already established artists mentioned here. Everyone gets reinvented and remixed in this kind of writing. There is a process of translation happening here, an attempt to negotiate the unfamiliar into the familiar. One common strategy in other responses to Lisbon batida has been to make comparisons with UK grime. Other genres have also been evoked, such as when UK music retailer Boomkat describes DJ Nervoso's 'Avacs' as 'like the maddest Chicago jack track you've never heard', or when Andy Beta writes, 'To an outsider such as myself, beyond the African sources, batida has an aesthetic that also brings to mind reggaeton, grime, baile funk, and footwork, i.e., electronic dance music made on the cheap (usually with Fruity Loops) that is still very much for its own urban community'.[2] This is one way for those who are listening to the music away from the context of a dance floor (e.g., those considering purchasing the records being released by Príncipe and other labels) to get a handle on this sound. There is also the information that comes with the releases via the Príncipe team, which has proven itself adept at providing compelling back stories and contextual spin (I use that word

[2]Uncredited product review for DJ Nervoso, *DJ Nervoso, Boomkat*, https:// boomkat.com/products/dj-nervoso, accessed 2 August 2021; Andy Beta, 'Lisbon's Batida Revolution', *Pitchfork*, 29 August 2014, https://pitchfork. com/features/electric-fling/9490-lisbons-batida-revolution/, accessed 2 August 2021.

in a positive way, both to acknowledge the need for PR and as a DJ-relevant term).

Translation, as Umberto Eco observed, is about negotiation.[3] How do I negotiate the communicative, signifying concepts emerging from your world through reference to my own? How do you begin to explain these things to me? The answer tends to be that we do so by finding the common ground, by looking for the concepts we both recognize, even if our signs for them differ. And because we often can't find precise equivalences, we negotiate. It's little wonder, then, that, given the task of explaining new music to their audiences, fans and journalists often reach for the already familiar. In the case of batida, the already familiar for the Anglophone writer and reader might be footwork from Chicago, grime from London, baile funk from Rio de Janeiro, gqom from Durban and so on. Sometimes, it is the reviewer or feature writer who makes the connections; sometimes, it is the artists themselves. If genres are in negotiation with each other, they are also influenced by each other. Angolan kuduro developed as a localized response to American house and techno music and that legacy doesn't disappear when kuduro gets reworked in Portugal. But the USA is not the dominant player here and, to start to understand the way such musics travel, we should look to parallel scenes (such as the dance music cultures of South Africa, Uganda or Mexico) and also to a connected global network of music, clubs and scenes, stitched together, however loosely, through festivals, club nights, samples, set lists, sound clouds and social media.

This is the kind of work being undertaken by writers such as Jace Clayton in his book *Uproot*, by the Norient team behind

[3]Umberto Eco, *Mouse Or Rat? Translation as Negotiation* (London: Weidenfeld & Nicolson, 2003).

the *Seismographic Sounds* project, by Jayna Brown in her work on the utopian impulse in global pop scenes and by Noel Lobley in his account of Chicago footwork, Shangaan Electro and gqom.[4] Lobley refers to the producers and consumers of these three as 'hyperactive communities', and part of that hyperactivity is the sheer speed with which these sounds travel around the world via global networks. The sounds, the files and the spin travel fast, prompting new negotiations and translations as sound cargoes are unloaded into new harbours.

Beyond and before writing lies the obvious ground for translating new, infectious musics. Perhaps the most immediate way we can theorize the translation of any new electronic dance music (EDM) genre is how well it translates to the dance floor. As Adam Bychawski noted of batida in *The Guardian*, 'although it might sound alien at first, this is party music: after the sense of disorientation subsides, your feet take over'.[5] The music finds dancers who are ready to take it on. As Dhanveer Singh Brar has noted of Chicago footwork, the strange cargoes of new dance genres can be unloaded more easily when the unloading is taken on by seasoned hands, or feet:

[4]See Theresa Beyer, Thomas Burkhalter and Hannes Liechti, eds, *Seismographic Sounds: Visions of a New World* (Bern, Switzerland: Norient, 2015); Jace Clayton, *Uproot: Travels in Twenty-First-Century Music and Digital Culture* (New York: Farrar, Straus and Giroux, 2016); Jayna Brown, 'Buzz and Rumble: Global Pop Music and Utopian Impulse', *Social Text* 28, no. 1 (2010): 125–46; Noel Lobley, 'Hyperactive Musical Communities On- and Offline: Dancing and Producing Chicago Footwork, Shangaan Electro, and Gqom', in *The Routledge Companion to the Study of Local Musicking*, ed. Suzel A. Reily and Katherine Brucher (New York: Routledge, 2018), 55–66.
[5]Adam Bychawski, 'Príncipe Discos: The New Club Sensation from the Portuguese Projects', *The Guardian* (27 October 2015), https://www.theguardian.com/music/2015/oct/27/principe-discos-batida-marfox-firmeza, accessed 2 August 2021

[DJ] Rashad's overabundant yet precise deployment of high-end scatter and low-end pulse allowed him to animate latent formations of Teklife in a range of other environments. The sense-memory London carries of jungle, for example, meant that it was suitably primed for the arrival of footwork.[6]

The dance floor, as a space of cosmopolitan encounter, is where translation happens. And not just the dance floor: to play the vinyl records or the digital files in any situation – home, car, office, neighbourhood, through open windows, across almost empty streets, in playgrounds and hanging-out spots – is to summon to affect the dance-primed mind. Explaining the international appeal of batida to Ryan Keeling in 2014, Pedro Gomes suggested:

> This can work in Africa. This can work in all of Latin and North America, in Asia and, of course, in Europe. This music has been brewing for centuries, through the slave trade, through immigration, and now through digital technology. Fruity Loops is a miracle for this secular brewing process, because finally you get this pristine percussive complexity translated directly to digital and then onto the vinyl. Now you can finally translate all these centuries of rhythmic advancement. Because it has that kind of richness to it, it can work. Because it's been brewing for so long, it can work anywhere. But it's not populist. It's not global in the sense of United Colours Of Benetton bullshit. It just works. People just react to it.[7]

[6]Dhanveer Singh Brar, 'Ghetto Thermodynamics', *Cesura//Acceso*, no. 1 (2014): 56–64.
[7]Pedro Gomes quoted in Ryan Keeling, 'The Ghetto Sound of Lisbon', *Resident Advisor* (10 March 2014), https://ra.co/features/2021, accessed 2 August 2021.

Here, translation gets placed in a different frame, as a process that happens when technology captures, stores and transmits what has been 'brewing for so long'.

In an interview with kuduro researcher Garth Sheridan in 2012, DJ Marfox connected the mostly non-verbal aspects of the batida sound to an ability of dancers unfamiliar with his culture or spoken language to translate his music: 'By my not singing … I am giving an opportunity for those who do not understand Portuguese to dance … [If I was] singing in Portuguese I imagine that I would not be at this international level.'[8] Marfox clearly recognizes the way in which his music is situated within a panoply of other global EDM and hip-hop genres and, beyond the connections that this provides dancers in nightclubs and at festivals, he is keen to see broader social links. As Sheridan reports, 'The lines that are drawn between grime and kuduro by DJ Marfox and Buraka Som Sistema highlight connections in the lived experience and material conditions of London and Lisbon's housing estates'.[9] Sheridan goes on to describe the club nights in Lisbon where kuduro and tarraxinha are played alongside Jamaican dancehall and reggaeton, and how the sounds of these latter genres have crept into Portuguese and Angolan kuduro, for example, via the ubiquitous 'Dem Bow' riddim. The process works in multiple directions: 'In selecting Dem Bow–based genres alongside Dem Bow–infused kuduro, DJs create an intertextual dialogue between kuduro, its roots and contemporary genres.

[8]Garth Sheridan, 'Hard Ass: Representation, Diaspora and Globalisation in Kuduro' (PhD, RMIT, 2014), 54.
[9]Ibid., 72. See also the numerous links made between the sonics and the social contexts of grime and batida in Vítor Belanciano' s *Não Dá Para Ficar Parado: Música Afro-Portuguesa: Celebração, Conflito e Esperança* (Porto, Portugal: Edições Afrontamento, 2020).

The adoption of kuduro signifiers in reggaeton artist Don Omar's 'Danza Kuduro' (2010) reflects a degree of porousness, emphasised by collaboration with French-Portuguese producer Lucenzo.'[10]

This 'porousness' remains a source of anxiety for many, however kuduro musicians in Angola are rightly upset that the genre they helped to establish gains its largest global audience via tracks such as 'Danza Kuduro', while they remain in relative obscurity and struggle to make a living from their music. There is also the issue of whether such a track, filtered as it is through so many layers of popular styles, has any right to use the word 'kuduro': surely something has been lost in translation? As noted earlier in this book, many commentators on the contemporary global EDM scene have raised concerns about the faddish nature of some global sounds; the works of Clayton and Wayne Marshall are exemplary in critiquing the kinds of distortions that can occur in such situations. Pedro Gomes, meanwhile, recognized similar risks right at the outset of the Príncipe project:

> Kuduro, as the blues, hip-hop, or any other popular vocabulary that has been part of a whole culture and time, should never ever be dismissed. Similar things can be said about the B-more sound and juke music – they're both part of very important continuums, and should be addressed in the grander scheme of things. If they get used up and tensely stylized for immediate, decontextualized, 'globalist' consumption, then that manifestation of the music and culture will give the

[10]Sheridan, 'Hard Ass', 76. On translation and reggaeton, see Wayne Marshall, 'Dem Bow, Dembow, Dembo: Translation and Transnation in Reggaeton', *Lied und populäre Kultur: Jahrbuch des Deutschen Volksliedarchivs//Song and Popular Culture: Yearbook of the German Folk Song Archive*, no. 53 (2008): 131–51.

illusion that that's all these genres and cultures have to offer, which couldn't be further from the truth.[11]

This is a reason to fix the music in various ways: not only to keep it playing on the dance floors, but also to write about it, to record it, to archive the history, as Príncipe does in extensive detail on its website. That website messes with the overly binary distinctions often made between 'static' archives and 'living' musicking events. It is both the place where those very events are announced (along with release schedules for the records, of course) and an ever-growing map of where the music has been and how it has been translated, both on the dance floor (there are many YouTube videos) and in the media.

There is still much, no doubt, that gets lost in translation. However, my own position on this has shifted in recent years. In the past, I was far more critical of attempts to translate genres in the kinds of cross-cultural manners described above, not least because the exercise always seemed to prioritize the Anglophone terms and genres, or at least to assume that these were the lingua franca for musical discourse. I became exercised about this when writing about fado in the early 2000s and constantly finding references to it as 'the Portuguese blues'. Even then, another part of me was vexed by the desire within fado discourse to fence it off in an often exclusionary way ('only Portuguese people can understand it', 'fado is the soul of Portugal', 'you have to be born a fadista, you can't learn it') even while wishing to claim it as a universal language ('you don't need to understand what I'm singing to

[11]Pedro Gomes quoted in Tony Poland, 'Príncipe: Discovering Lisbon's Hidden Nobility', *Juno Daily* (blog), 4 April 2012, https://www.juno.co.uk/junodaily/2012/04/04/principe-discovering-lisbons-hidden-nobility/, accessed 2 August 2021. 'B-more' refers to Baltimore club music.

get the music', 'fado is universal'). At that time, because I was working on music and nostalgia, I became inspired by Svetlana Boym's work, where she talks about a European 'grammar of nostalgia' and points out that many European countries have supposedly 'untranslatable' words which are in fact synonyms for each other (words like *saudade, dor, sehnsucht*).[12] Since then, I've been fascinated by the paradoxes thrown up by the simultaneous desire to fence cultural terms and practices off while also claiming equivalency and even universality for them.

When I started researching and writing about batida, I was interested to see this process emerge again. At first, I was still critical of the seeming need to translate the terms and the genres into Anglo equivalents. However, as I spent more time researching and as I spoke to people in Quinta do Mocho, I started to move towards a more fluid position, inspired in part by Kwame Anthony Appiah's work on cosmopolitanism. Appiah refers to 'color language', noting that recognition of colour may be universal but the complexities of naming colour(s) move towards the local and specific, 'Whether you have a word for the color purple', writes Appiah, 'won't just depend on whether you've ever seen something purple; it will depend, too, on the resources of your language.' He goes on:

> The points of entry to cross-cultural conversations are things
> that are shared by those who are in the conversation. They
> do not need to be universal; all they need to be is what these
> particular people have in common. Once we have found
> enough we share, there is the further possibility that we will
> be able to enjoy discovering things we do not yet share.[13]

[12]Svetlana Boym, *The Future of Nostalgia* (New York: Basic Books, 2001).
[13]Kwame Anthony Appiah, *Cosmopolitanism: Ethics in a World of Strangers* (London: Allen Lane, 2006), 96–7.

I now prefer to work with this inspiring idea of difference and different languages as an invitation to find what we have in common than the previous stance I often took – and which I think is common to many of us who have read our ethnomusicology and thought critically about issues of representation – which was a more critical standpoint that worried constantly about 'othering' and misrepresentation. While it is still necessary to be vigilant about such matters, the worry can sometimes be disenabling and stop us from doing the practical work of understanding each other and building community. I found that what I was reading as 'theory' in Appiah (theory for me; practical guidance backed up by life experience and learning for him) played out in practical terms when I visited Quinta do Mocho and experienced the attempts at translation and representation happening there. This is true of the art projects happening there and the tours that accompany them, where appeals are made to the common languages (e.g., knowledge and appreciation of art) that are used as the basis for explaining how the artworks represent local issues. It's also there in the way that some of the musicians talk about the music. When I interviewed DJ Marfox, he talked about his music as taking something that was already known (referring both to Lusophone African styles but also American house and techno and British grime) and adding something to it, or twisting it in new ways. Clayton provides complementary ways of thinking about strangeness and how to deal with it, writing that

> experiencing the world via music or travel is *supposed* to be strange. Acknowledging that you don't know what's going on while being willing to linger, listen, and learn is all it takes. Noise appreciated as poetry becomes music. Foreign languages learned turn familiar. Allegedly exotic sounds

approached in their own terms … can reemerge as soul and set up camp inside yours.[14]

The willingness to linger and learn sits well with what I was feeling on my visits to Quinta do Mocho. Of course, there is always more to learn.

***

Once we establish dancing, lingering and 'color language' as ways of translating the sounds of batida, or indeed any other forms of music, we are ready to reconsider the written response to it. Despite the declarations of strangeness, in fact the music finds journalists who are ready to use language to express what they hear as new in batida, while using terms with which their readers are familiar. One way to do this is through metaphors. In this book, I have brought some of my own to bear on my earlier attempts to describe the sounds of *DJs do Guetto* (*DJDG*), and I have reported those of others as they responded to later recordings by the artists who continued the *DJDG* story. Another strategy to consider would be to employ the kinds of neologisms that make Kodwo Eshun's writing on sonic fiction so enjoyably strange. Through enstranging the language available for music criticism, Eshun enables his readers to read about his examples as if for the first time. For him, translating strangeness requires multiple neologisms, even suggesting the need for a whole new language. But there's a sense in his account that the music is doing the same through its deployment of what he calls hip-hop's '-abulary machine'. 'The cosmophonic engine is driven by neologisms,' Eshun writes, 'by terms like [the Ultramagnetic MCs'] "exquisitive", which joins

14Clayton, *Uproot*, 92.

exquisite to inquisitive. *Brainiac*'s syntactic -abulary machine sparks new synaptic junctions, new pathways for "fuel" to "ignite blood pressure above the brain level".[15] A common strategy is to combine existing terms in new combinations, which sounds a little bit like dancing, which means, perhaps – building on Brar's identification of the architectural qualities of Chicago footwork[16] – that writing about music really *is* dancing about architecture, after all. Which dancers will get to delineate the architecture for batida and what comes after translation are matters that still need to be negotiated. The music has had its moment of quick-fire journalistic response and had its strangeness marked, measured and metaphorized. It now awaits the more extensive multi-stranded narratives that have begun to emerge around grime, British bass culture, Chicago footwork and other elements of global bass and DJ cultures. The shape of its journey is still to be negotiated, the voices of many of its various actors still to be heard.

[15]Kodwo Eshun, *More Brilliant than the Sun: Adventures in Sonic Fiction* (London: Quartet Books, 1998), 027.
[16]Dhanveer Singh Brar, 'Architekture and Teklife in the Hyperghetto: The Sonic Ecology of Footwork', *Social Text* 34, no. 1126 (March 2016): 21–48.

10 An ending

My third – and, for a while, final – visit to Quinta do Mocho occurs on the morning of Thursday, 9 January 2020. I meet Kally Meru at the Casa de Cultura de Sacavém and we talk for an hour or so. Kally's not feeling well and we have to pause our conversation a few times. Even so, we manage to discuss a bit more about the neighbourhood, the creation of the public art projects and the guided tours that he and other community members have been running. When we leave the Cultural Centre, Kally offers to take me to DJ Firmeza's house to see if he's at home. As we cross the roundabout separating this part of Sacavém from the streets of Quinta do Mocho, we read a notice announcing the clearing of some adjacent land. This is where some residents grow sugarcane and where goats can be found tethered, a splash of rurality out on the edge of the city and its busy airport. The previous year the canes had been allowed to dry out and there had been a major fire. Firmeza isn't home and so Kally offers to try and locate him and DJ Lilocox for a possible meeting the next day. I tell him to rest and we hug and say goodbye.

Over the following months, a global pandemic locks down much of the world's population. Travel becomes impossible and my planned follow-up visits to Quinta do Mocho don't happen. I continue to observe the batida scene from a distance, with the strange intimacy that comes with newly mediated online events. Lisbon's batida DJs, like their Angolan counterparts and like so many DIY producers around the world, have long made their bedrooms the site of production for their sounds. Now, with so many confined to their homes and with nightclubs and in-person festivals shut down, bedrooms and other domestic spaces become stages. DJ Marfox and others take part in various performances during 2020 and 2021, beaming beats out to remote audiences from a variety of domestic spaces. Away from the dance floor, the music is forced to become detached from obvious context, something its recorded presence had always held as a possibility. But any brief feeling that this justifies my treatment of the sounds of batida as separable from the dance floor is quickly subsumed, as the pandemic drags on, by the realization that this music needs to be reconnected with its 'home' space as soon as possible so that the opportunities opened for musicians such as Marfox do not get swept away along with so much else.

Meanwhile, features continue appearing in the press, including *Pitchfork*'s July 2020 retrospective homage to Príncipe Discos.[1] Vítor Belanciano's book on Afro-Portuguese music appears, offering a statement of presence for this under-represented part of Portuguese culture. Marfox, one of the subjects of the book, is among the guests at a launch event that is streamed online. Príncipe continues releasing music, though it becomes harder to keep up

---

[1] Madison Bloom, 'A Guide to Portugal's Príncipe Discos, One of the Most Exciting Dance Labels on Earth', *Pitchfork*, 30 July 2020, https://pitchfork.com/thepitch/principe-discos-portugal-dance-label-guide-dj-marfox-nidia/, accessed 2 August 2021.

with the schedule of vinyl releases with everything locked down. When P040 appears in July 2020, it is a digital-only compilation featuring over thirty DJs (some familiar to the label's followers, some less so). In a tradition established by the label's 2013 reissue of *DJs do Guetto* (*DJDG*) and the 2016 compilation *Mambos Levis D'Outro Mundo*, *Verão Dark Hope* serves as both a showcase of talent and a statement on a moment in time (most notably the global pandemic and the unfolding Black Lives Matter movement), as described in the accompanying liner notes:

> They say there were two Summers of Love before, but maybe every Summer is just that, and maybe every Season should be. This one right now demands reflexion and calls for hope. Concrete action too: we selected 32 standalone tracks culled from an ever expanding realm of fresh and archive material. 100% of the earnings from the album shall be distributed in equal parts between all the artists involved. What we do would never become a fact without them, their drive, imagination and talent. Let's keep focused on Change.[2]

***

Prior to starting to negotiate my understanding of batida, first as a record buyer, later as a researcher, my encounters with the musical life of Lisbon had mostly been connected to the city's fado music, which I started researching in earnest around 2004. My work on fado sought to emphasize the connection between fado and the city of Lisbon, as did the work of other

---

[2]Uncredited notes to Various Artists, *Verão Dark Hope* (Digital release, Príncipe Discos P040, 2020), https://principediscos.wordpress.com/2020/07/03/p040-v-a-verao-dark-hope/, accessed 2 August 2021.

scholars such as Michael Colvin and Lila Ellen Gray.[3] This work challenged stereotypes about fado as Portugal's national music, but ultimately maintained such identifications. With regard to the world music network that developed in the 1980s and 1990s,[4] I've often felt that the end result is a kind of United Nations General Assembly, where each country or region is entitled to one representative artist, genre or style who stands in for that body. Genre and nation are often conflated in this process so that Spain is mostly represented by flamenco, Greece by rembetiko, Argentina by tango, Mali by kora players or griots, Tuva by throat singers, Cabo Verde by morna and Portugal by fado.[5] As an example of 'World Music 2.0', batida has the potential to challenge the world music network as it threatens to displace fado as the music representative of Lisbon/Portugal. However, rather than thinking that the torch has been passed from Mariza to Marfox, it is probably more accurate to suggest that these sounds of Lisbon are heard on parallel networks, other channels, where what many have been calling 'World Music 2.0' or 'outernational music' is hipper and more important than the trad tendencies of world music. Even though *Pitchfork* described DJ Marfox in 2014 as 'ambassador for this music around the world' – a role which

[3]Michael Colvin, *The Reconstruction of Lisbon: Severa's Legacy and the Fado's Rewriting of Urban History* (Lewisburg, PA: Bucknell University Press, 2008); Richard Elliott, *Fado and the Place of Longing: Loss, Memory and the City* (Farnham, UK: Ashgate, 2010); Lila Ellen Gray, *Fado Resounding: Affective Politics and Urban Life* (Durham, NC: Duke University Press, 2013).
[4]By which I mean the connected print, broadcast and online media, the concert and festival promoters, the specialist record labels and retailers, and a curious world music audience.
[5]For an account of how Cape Verdean music became understood globally through the music of Cesária Évora, see Fernando Arenas, *Lusophone Africa: Beyond Independence* (Minneapolis: University of Minnesota Press, 2011), 45–102.

artists such as Mariza and Ana Moura had previously taken on for fado – these worlds have been unlikely, for the most part, to meet.

Fado and batida are generally mapped onto different parts of the city: the former in the central and downtown areas, the latter in the peripheral neighbourhoods such as Quinta do Mocho. This geographical aspect is what most commentators

Figure 10.1 *Saudade, a mural by UNTAY (Boaz Sides), Quinta do Mocho, 2016. Photograph by Richard Elliott.*

on the batida scene highlight when tracing its origins, noting the disconnections that exist between the city centre and the outskirts in terms of public transport and other infrastructural elements. To move between downtown tourist spots of Baixa-Chiado and Alfama and the 'social' neighbourhoods of Quinta do Mocho and Cova da Moura is to move through multiple Lisbons. The latter areas haven't been completely immune from the massive rise in tourism that Lisbon has witnessed over the past decade – tours of the former ghettos are available for those willing to seek them out – but the geo- and demographic fragmentation of these spaces remains a powerful reminder of the legacies of postcolonialism.[6]

Within Quinta do Mocho, attempts are being made to address the fragmentation via three locally organized strategies: to bring people to the neighbourhood; to export knowledge of the neighbourhood to the world and to create local jobs. The first of these has been quite successful: the tours of the former ghettos which, for Quinta do Mocho, involve taking visitors to see the artworks that adorn the neighbourhood's buildings (see Figure 10.1). Connections between music and space are remembered here, as in the murals depicting DJ Nervoso and fado star Amália Rodrigues (this is one way in which those worlds meet). If the first aim of bringing visitors to a once-feared neighbourhood has been a success, then there is less certainty around the other aims of increasing its visibility outside of Lisbon and of securing work

[6]The touristification that has occurred in recent years in Lisbon's former ghettos is minor compared to what has taken root elsewhere in the city, meaning that there is not really a major contradiction between noting the increased visibility and audibility of the peripheries and highlighting the isolation in which most of the music discussed in this book was made.

for its residents. Nevertheless, the neighbourhood provides a compelling example of an attempt at 'reassembling the social'.[7] In adopting that term from Bruno Latour's account of Actor-Network-Theory, I am thinking of the necessity to recognize the multiple actors who create, maintain and narrate a scene like batida and negotiate the translation of its localized spaces to its globalized configurations. I am also thinking of the designation of Quinta do Mocho as a 'social neighbourhood' and how this further connects batida to UK grime, US footwork and Brazilian baile funk; this is part of what Marfox and the Príncipe team mean, after all, when they say 'this is our grime'.

There are concerns about a too-swift move from the local to the global, with some DJs expressing anxiety about the scene changing as it becomes more visible and audible to outside eyes and ears. Similar concerns come from residents who have tourists traipsing past their houses, peering through their doorways and windows, treating them as spectacles. But there's also a recognition that the forced segregation brought about by 'social policies' was and would be much worse than this new attempt at translating experience. The way to reassemble the social, for many, is through gradual translation of the spaces and places and cultural practices of the neighbourhoods for the benefit of those who would otherwise perpetuate divisions through fear and prejudice. This is translation as education. To connect this to the points made in this book about responses to batida, translation can be thought of as a route to cosmopolitanism, in the sense that Kwame Anthony Appiah develops the term.[8]

[7]Bruno Latour, *Reassembling the Social: An Introduction to Actor-Network-Theory* (Oxford, UK: Oxford University Press, 2007).
[8]Kwame Anthony Appiah, *Cosmopolitanism: Ethics in a World of Strangers* (London: Allen Lane, 2006), 97.

The members of the Príncipe team, like those of fellow label Enchufada, recognize the inequalities at work between metropolitan centres and the colonies that helped to make them metropolitan. Yet they also draw strength from the cultural legacies of the Lusophone Black Atlantic and simultaneously tap into the networks of the present and future. The music they release is tied to place and circumstance, but also Afrofuturist, an ever-expanding collection of what Kodwo Eshun has called 'sonic fictions'.[9] As the 2016 Príncipe compilation *Mambos Levis d'Outro Mundo* would have it, this is music from another world, both in emanating from a world that had virtually no representation in mainstream Portuguese culture and in being futuristically otherworldly.[10] It's also otherworldly in its multi-mundiality, sampling musics and beats from all over. 'For me,' says Marfox, 'the most important quality of this music is that it allows me to go and drink from other sound sources and integrate what I want … You can influence yourself and draw upon other strains of music and use what you see fit. I think that's the most fantastic and admirable quality.'[11]

In a short documentary video from *Rimas and Batidas* in 2015, Marfox reflected on success in the context of the neighbourhood: 'For me, this is success: being able to enjoy my neighbourhood, having my music, having you at my place, talking to you in my room, showing you the surroundings, grabbing a coffee and having a laugh. That's success. Living life to the fullest.'[12] This was how it felt when I visited Quinta do Mocho and was invited by Marfox into his house for a long conversation about *DJDG*, before being taken for lunch at one of the local African cafes. Marfox's observations on the role of music in the community also resonate with what Caspar Melville has written at the start of his exploration of Black music in London:

> It is art that creates the conditions for community (though it doesn't always achieve this) and that reflects but also moves beneath and beyond the social and political conditions in which it is born. It is an art defined, in Arthur Jafa's words, by its 'beauty, power and alienation' … While black music's more experimental manifestations – from the music of Sun Ra to jungle and grime – can sound alien, alienated, alienating (Eshun 1998), it can also work to 'unmake alienation' and allow the emergence of a repertoire of new cultural and political possibilities (Spillers 2006: 25). The stories and histories that this book tells matter, and not just as a contribution to black history, but to London history and the story of the nation.[13]

I have written my own much smaller book with something similar in mind. Alive both to the kind of alienation brought so excitingly to life by Eshun in his enstranging text and to the unmaking of alienation that Melville alludes to via the work

[12]DJ Marfox in 'RBTV apresenta… DJ Marfox', uploaded to YouTube by Rimas e Batidas on 20 April 2015, https://www.youtube.com/watch?v=4SRv2yi6x1c, accessed 2 August 2021.
[13]Caspar Melville, *It's a London Thing: How Rare Groove, Acid House and Jungle Remapped the City* (Manchester, UK: Manchester University Press, 2020), 23.

of Hortense Spillers, I have wanted to show how something as almost ephemeral as a set of rhythmic instrumental tracks uploaded to the internet by a group of teenagers in 2006 can be understood to have lasting meaning. More so than many other 'albums', *DJDG* feels like it wasn't supposed to last beyond its immediate functions of starting the 2006–7 school year off with a bang, getting some gigs at parties, perhaps getting six names known a bit beyond their immediate neighbourhoods. And yet, so much came after it that it was perhaps inevitable that a foundation stone would be needed, a real and mythological point X to mark the moment where a bunch of young people from the edges of the city asserted their presence and found new pride in their community.

Bibliography

Alisch, Stefanie, and Nadine Siegert. 'Angolanidade Revisited: Kuduro'. *Norient*, 6 June 2011, https://norient.com/academic/kuduro, accessed 2 August 2021.

Anniss, Matt. *Join the Future: Bleep Techno and the Birth of British Bass Music*. London: Velocity Press, 2019.

Appiah, Kwame Anthony. *Cosmopolitanism: Ethics in a World of Strangers*. London: Allen Lane, 2006.

Arenas, Fernando. *Lusophone Africa: Beyond Independence*. Minneapolis: University of Minnesota Press, 2011.

Bateman, Jessica. 'Quinta Do Mocho: How This Crime-Plagued Lisbon Estate Became the City's Coolest Open Air Gallery'. *The Independent*, 9 August 2018, https://www.independent.co.uk/travel/europe/quinta-do-mocho-lisbon-estate-street-art-festival-gallery-portugal-immigration-crime-a8484161.html, accessed 2 August 2021.

Baudrillard, Jean. *Simulacra and Simulation*. Translated by Sheila Faria Glaser. Ann Arbor: University of Michigan Press, 1994.

Belanciano, Vítor. *Não Dá Para Ficar Parado: Música Afro-Portuguesa: Celebração, Conflito e Esperança*. Porto, Portugal: Edições Afrontamento, 2020.

Beta, Andy. 'Lisbon's Batida Revolution', *Pitchfork*, 29 August 2014,https://pitchfork.com/features/electric-fling/9490-lisbons-batida-revolution/, accessed 2 August 2021.

Beyer, Theresa, Thomas Burkhalter and Hannes Liechti, eds. *Seismographic Sounds: Visions of a New World*. 1st edition. Bern, Switzerland: Norient, 2015.

Bloom, Madison. 'A Guide to Portugal's Príncipe Discos, One of the Most Exciting Dance Labels on Earth'. *Pitchfork*, 30 July 2020, https://pitchfork.com/thepitch/

principe-discos-portugal-dance-label-guide-dj-marfox-nidia/, accessed 2 August 2021.

Boakye, Jeffrey. *Hold Tight: Black Masculinity, Millennials and the Meaning of Grime*. London: Influx Press, 2017.

Bolter, Jay David, and Richard Grusin. *Remediation: Understanding New Media*. Cambridge, MA: MIT Press, 2000.

Boym, Svetlana. *The Future of Nostalgia*. New York: Basic Books, 2001.

Brar, Dhanveer Singh. 'Architekture and Teklife in the Hyperghetto: The Sonic Ecology of Footwork'. *Social Text* 34, no. 1 126 (2016): 21–48, https://doi.org/10.1215/01642472-3427117.

Brar, Dhanveer Singh. 'Ghetto Thermodynamics'. *Cesura//Acceso*, no. 1 (2014): 56–64.

Brown, Jayna. 'Buzz and Rumble: Global Pop Music and Utopian Impulse'. *Social Text* 28, no. 1 (2010): 125–46, https://doi.org/10.1215/01642472-2009-063.

Burkhalter, Thomas. 'Sound Studies across Continents: A Multidisciplinary Research Approach', in *Sound as Popular Culture: A Research Companion*, edited by Jens Gerrit Papenburg and Holger Schulze, 89–95. Cambridge, MA: MIT Press, 2016.

Bychawski, Adam. 'Príncipe Discos: The New Club Sensation from the Portuguese Projects'. *The Guardian*, 27 October 2015, https://www.theguardian.com/music/2015/oct/27/principe-discos-batida-marfox-firmeza, accessed 2 August 2021.

Chaves, Henrique. 'Clickbaits, Violência e Arte Pública Na Quinta Do Mocho, Loures'. *Trabalhos de Antropologia e Etnologia* 57 (2017): 197–210.

Clayton, Jace. *Uproot: Travels in Twenty-First-Century Music and Digital Culture*. New York: Farrar, Straus and Giroux, 2016.

Colvin, Michael. *The Reconstruction of Lisbon: Severa's Legacy and the Fado's Rewriting of Urban History*. Lewisburg, PA: Bucknell University Press, 2008.

Eco, Umberto. *Mouse or Rat? Translation as Negotiation*. London: Weidenfeld & Nicolson, 2003.

Elliott, Richard. *Fado and the Place of Longing: Loss, Memory and the City*. Farnham, UK: Ashgate, 2010.

Elliott, Richard. *The Sound of Nonsense*. New York: Bloomsbury Academic, 2018.

Epalanga, Kalaf. *Também Os Brancos Sabem Dançar: Um Romance Musical*. Alfragide, Portugal: Caminho, 2017.

Eshun, Kodwo. *More Brilliant than the Sun: Adventures in Sonic Fiction*. London: Quartet Books, 1998.

Feld, Steven. 'A Sweet Lullaby for World Music'. *Public Culture* 12, no. 1 (2000): 145–71.

Fintoni, Laurent. *Bedroom Beats & B-Sides: Instrumental Hip Hop & Electronic Music at the Turn of the Century*. London: Velocity Press, 2020.

Flaherty, Eden. 'A Decade of Change Part Two: Quinta Do Mocho'. *Atlas Lisboa*, 15 May 2018, https://www.atlaslisboa.com/quinta-do-mocho/, accessed 2 August 2021.

Gallope, Michael. 'World Music Without Profit'. *Twentieth-Century Music* 17, no. 2 (June 2020): 161–95, https://doi.org/10.1017/S1478572220000018.

Gendron, Bernard. 'Theodor Adorno Meets the Cadillacs'. In *Studies in Entertainment: Critical Approaches to Mass Culture*, edited by Tania Modleski, 18–36. Bloomington: Indiana University Press, 1986.

Gray, Lila Ellen. *Fado Resounding: Affective Politics and Urban Life*. Durham, NC: Duke University Press, 2013.

Gray, Lila Ellen. 'Listening Low-Cost: Ethnography, the City, and the Tourist Ear'. In *The Routledge Companion to the Study of Local Musicking*, edited by Suzel A. Reily and Katherine Brucher, 417–28. New York: Routledge, 2018.

Greene, Paul D., and Thomas Porcello, eds. *Wired for Sound: Engineering and Technologies in Sonic Cultures*. Music/Culture. Middletown, CT: Wesleyan University Press, 2005.

Hancox, Dan. 'A History of Grime, by the People Who Created It', *The Guardian*, 6 December 2012, https://www.theguardian. com/music/2012/dec/06/a-history-of-grime, accessed 2 August 2021.

Hancox, Dan. *Inner City Pressure: The Story of Grime*. London: William Collins, 2018.

Houghton, Edwin STATS. 'Ghetto Palms: DJ Znobia/Angolan Kuduro'. *The Fader*, 11 June 2008, http://www.thefader. com/2008/6/11/ghetto-palms-dj-znobia-angolan-kuduro, accessed 19 April 2021.

Ismaiel-Wendt, Johannes. 'Track Studies: Popular Music and Postcolonial Analysis'. In *Postcolonial Studies across the Disciplines*, edited by Jana Gohrisch and Ellen Grünkemeier, 89–107. Amsterdam: Rodopi, 2013.

Jiménez Sedano, Livia. 'Kizomba beyond Angolan-Ness and Lusofonia: The Transnational Dance Floor'. *Atlantic Studies* 17, no. 1 (2 January 2020): 91–109, https://doi.org/10.1080/14788 810.2019.1696081.

Kabir, Ananya Jahanara. 'Oceans, Cities, Islands: Sites and Routes of Afro-Diasporic Rhythm Cultures'. *Atlantic Studies* 11, no. 1 (2014): 106–24, https://doi.org/10.1080/14788810.2014.8690 10.

Keeling, Ryan. 'The Ghetto Sound of Lisbon'. *Resident Advisor*, 10 March 2014, https://ra.co/features/2021, accessed 2 August 2021.

La Barre, Jorge de. 'Sampling Lisbon: Kuduro and the Lusophone Imagination'. *Journal of Popular Music Studies* 31, no. 1 (2019): 109–30, https://doi.org/10.1525/jpms.2019.311010.

Latour, Bruno. *Reassembling the Social: An Introduction to Actor-Network-Theory*. Oxford, UK: Oxford University Press, 2007.

Lobley, Noel. 'Hyperactive Musical Communities On- and Offline: Dancing and Producing Chicago Footwork, Shangaan Electro, and Gqom'. In *The Routledge Companion to the Study of Local Musicking*, edited by Suzel A. Reily and Katherine

Brucher, 55–66. New York: Routledge, 2018, https://doi.
    org/10.4324/9781315687353-6.
Marcon, Frank. 'O kuduro como expressão da juventude em
    Portugal: estilos de vida e processos de identificação'.
    Sociedade e Estado 28, no. 1 (April 2013): 75–90, https://doi.
    org/10.1590/S0102-69922013000100005.
Marshall, Wayne. 'Dem Bow, Dembow, Dembo: Translation and
    Transnation in Reggaeton'. *Lied und populäre Kultur: Jahrbuch
    des Deutschen Volksliedarchivs//Song and Popular
    Culture: Yearbook of the German Folk Song Archive*, no. 53
    (2008): 131–51.
Marshall, Wayne. 'Sounds of the Wide, Wired World'. *The National*,
    29 October 2010, https://www.thenationalnews.com/arts-
    culture/music/sounds-of-the-wide-wired-world-1.516526,
    accessed 2 August 2021.
McClary, Susan. 'Rap, Minimalism, and Structures of Time in
    Late Twentieth-Century Culture'. In *Audio Culture: Readings
    in Modern Music*, edited by Christoph Cox and Daniel
    Warner, revised edition, 455–64. New York: Bloomsbury
    Academic, 2017.
McGlynn, Declan, 'How FL Studio Changed Electronic Music
    Forever'. *DJ Mag*, 20 April 2020, https://djmag.com/longreads/
    how-fl-studio-changed-electronic-music-forever, accessed 2
    August 2021.
Melville, Caspar. *It's a London Thing: How Rare Groove, Acid House
    and Jungle Remapped the City*. Manchester, UK: Manchester
    University Press, 2020.
Max Mertens, 'DJ Marfox Levels Up', *Thump/Vice* (later
    incorporated into Noisey/Vice), *Vice/Noisey* (5 April 2016),
    https://www.vice.com/en/article/78j4dz/dj-marfox-spotlight-
    interview-chapa-quente, accessed 19 April 2021.
Moorman, Marissa J. 'Anatomy of Kuduro: Articulating the
    Angolan Body Politic after the War'. *African Studies Review*

57, no. 3 (December 2014): 21–40, https://doi.org/10.1017/asr.2014.90.

Mudede, Charles. 'The Turntable', *CTheory*, 24 April 2003, https://journals.uvic.ca/index.php/ctheory/article/view/14561, accessed 20 February 2020.

Novak, David. 'The Sublime Frequencies of New Old Media'. *Public Culture* 23, no. 3 (2011): 603–34, https://doi.org/10.1215/08992363-1336435.

Nunes, Fábio. 'Em Portugal Parece que Estão a Ver Até Quando Duram as Nossas Pilhas'. *Notícias ao Minuto*, 6 February 2018, https://www.noticiasaominuto.com/vozes-ao-minuto/940172/em-portugal-parece-que-estao-a-ver-ate-quando-duram-as-nossas-pilhas, accessed 2 August 2021.

Pardue, Derek. 'Lisbon Is Black: An Argument of Presence'. In *The Routledge Handbook of Anthropology and the City*, edited by Setha Low, 475–91. London: Routledge, 2019.

Pereira, Pedro Schacht. '"Dance Is a Disguise": Batida and the Infrapolitics of Dance Music in Postcolonial Portugal'. In *Challenging Memories and Rebuilding Identities: Literary and Artistic Voices That Undo the Lusophone Atlantic*, edited by Margarida Rendeiro and Federica Lupati, 121–38. New York: Routledge, 2020.

Pinho, Jorge. 'A Música Africana Reinventa-se nos Guetos de Lisboa', *Rede Angola*, 12 February 2015, http://www.redeangola.info/especiais/a-musica-africana-reinventa-se-nos-guetos-de-lisboa/, accessed 2 August 2021.

Ratliff, Ben. *Every Song Ever: Twenty Ways to Listen in an Age of Musical Plenty*. New York: Farrar, Straus and Giroux, 2016.

Regev, Motti. *Pop-Rock Music: Aesthetic Cosmopolitanism in Late Modernity*. Cambridge, UK: Polity, 2013.

Rhensius, Philipp. 'Dance Away Your Origin: Nidia'. *Norient*, 19 September 2017, https://norient.com/stories/nidia, accessed 20 April 2021.

Rocha, Camilo. 'Global Ghettotech'. *Norient*, 13 June 2009, https://
     norient.com/stories/rochaglobalghettotech/, accessed 2
     August 2021.
Sánchez Fuarros, Iñigo. '"Ai, Mouraria!" Music, Tourism, and Urban
     Renewal in a Historic Lisbon Neighbourhood'. *MUSICultures* 43,
     no. 2 (2016): 66–88.
Sherburne, Philip. Review of DJ Marfox, *Eu Sei Quem Sou*
     EP. *Resident Advisor*, 27 January 2012, https://www.
     residentadvisor.net/reviews/10337, accessed 2 August 2021.
Sherburne, Philip. 'Control Voltage's Friday Five: Damaged Beats
     from Blawan and Theo Parrish', *SPIN*, 21 September 2012,
     https://www.spin.com/2012/09/damaged-beats-from-
     blawan-and-theo-parrish/, accessed 2 August 2021.
Sherburne, Philip. 'Draw a Straight Line and Follow
     It: Minimalism in Contemporary Electronic Dance Music'.
     In *Audio Culture: Readings in Modern Music*, edited by
     Christoph Cox and Daniel Warner, revised edition, 465–76.
     New York: Bloomsbury Academic, 2017.
Sheridan, Garth. 'Fruity Batidas: The Technologies and Aesthetics
     of Kuduro'. *Dancecult* 6, no. 1 (2014): 83–96, https://doi.
     org/10.12801/1947-5403.2014.06.01.05.
Sheridan, Garth. 'Hard Ass: Representation, Diaspora and
     Globalisation in Kuduro'. PhD, RMIT, 2014, https://
     researchrepository.rmit.edu.au/esploro/outputs/doctoral/
     Hard-ass-representation-diaspora-and-globalisation-in-
     kuduro/9921863836601341.
Shklovsky, Viktor. 'Art as Device'. In *Viktor Shklovsky: A Reader*,
     edited by Alexandra Berlina, 73–96. New York: Bloomsbury
     Academic, 2017.
Sicko, Dan. *Techno Rebels: The Renegades of Electronic Funk*, revised
     second edition. Detroit, MI: Wayne State University Press, 2010.
Small, Christopher. *Musicking: The Meanings of Performing and
     Listening*. Music/Culture. Hanover, NH: University Press of New
     England, 1998.

Tomás, António. 'Becoming Famous: Kuduro, Politics and the
    Performance of Social Visibility'. *Critical Interventions* 8, no. 2 (4
    May 2014): 261–75, https://doi.org/10.1080/19301944.2014.9
    38987.
Tucker, Boima. 'Kuduro's International Wave'. *Africa Is a Country*,
    24 December 2012, https://africasacountry.com/2012/12/
    kuduros-international-wave, accessed 2 August 2021.
van Veen, tobias c. 'Vessels of Transfer: Allegories of
    Afrofuturism in Jeff Mills and Janelle Monáe'. *Dancecult* 5,
    no. 2 (2013): 7–41, https://doi.org/10.12801/1947-
    5403.2013.05.02.02.
Young, Hershini. '"Sound of Kuduro Knocking at My
    Door": Kuduro Dance and the Poetics of Debility'. *African
    American Review* 45, no. 3 (2012): 391–402, https://doi.
    org/10.1353/afa.2012.0037.

Discography

Buraka Som Sistema. *From Buraka to the World.* CD EP. Enchufada
    ENCD002, 2006.
Buraka Som Sistema. *Black Diamond.* CD. Enchufada/Sony BMG
    Portugal 88697398072, 2008.
DJ Amorim. *Kumix 3.* CD. Sons D'África CD336, 2000.
DJ Amorim. *Ku Mix 4.* CD. iPlay IP14022, 2008.
DJ Marfox. *Revolução: 2005–2008.* CD. Nos Discos NOS#05, 2015.
    Also released on vinyl as a double 12-inch by Boomkat
    Editions BKEDIT01, 2016.
DJ Marfox. *Eu Sei Quem Sou.* 12-inch and digital release. Príncipe
    Discos P001, 2011.
DJ Nervoso. *DJ Nervoso.* 12-inch and digital release. Príncipe
    Discos P016, 2016.
DJ Nigga Fox. *O Meu Estilo.* 12-inch and digital release. Príncipe
    Discos P004, 2013.

DJ N.K. *DJ do Ghetto*. Digital album. Lit City Trax, 2016, https://
    litcitytrax.bandcamp.com/album/dj-do-ghetto, accessed 2
    August 2021.
Galliano, Frederic. *Frederic Galliano Presents Kuduro Sound System*.
    CD. Frikyiwa FKW 038, 2006.
Various Artists. *9 Bairros, Novos Sons*. CD and digital release.
    Calouste Gulbenkian Foundation/Enchufada, 2007.
Various Artists. *African Dance Music: New Beat of Angola 2006*. CD.
    Som Livre, 2006.
Various Artists. *Cargaa 1*. 12-inch EP. Warp WAP378, 2015.
Various Artists. *Cargaa 2*. 12-inch EP. Warp WAP379, 2015.
Various Artists. *Cargaa 3*. 12-inch EP. Warp WAP380, 2015.
Various Artists. *DJs do Guetto Vol. 1*. No physical release. Originally
    released online as downloadable zip files in 2006. Reissued
    by Príncipe Discos in 2013 via links made available at the
    Príncipe WordPress site, https://principediscos.wordpress.
    com/2013/02/10/pr001-va-djs-do-guetto-vol-1/. Also released
    in 2013 via Príncipe's SoundCloud site at https://soundcloud.
    com/principepromos/sets/dj-s-di-guetto-vol-1_2013 (CD1)
    and https://soundcloud.com/principepromos/sets/dj-s-
    di-guetto-vol-1_2013-1 (CD2). All URLs last accessed on 2
    August 2021.
Various Artists, *Kuduro Style*. CD. EMI France 5099926738123, 2008.
Various Artists. *Mambos Levis D'Outro Mundo*. CD. Príncipe Discos
    P015, 2016.
Various Artists, *Verão Dark Hope*. Digital release, Príncipe Discos
    P040, 2020.

Index

alien 10, 12, 59, 107, 114, 131
Amado, Tony 18–19, 26, 103
Angola 17–27, 31, 48, 67,
    71, 75, 76, 80–1, 102–3,
    113, 116–17
Appiah, Kwame Anthony
    119–20, 129
Artist Unknown (DJ Marfox) 111

baile funk 26, 112, 113, 129
Bandcamp 3, 12, 45, 96, 109
batida
    tracks, *see* tracks
    uses of term 17–35
Batida (Pedro Coquenão) 17, 26
bedroom 12–13, 42, 55, 124
Belanciano, Vítor 23, 54–6,
    102–3, 116, 124
Black Atlantic 7, 29, 71, 130
Black Lives Matter 125
Blacksea Não Maya (B.N.M.) 104
bleep techno, *see* techno
Brazil 7, 25, 26, 33, 113, 129
Buraka Som Sistema 21, 23,
    26–8, 90, 116

Chicago footwork, *see* footwork
Clayton, Jace 7–8, 12, 31, 33–4,
    67–70, 113–14, 117, 120–1
community 4–7, 13, 53, 55,
    59, 90, 102, 112, 114, 120,
    123, 131–2

cosmopolitanism 7, 110, 115,
    119, 129
Covid–19 8, 123–5

dancing 6–7, 19, 25, 43, 66,
    78, 121–2
DJ Amorim 22–4, 28
DJ Firmeza 55, 83, 101, 103, 123
DJ Fofuxo 2, 29, 40, 71, 78–80, 84
DJ Jesse 2, 29, 39, 79–80, 84
DJ Lilocox 30, 123
DJ Marfox
    branding and
        promotion 76–7
    early life 73–7
    influence of kuduro on 22–5,
        32, 74–7
    post-*DJDG* career 87–96,
        102–7
    as representative of batida
        54–6, 102–7, 124, 126–7,
        130–1
    reviews of his work 111–16
DJ N.K. 2, 14, 29, 37–8, 40, 45,
    71, 80–4
DJ Nervoso 2, 25, 29, 56–8, 61,
    66, 78–84, 88, 91–2, 101–4,
    112, 128
DJ Nigga Fox 83, 101, 103,
    105, 107–8
DJ Pausas 2, 29, 37, 71, 78–82, 84
DJ Rashad 108, 115

DJ Znobia 22–5, 28–9, 103
DJs do Guetto (album)
    as album 1–14, 45, 82–3
    individual tracks, *see* tracks
    making of and original
        release 77–83
    reissue by Príncipe Discos
        1–4, 98–9
DJs do Guetto (crew) 38,
    57, 77–85
dub 37, 40, 71, 87

EDM, *see* electronic dance music
electronic dance music (EDM)
    5–7, 11, 18, 31, 33, 54, 61,
    64–6, 90, 93, 105, 109–10,
    114, 116–17
Enchufada (record label) 3, 21,
    88, 130
encounter 7–8, 11–14, 37–45,
    49, 55, 61–71, 89, 115, 125
enstrangement 62–63, 121, 131,
    see also strangeness
Epalanga, Kalaf 21, 23
Eshun, Kodwo 10–11, 13, 24,
    35, 43–4, 57–8, 62, 69,
    121–2, 130–1

fado 47, 98, 118–19, 125–8
Ferreira, André 93
Filho Único 88–90, 92–3
FL Studio, *see* FruityLoops
Flur (record shop) 89, 92, 94, 96
footwork 109–10, 112–15,
    122, 129
formats 1–2, 5, 21, 44–5, 82–3,
    95–6, 98–9, 124

FruityLoops (aka FL Studio) 4, 18,
    20–2, 27, 42, 62, 65, 68, 70,
    76, 82, 112, 115
funaná 2, 75, 87–9
futurity 3–4, 7, 10, 42, 59, 61,
    106–9, 130

gaming 39, 41–2, 76
glitch 42, 67, 70
Gomes, Nelson 88–9, 92
Gomes, Pedro 23, 29, 88–9, 92–4,
    107–8, 115, 117–18, 130
gqom 32, 109–10, 113–14

hip-hop 10, 20, 23, 35, 55, 57–8,
    64, 77, 105, 116–17, 121

jungle 65, 115, 131

Kally Meru (José Carlos de
    Andrade Ribeiro) 49–52,
    54, 123
Keeling, Ryan 30, 66, 89, 105, 115
kizomba 2, 19, 22, 29, 31–2,
    75, 84
kuduro, *overview* 18–30

Lisbon 7–8, 13, 18, 21–32, 47–59,
    73–4, 88–96, 116–18, 125–
    8, *see also* place, Quinta da
    Vitória, Quinta do Mocho
loops 14, 20, 24, 29, 38, 40, 44,
    61–71, 91, 95

Mambos Levis d'Outro Mundo
    (compilation) 125, 130
Marshall, Wayne 8, 12, 31, 117

Matos, Márcio 1–2, 89, 92–
    4, 96–8
migration 11, 17–35, 47–8, 53,
    73, 75, 115
minimalism 20, 29, 63–6, 71, 91
Moorman, Marissa 19, 21
Moura, José 89, 92–3
MP3, *see* formats
murals 50–3, 57–8, 127–8
musicking 6, 118

narrative 61–71
Niagara 89, 103
Nídia (aka Nídia Minaj) 9–11, 56,
    101, 105

O Meu Estilo (DJ Nigga Fox)
    103–4, 107
objects 6–7, 9, 12–13, 35, 99

Photonz 89, 93–5
Pinheiro da Silva, Tó
    (António) 97–8
Piquenos DJs do Guetto
    (P.D.D.G.) 104
place 47–59, 73–4, 123–9
post-humanism 10–11, 13, 38,
    66–7, 69
presence 38, 48, 55–9, 74, 98–9,
    102, 124, 132
Príncipe Discos (record label)
    1–4, 12, 14, 30, 44–5, 73–4,
    83–4, 89, 92, 104, 109, 112–
    14, 117–18, 124–5, 129–30

Quinta da Vitória 54, 57, 73–4,
    87–8

Quinta do Mocho 8, 22, 47–59,
    73, 78–9, 92–9, 101–6,
    119–21, 123–4, 127–9

reggaeton 84, 112, 116–17
repetition, 25, 63–7, 70–1, *see
    also* loops
Revolução (DJ Marfox) 91–2,
    101

Sebem 19, 22
Sherburne, Philip 65, 95, 103–4,
    107, 111–12
Sheridan, Garth 18, 20–1, 26–
    8, 116–17
sonic catharsis 33
sonic delinking 9, 11, 32, 62
sonic fiction 10
SoundCloud 3, 45, 67, 96, 109
South Africa, *see also* gqom 32,
    109, 113–14
space, *see* place
strangeness, *see also*
    enstrangement 3–4, 7, 10–
    12, 14, 38, 43–4, 61–3, 70,
    106–10, 114, 120–2, 124
streaming, *see* formats
street art, *see* murals

tarraxinha 2, 19, 22, 29, 31, 39,
    78–9, 116
techno 2, 10, 18–20, 23–4, 28–9,
    31, 33, 37, 41, 57–8, 71, 87–
    8, 95, 108, 111, 113, 120
tracks
    'Alarme Noturno' (DJ
        N.K.) 40, 71

'Danza Kuduro' (Don
Omar) 117
'Do You Think You're Better'
(DJ N.K.) 29
'Drift Furioso' (DJ Marfox) 91
'É Africa' (DJ Fofuxo) 71
'Estão a Dar Medo' (DJ N.K.)
38–9, 41
'Eu Sei Quem Sou' (DJ
Marfox) 94–6
'Funk em Kuduro' (DJ
Marfox) 91
'Horáá' (DJ Pausas) 71
'Hwwambo' (DJ Nigga
Fox) 107
'Intro di Guetto' (DJ N.K and DJ
Pausas) 37–8
'Keep Your Hands in the Air'
(DJ N.K.) 29
'Me Respeitam' (DJ Pausas) 71
'MSN Kuduro' (DJ N.K.) 80
'Noddy di Ghetto' (DJ
Fofuxo) 40–1
'O Badaah' (DJ Nigga Fox) 107
'Pimp My Ragga' (DJ
Jesse) 39–40
'Sem Fronteiras' (DJ
Marfox) 91–2

'Sirene' (DJ Marfox and DJ
N.K.) 40, 45
'Tarracho do Guetto' (DJ
Fofuxo) 29
'Tarracho Exxelentt' (DJ Pausas
and DJ Fofuxo) 29
'Tarracho Nervoso' (DJ
Nervoso) 29
'Tecnho' (DJ Jesse) 29
'Tukiza' (DJ Jesse) 29
'Um Bes Bai' (DJ Marfox)
87–8, 91
translation 10, 43–4, 61, 111–
22, 129

utopia 114

Verão Dark Hope
(compliation) 125
video games, see gaming
vinyl, see formats

witnessing, see presence
World Music 2.0 8, 12, 69,
108–9, 126
world music, 34, 108–9, 126–7,
see also World Music 2.0

33 1/3 Brazil

Series Editor: Jason Stanyek

Covering the genres of samba, tropicália, rock, hip hop, forró, bossa nova, heavy metal and funk, among others, 33 1/3 Brazil is a series devoted to in-depth examination of the most important Brazilian albums of the twentieth and twenty-first centuries.

Published Titles:

Caetano Veloso's *A Foreign Sound* by Barbara Browning
Tim Maia's *Tim Maia Racional Vols. 1 &2* by Allen Thayer
João Gilberto and Stan Getz's *Getz/Gilberto* by Brian McCann
Gilberto Gil's *Refazenda* by Marc A. Hertzman
Dona Ivone Lara's *Sorriso Negro* by Mila Burns
Milton Nascimento and Lô Borges's *The Corner Club* by Jonathon Grasse
Racionais MCs' *Sobrevivendo no Inferno* by Derek Pardue
Naná Vasconcelos's *Saudades* by Daniel B. Sharp

Forthcoming titles:

Jorge Ben Jor's *África Brasil* by Frederick J. Moehn
Chico Buarque's *Chico Buarque* by Charles A. Perrone

33 1/3 Europe

Series Editor: Fabian Holt

Spanning a range of artists and genres, 33 1/3 Europe offers engaging accounts of popular and culturally significant albums of Continental Europe and the North Atlantic from the twentieth and twenty-first centuries.

Published Titles:

Darkthrone's *A Blaze in the Northern Sky* by Ross Hagen
Ivo Papazov's *Balkanology* by Carol Silverman

Heiner Müller and Heiner Goebbels's *Wolokolamsker Chaussee* by
   Philip V. Bohlman
Modeselektor's *Happy Birthday!* by Sean Nye
Mercyful Fate's *Don't Break the Oath* by Henrik Marstal
Various Artists' *DJs do Guetto* by Richard Elliott
Bea Playa's *I'll Be Your Plaything* by Anna Szemere and András Rónai
Czesław Niemen's *Niemen Enigmatic* by Ewa Mazierska and Mariusz
   Gradowski

Forthcoming Titles:
Los Rodriguez's *Sin Documentos* by Fernán del Val and Héctor Fouce
Massada's *Astaganaga* by Lutgard Mutsaers
Nuovo Canzoniere's *Bella Ciao* by Jacopo Tomatis
Amália Rodrigues's *Amália at the Olympia* by Lilla Ellen Gray
Ardit Gjebrea's *Projekt Jon* by Nicholas Tochka
Vopli Vidopliassova's *Tantsi* by Maria Sonevytsky
Édith Piaf's *Recital 1961* by David Looseley
Iannis Xenakis' *Persepolis* by Aram Yardumian

Modeselektor's Happy Birthday!

Sean Nye

Series Editor: Fabian Holt

BLOOMSBURY ACADEMIC

NEW YORK · LONDON · OXFORD · NEW DELHI · SYDNEY

BLOOMSBURY ACADEMIC
Bloomsbury Publishing Inc
1385 Broadway, New York, NY 10018, USA
50 Bedford Square, London, WC1B 3DP, UK
29 Earlsfort Terrace, Dublin 2, Ireland

BLOOMSBURY, BLOOMSBURY ACADEMIC and the Diana logo are
trademarks of Bloomsbury Publishing Plc

First published in the United States of America 2022

Copyright © Sean Nye, 2022

For legal purposes the Acknowledgments on p. ix constitute an
extension of this copyright page.

A catalog record for this book is available from the Library of Congress.

ISBN: HB: 978-1-5013-4624-8
PB: 978-1-5013-4625-5
ePDF: 978-1-5013-4627-9
eBook: 978-1-5013-4626-2

Typeset by Deanta Global Publishing Services, Chennai, India

Series: 33 1/3 Europe

To find out more about our authors and books, visit www.bloomsbury
.com and sign up for our newsletters.

Contents

Acknowledgments ix
Track Listing x
Prelude: Transatlantic Vertigo xi

Part I **Different Voices** 1

1 **The Former East** 3

2 **Title Track: Birthday Noise** 18

3 **The 200000 Decade: Russian Crunk, Or Genre Fun** 26

4 **Moderat Beginnings** 36

5 **Radiohead Stardust** 44

Part II **Rave Chronicles** 53

6 **Arena Techno Heritage** 55

7 **Cover I: Scooter Studies** 65

8 **Interlude: What about Breakcore?** 76

9 **Cover II: Rave Rebirth** 83

10 **Arena Techno to Anti-EDM** 92

Postlude: Wall Ghosts 99
Bibliography 103
Index 110

Contents

Acknowledgments

This specific project is indebted to many friends and colleagues at different stages of my life. My thanks to Vanessa Bhark, Ben Lukas Boysen, Nicolas Chevreux, Robert Crouch, Elliott De Aratanha, Joanna Demers, Enduser, Georg Fischer, Luis-Manuel Garcia, Christian Giraldo, Sumanth Gopinath, Jürgen Große, Mirko Hall, John Held, Melissa Herman, Ronald Hitzler, Rembert Hüser, Jan Klesse, Felix Knoke, Daniela Knuth, Jordan Kraemer, Richard Leppert, Stefan Meyer, Mathis Mootz, Yann Novak, Daniel Reisser, Daniel Schneider, Uwe Schütte, Lukas Seel, and Michail Stangl. And to Kim Dohlich, in memoriam. For interviews and discussions that helped with this project, my thanks to Frank Bretschneider, Jan Kummer, Oliver Lieb, Uwe Schmidt, Claudia Schneider, and Adam X. For advice on the text, many thanks to Christian Chico, Vera Maria Fleischer, Thomas Kwong, Chris Manik, Matthias Pasdzierny, Marit Posch, Nate Sloan, Aaron Thompson, and Lisa Cooper Vest—and special thanks to Fabian Holt, Leah Babb-Rosenfeld, Rachel Moore, and Mohammed Raffi at Bloomsbury.

My time in Berlin was supported by the German Academic Exchange Service (DAAD) and the Berlin Program for Advanced German and European Studies: thanks to Peter Wicke and Jens Papenburg at the Humboldt University of Berlin, and to Karin Goihl at the Berlin Program for Advanced German and European Studies. Additional thanks to my students at USC's Thornton School of Music, to the VOLUME collective, and to the Archiv der Jugendkulturen in Berlin. This book is dedicated to my family and friends on multiple coasts; the conclusions are, in the end, my own, though I hope you will enjoy them.

Track Listing

1. Happy Birthday!

2. Godspeed

3. 2000007, *feat. TTC*

4. Let Your Love Grow, *Moderat feat. Paul St. Hilaire*

5. Em Ocean

6. Sucker Pin

7. Edgar

8. Hyper Hyper, *feat. Otto von Schirach*

9. B.M.I.

10. The Dark Side of the Frog, *feat. Puppetmastaz*

11. The Dark Side of the Sun, *feat. Puppetmastaz*

12. Déboutonner, *feat. Siriusmo*

13. The Black Block

14. The First Rebirth

15. The White Flash, *feat. Thom Yorke*

16. Late Check-Out

17. The Wedding Toccata Theme

18. (I Can't Sleep) Without Music, *feat. Maxïmo Park*

Prelude
Transatlantic Vertigo

The time is the month of May 2017. I am sitting in the back of an Airbus A330-200, on an overnight, reasonably priced *Air Berlin* flight from New York's JFK to Berlin's Tegel Airport. We have been in the air for about an hour. The plane's departure was in the early evening, and so the sun is close to setting. I look out at the horizon so as to catch a glimpse of the Canadian border. As is tradition, I have paid the extra service charge to secure a window seat, in order to observe the sky at roughly 35,000 feet. But the coast is hazy and difficult to spot. I imagine that this flight away from the sun, toward Greenwich time, is speeding up the sunset. It will also speed up the night. Still, at the moment, given that the coast can be spotted, it is obviously toward the beginning of this flight—estimated at 7 hours and 45 minutes.

Soon it will essentially be dark. The moon and stars will be shining over the Atlantic. The screens of inflight entertainment will shut off as passengers try to rest. These attempts emerge soon on this flight. The passengers curl up after watching their little screens. I wonder here in juvenile fashion, and as many have wondered, how quickly humans accustom themselves to the experience of flight, with a mix of nonchalance, boredom, and mild discomfort. Clichéd as this musing is, it shocks me.

For, no matter how many flights I take, I must book a window seat. The ability to see the horizon is vital. To be sure, those in the aisle seats and the middle of the plane might prefer *not* to know where they are—high up in the air—or they simply had the ill-luck of booking too late. In the duty-free zone, money can also be tight.

Nonetheless, my fascination with sitting at the window remains. And so, with that tingly feeling of 35,000 feet in mind, let's tarry with this idea, as we move into the world of electronic sounds and gradually approach a twenty-first-century duo from the city of Berlin (or as we'll see, from the periphery of Berlin): Modeselektor. Let's propose, perhaps this fascination with flight is analogous to the sustained fascination with audio technology, as is the case with so many fans of electronic music. Whether it is an aircraft or a synthesizer, it grounds the taste for electronic sounds—also in 2017.

I was born in 1978, and so, as with many of my generation, I have been listening to these sounds since childhood: from multiple sources—computer games, sci-fi films, and cartoon soundtracks; and from multiple decades—disco to synthpop to hardcore. However, the refusal to grow accustomed to these sounds remains. Electronic music continues to put clubbers, also of my generation, into a frenzy on both sides of the Atlantic. In this spirit, I'll soon be approaching the members of Modeselektor—Sebastian Szary and Gernot Bronsert—through the lens of generational experiences. For they are of relatively the same age: born in 1975 and 1978, respectively. This issue of generations will repeatedly come up.

Still, as I sit in the Airbus and approach middle age, it has to be admitted: something has changed. The experience with electronic music in 2017 is like the experience with new updates in technology—a vertigo of exuberance and banality; the future and the everyday. It also can't be denied, as we head out on *Air Berlin* over the Atlantic Ocean, that this jet-set experience has become a tradition.

This flight is part of the trajectory of a familiar transatlantic journey—a late stage of well-established patterns of flight. My experience at this moment is anything but special; indeed, it has been routine, and quite excruciating, for the numerous DJ-producers of the jet-set generations, or what Tobias Rapp coined in 2009 as the *EasyJet Set*, in reference to the new economies of bargain-airline club tourism in Berlin.[1] These various jet-set patterns developed before I—or Modeselektor—were born. The age was marked by events such as the mass production of the Boeing 707 in 1958 and the introduction of the jumbo-jet in 1970 with the Boeing 747.[2]

In this era of jet-set banality, with greater focus on carbon footprints than cosmic excitement, I am also only a minor part of a generation trying to maintain a long tradition—that of transatlantic relationships and links between the United States and Germany, in this year of political crisis: the year 2017.

But let's pause with this generational history, for now. As the transatlantic flight continues, out into the ocean, I prepare to catch a few hours of sleep. Yet, sleep won't come. The sense of awe beyond the window keeps me alert, despite the routine. Bizarre as it might sound, at this moment, I am a middle-aged

---

1 Tobias Rapp, *Lost and Sound: Berlin, Techno, und der Easyjetset* (Frankfurt: Suhrkamp, 2009).
2 For a cultural history of air travel, see Marc Dierikx, *Clipping the Clouds: How Air Travel Changed the World* (Westport: Praeger, 2008).

raver in the air, with a millennial longing. So, I do something clichéd for the techno world, but also soothing next to the window portal in the back of the Airbus: I put on the music of the British electronic artist Burial, making selections on my iPhone, especially from the 2007 album *Untrue*, as well as the 2013 EP *Rival Dealer*. Trust me . . . hearing Burial, the audio ghosts in the middle of the night, and in the middle of the Atlantic Ocean—it is breathtaking. This is the inflight-entertainment version of the underground club.

To be sure, I'm not listening to Modeselektor yet, though the album I'll be writing about—*Happy Birthday!*—also has much to say about the time of 2007, in related, though distinct, ways from *Untrue*. The year 2007 will be an important one—not to mention that some of the styles of Burial and Modeselektor will later intersect.

So, I nestle into the seat and look out at the moon and stars. I know that I am getting my money's worth from that extra service charge for this window seat. As night proceeds, I fade back and forth between sleep and the silver hints of the Atlantic.

*　*　*

And rubbing my eyes, early Friday morning, I arrive in Berlin Tegel in an entirely expected, exhausted haze. The Airbus glides by the Berlin cityscape and the prominent TV Tower, symbol of the East German past, as we proceed to land at Tegel Airport, located in the former West. Now, to be precise, the date of this landing is May 25, 2017. It should be noted that this Friday is significant in the United States because it leads into Memorial Day weekend—or also, what in the world of electronic music, more specifically Detroit techno, is called the weekend of the *Movement Festival*, formerly known as the *Detroit Electronic Music Festival* (DEMF). This festival is arguably the most important annual event for electronic dance music in the United States.

Memories surface here, because during the previous year, I had been in Detroit for the Movement Festival. I thus arrive in Berlin with some sadness, since I might have attended Movement also in 2017. It would have involved waiting a week longer before flying to Berlin. But with the time and money, as the cliché goes: it was not meant to be.

Heading into Berlin on the morning bus, I am now completely and utterly exhausted—squinting with bags under the eyes. I eventually arrive at a friend's apartment in the district of Neukölln, where I catch up on sleep. But here, I should explain that, as long as the NYC flight was, I usually fly the ten plus hour routes from the West Coast, because I have been based in Los Angeles since 2013—where Berlin is at a yet further distance.

Memories are rushing back, for I am arriving in a city where I resided from 2008 to 2011. To situate my West Coast perspective (I also grew up near San Francisco), my experiences with Germany extend back to the 1990s—specifically, to 1995, when, as a high school exchange student, I lived in the quite non-tourist (though historic) city of Braunschweig. During that summer, together with my host family, I visited Berlin for the first time. That year, as a sixteen-year-old American exchange student, I was hearing vague rumors about something in Berlin called the Love Parade, the largest techno event in the world at that time (it would reach over a million attendees by the end of the decade). Echoes of other rave events across the landscape were also heard.

While techno was rising in popularity, my first visit to Berlin was marked by a special event in 1995: Christo and Jeanne-Claude's public art installation in the form of a government building, *the Wrapped Reichstag.* The entire Reichstag was covered in fabric for two weeks; its silver sheens marked a new European experience, especially for the once-divided city.[3] My host family and I arrived in Berlin to view this site following a road trip where we passed through the remains of the guard structures of the Former East, and swiftly by Magdeburg, and then gradually weaved our way into the former heart of "West Berlin."

That morning, it had rained, so the blinding brightness of the Wrapped Reichstag was glistening in the sun. I, as a teenie-traditionalist American, had neglected modern art and was looking for old Europe in my exchange year—but then, squinting at the massive silver wrappings proved to be one of my early lessons in appreciating modern art—an acknowledgment of Europe as a hypermodern site on the road to the twenty-first century.

*   *   *

With this Airbus arrival in the year 2017, these multiple memories came flooding back. However, more than Berlin and the Wrapped Reichstag in 1995, my mind became focused on Detroit and those euphoric weekends of the Movement

---

3 Peter Jelavich, "The *Wrapped Reichstag*: From Political Symbol to Artistic Spectacle," *German Politics and Society* 13, no. 4 (1995): 110–27.

Festival, on account of a special moment. It took the form of a surprise encounter in Berlin. What was shocking is that this encounter happened so soon after my arrival.

For, while I could barely move on Friday, it was time (as is the custom when one shifts to Berlin time) to experience music and dance on Saturday evening. I thus quickly met a fellow academic techno-enthusiast, and we biked to the border of the now-famous clubbing districts of Kreuzberg and Friedrichshain.

On the way to that former border, now clubland, suddenly—and after just a few hours in the city—I received some news that would make the weekend fateful. My techno colleague casually mentioned: "A member of Modeselektor might be where we are headed tonight." We were headed, namely, to the RAW Tempel by the river Spree. The RAW Tempel, a collection of old warehouses and buildings, is now a partial industrial playground of bars, clubs, and bass music, a memory of (now gentrified) Berlin's more rugged past. At RAW Tempel, we were arriving to see a performance by the Miami mashup, a.k.a. breakcore, artist Otto von Schirach.

This Otto von Schirach party was a kind of Berlin replacement for the Movement Festival weekend. I had just posted on social media to a circle of Detroit buddies about my intense regret at missing Movement, where the year prior Modeselektor had performed at a peak hour on the main stage . . . but then, Detroit 2016 circled back with Berlin 2017. As we arrived at the party, standing in front of me by the dusty entrance to the club, relaxed and cool, was none other than Gernot Bronsert. As mentioned, he, together with Sebastian Szary, makes up the Berlin duo known as Modeselektor.

This moment was, in bizarre fashion, a kind of transatlantic déjà vu. I was now in Berlin with a member of Modeselektor, whom I had seen in a distant city exactly one year prior. I was thus struggling to place Detroit in Berlin that weekend. Moreover, I had been introduced to Modeselektor by seeing the duo perform live when I first moved to Berlin in 2008. Biographical years and places became a confusing jigsaw puzzle.

Yet, here in the year 2017, it was also a challenging moment. A final issue must be pointed out here for this occasion: the encounter with Bronsert was, essentially, my first conversation with a European about President Donald Trump—a little over twenty-four hours after arriving in Berlin—on my first trip to Germany since the 2016 election. It amounted to a quick opening question: "Are you ashamed?" A discussion with Bronsert about transatlantic political shock and its fearful developments immediately followed, which was difficult but necessary. And while I was experiencing this personal encounter, I was wondering what the hell would happen to these transatlantic links and connections, whether in the forms of friendship, music, or politics, in the coming years.

Soon after, however, our conversation about these issues and other topics was cut short (as so often happens). The breakcore set had begun, and we headed in to be blasted by the mashed-up-Miami chaos of Bronsert's noise colleague, Otto von Schirach. My speech thus moved to the rhythmic patterns of coughing, as we became immersed in a haze of cigarettes, weed, and dust. At some point later that evening, amid the haze, Bronsert disappeared.

Intro 1.0: The Album

It was this weekend of transatlantic vertigo that sparked the thought of writing about Modeselektor. A network of memories and culture became connected to that weekend; and this network became fixed in my mind thereafter. It represents a transnational musical experience that will hopefully be intriguing to many who are reading this book, whether they have traveled across the Atlantic or not.

Thus, with the memory of that weekend in mind, and the choice of artist having been made, a new task presented itself—an album needed to be selected. In making that choice, I chose an album that works as a crossroad to the Berlin histories that I wish to highlight (and which relates to these weekend memories): Modeselektor's album from 2007, *Happy Birthday!* It could be no other. For, what I hope to achieve in this little book is to explore through *Happy Birthday!* a particular moment in those mid- and late 2000s, leading into the next decade—the gradual aging of techno culture and Berlin. Even if you don't yet know Modeselektor's music, ongoing questions of East and West, whether with respect to Germany or Europe, remain in the reception of electronic music. In particular, post–1989 German techno culture remains an intricate web of history that is shrouded in some mystery, especially for American fans.

Furthermore, a certain romanticizing of the post-1989 era and the Fall of the Wall is ongoing. Berlin has become a global fantasy and brand as much as a city (though this reputation also has substantive reasons for having developed). Engaging this past with particular wit, Modeselektor's *Happy Birthday!* will uncover ongoing questions of post–1989 electronic history. In this mode, I plan to connect the stories often told about techno history in new ways.

With *Happy Birthday*, new intersections of techno in Berlin and beyond, and of electronic coolness, parties, irony, and wit, will gradually emerge. One aspect that is also crucial for American readers to be aware of is the following: this story will, in part, be a counter history of (East) German music in the 1990s, especially as has been received in popular form in the United States. For example, it will not center on the notorious East German metal band Rammstein, a group that has been massively popular in the United States since the 1990s—indeed, their perpetual reception lingers like the bad ringing in one's ears after a club night. In fact, one of my goals with this book is to help update the American reception of post–1989 German popular music. I thus have the basic aim of introducing other (East) German stories with a transatlantic dimension.

The history of electronic music and club culture is key here. As mentioned, *Happy Birthday!* was released in the year 2007, in the same era as Burial's dual magnum opuses *Burial* (2006) and *Untrue* (2007). These two albums marked a moment of reflection specifically for British rave memories, or, as one might describe it, these albums were "almost a requiem or funeral eulogy for rave culture."[4] Such moments could be glimpsed across the Channel in continental Europe during the late 2000s, where in Germany reflective albums and new editions—and from a techno scene now a couple of decades

---

4 Simon Reynolds, *Energy Flash: A Journey through Rave Music and Dance Culture* (Berkeley: Soft Skull Press, 2012), 515.

old—were also being released. These included Gas's box collection *Nah und Fern,* Atom™'s *Liedgut*, Shed's *Shedding the Past*, and more.[5] *Happy Birthday!* can be viewed as having a particular spin on this late 2000s moment, with wit and humor.

However, this reflective mood was accompanied by new and surprising developments. A tidal wave of electronic pop and dance hit multiple shores around the year 2007. For, also in France that same year, Daft Punk's *Alive 2007* and Justice's *Cross* heralded a new age of maximalist freakouts with a French touch. These albums—and Daft Punk's legendary 2006 "pyramid performance" in Coachella, CA[6]—would be some of the key transatlantic influences on a new commercial and generational juggernaut: the sonic simulations that would eventually be dubbed "American EDM," and be linked to an alternate dance history under the coordinates of, as traced by Simon Reynolds, "digital maximalism."[7] That Modeselektor is the primary group from Berlin's second wave that hinted at this maximal future in 2007 is already intriguing.

The question of techno as arena performance versus underground club is a key tension here. I'll explain these historical connections more in a bit. But let's first return to the album choice. Modeselektor fans in particular might be surprised by my selection of *Happy Birthday*, the duo's sophomore album. I will thus explore a few questions about

---

5 I explore Gas and Atom™ in "Minimal Understandings: The Berlin Decade, The Minimal Continuum, and Debates on the Legacy of German Techno," *Journal of Popular Music Studies* 25, no. 2 (2013): 154–84.

6 Michaelangelo Matos, *The Underground Is Massive: How Electronic Dance Music Conquered America* (New York: Dey Street, 2015), 313–38.

7 Simon Reynolds, "Maximal Nation," *Pitchfork*, December 6, 2011. https://pitchfork.com/features/article/8721-maximal-nation/.

this choice. As I proceed, this discussion will hopefully work as an explanation for Modeselektor fans *and* as a general introduction for the newly acquainted. So, let's take a brief dive into this duo's past, as I work to weave a kind of musical thread that will address readers and topics on multiple coasts.

As a duo involved in live performance and DJ culture, Modeselektor's history stretches back to the early 1990s, when Bronsert and Szary were, among other activities, experiencing parties at Berlin venues such as the legendary club Tresor. During the mid-1990s, the older Szary began organizing rave parties in towns just east of Berlin, in the "Former East," as it is now peculiarly called, where they both grew up. Bronsert also attended these parties and the duo's musical worlds gradually became intertwined. An eclectic mix of DJ culture and studio production became foundational here, as the duo refined their techniques following their move to the Berlin city center in the late 1990s.

The first Modeselektor EPs were released in the early 2000s, and from the beginning, a post-rave mashup of styles, from hardcore to hip-hop to techno, marked their music. Beyond this mashup, it was especially their mix of humor and excess that first intrigued me and many other listeners, for Modeselektor's style evolved in the midst of a decade in Berlin that was marked by club coolness, or what became dubbed "Berlin minimal" at its cool peak in the mid-2000s.[8] Right in the middle of this later history, the duo's first album appeared

____

8 See Mark Butler, *Playing with Something that Runs: Technology, Improvisation, and Composition in DJ and Laptop Performance* (New York: Oxford University Press, 2014), 18–19.

in 2005 and surprised audiences with its humorful mashups reflected in the title: *Hello Mom!*

So, let's ask an opening question: Why not focus on their first album? After all, *Hello Mom!* had an equal, if not greater, musical impact than 2007's *Happy Birthday!*—partly for the obvious reason that it was Modeselektor's debut, and it provided a model for the sophomore album. However, this is where the intertwining history of the two albums becomes intriguing: *Happy Birthday!* makes some of the initial musical and cultural winks on *Hello Mom!* more explicit. In other words, new understandings of *Hello Mom!* will emerge in retroactive fashion.

Modeselektor's career in the 2010s would also continue to evolve. The duo has released three more albums to date: *Monkeytown* (2011), *Who Else* (2019), and *Extended* (2021). *Monkeytown* signified a new phase in the duo's work and reputation with the founding of record labels. The title was the same as the name for their main label, which they had founded in 2009. Monkeytown would be paired with another influential label, 50Weapons, which they also put into full gear around this time. Indeed, the labels represented Modeselektor's new status as Berlin scene promoters and representatives. These foundations had already been laid through the releases of *Hello Mom!* and *Happy Birthday!* on one of the city's quintessential labels: *BPitch Control* (about which more later).

There are still more tales to tell in the duo's career—or, in fact, also the *trio's* career. Indeed, for many readers, Modeselektor's later career in the group *Moderat* is likely more familiar. Moderat has quite a legacy, to say the least. To explain: Moderat is a trio consisting of Modeselektor together with fellow producer

Sascha Ring, a.k.a. Apparat. The name of this supergroup is a techno portmanteau: Modeselektor + Apparat = Moderat. The Moderat albums that followed in *Happy Birthday*'s wake, *Moderat* (2009), *II* (2013), and *III* (2016), represented repeated commercial-critical successes, and on international levels that *Happy Birthday!* never quite reached. There is also a sleekness and an emotional depth to the productions by Moderat, with an alternate mashup of pop vocals and emotions, highly informed by Apparat.

Indeed, these are all intriguing and valid examples for study. I will even admit here that *Happy Birthday!* is not necessarily my favorite album in terms of a continuous listening experience . . . and yet, the choice of *Happy Birthday!* represents an answer to a series of fundamental issues. To start: *Happy Birthday!* is the perfect *transitional* album—and party album. Through this album, I will address a range of topics that the other albums do not touch in the same way. The album combines threads of the earlier and later works in compelling fashion, both as Modeselektor and Moderat. It also tunes into larger currents involving post–1989 dance culture and Berlin.

In the spirit of these multiple threads and memories, I thus won't be viewing *Happy Birthday!* so much as a work, but as a *network*.[9] In other words, rather than as a unified product to be analyzed as an individual album, it is the notion of an intersection that attracts me to this work. Indeed, it is the

---

9 Butler, *Playing with Something that Runs*, 28–30. This approach is related to Butler's analysis of "work-concepts" in his theorizing of DJ and laptop performance. See the chapter "Remixing One's Self: Ontologies of the Provisional Work," 25–64.

mix of genres, collaborations, and covers that will lead us on an electronic journey beyond the album's own horizons. For, I return to this crucial point: I am eager to reveal broader histories of techno and explore post–1989 rave culture in Germany.

In the spirit of this transatlantic journey—especially for American readers—*Happy Birthday!* will provide new understandings of the currents of popular and electronic music in Germany and Europe. In this album, I will explore its pop references to raves, rock, and electronic music during both the 1990s and 2000s. The album plays with genre categories from techno to glitch to hip-hop, as well as the tension between dance-pop and the underground, and between urban and provincial history. Indeed, as a scholar of German popular music, I've been concerned about some of the standard receptions of European techno in the United States—which include electronic traditions that I have highlighted in my own research, such as the aforementioned focus on "minimal techno." Precisely through its mix of genres, *Happy Birthday!* highlights some of the international currents of Berlin electronic music in the twenty-first century.

New tales of post–1989 electronic music history can here be envisioned. As a collective scene more complicated than often imagined, Berlin has obviously had an impact. "Berlin techno" and its club culture have become an iconic juggernaut in global electronic music. Yet, the framing of European and Berlin memories—sometimes in the form of emphasizing post–1989 East Germans as "liberated dancers" rather than musicians—is one issue that needs addressing. Modeselektor will be one mode of exploring techno production and scenes in the "Former East."

Happy Birthday! as a *network* of musical references proves, in fact, more striking than one might imagine. As indicated, beyond histories of the "Former East," the international tension between pop fodder and underground is presented at a new level of playfulness. The album is, in a certain sense, more extreme and fascinating than Modeselektor's usual hallmark of casual play with music genres and rave references.

One example truly stands out.

Here it is: *Happy Birthday!* is the only electronic album I know that has links to two quite contrasting musical groups: first, *Radiohead*, the British legends of post-rock, and second, *Scooter*, which is, well, a notorious German trio that specializes in, let us call it, hardcore rave-pop (if you don't know about Scooter, please wait until Chapter 7).

Despite this, *Happy Birthday!* still garnered critical praise as a cohesive work, and network.

That fact is intriguing, to say the least.

*   *   *

Intro 2.0: The Research

But, before we get to the album, there is more that we can explore in the post–1989 traditions of electronic music. Let's return to laying the foundations for the network surrounding this duo, and the larger traditions of rave. These will have some consequences for the methods of this book. After all, beyond the question of Modeselektor or Moderat albums, many other German techno albums could have been chosen. Yet here, there is another matter: in exploring the Berlin history of techno and electronic music, the very idea of the album poses a challenge—certainly a concern for 33 1/3.

Techno albums, or more specifically *rave albums*, present special challenges for analysis. Dance culture has repeatedly struggled with or questioned the album format since its inception. Audiences accustomed to concept albums or rock operas may need some initiation in techno albums. Influential artists in rave culture can make captivating EPs and 12" singles. However, creating a successful dance album has sometimes proved elusive, depending on the artist. To this issue, Simon Reynolds reminds us in *Energy Flash*, his classic history of rave culture, that writing about dance music requires some shifts in focus when compared with rock. First, the preferred format for dance culture in the context of clubs and raves is usually not the album. Addressing his 1990s experiences at British raves and clubs, Reynolds states:

> It was an entirely different and un-rock way of using music: the anthemic track rather than the album, the total flow of the DJ's mix, the alternative media of pirate radio and specialist record stores, music as a synergistic partner with drugs, and the whole magic/tragic cycle of living for the weekend and paying for it with the midweek comedown.[10]

These observations remain relevant today. Moreover, they could describe not just British, but German raves as well in the 1990s, which is where Modeselektor has its roots.

---

10 Reynolds, *Energy Flash*, xxi.

To be sure, Reynolds practically contradicts some of these claims by going on in *Energy Flash* to write expertly about dozens of electronic albums, ranging from Autechre to Aphex Twin to the Prodigy—all of whom would become inspirations for Modeselektor. Detroit techno has also been singularly adept at merging concept album and Afrofuturist science fiction ever since Cybotron's *Enter* (1983). And in the context of German electronic music, the reputation of Kraftwerk rests on concept albums from *Radio-Activity* (1975) to *Computer World* (1981), as much as it rests on their sampled legacy. Berlin techno, not to mention Frankfurt or Cologne techno, also features compelling albums since the 1990s. By the time Modeselektor came on the scene, the dance album had evolved into a refined form. So, to qualify Reynolds's statement: the techno album actually occupies a tradition as rich as the parallel history of 12" record labels and producer networks.

Nevertheless, Reynolds's reminders about clubs, formats, and DJ culture require consideration. More recently, Mark Butler has provided a scholarly analysis of digital live-PAs that similarly unsettles the fixed musical work. In *Playing with Something That Runs,* Butler considers twenty-first-century developments in equipment and performance styles, especially in Berlin, as well as the blurred and multiple functions of digital audio workstations (DAWs).[11] In sum, like a history of prose that would focus only on novels rather than essays and short stories, a history of dance culture that only focuses on albums would be missing the point.

These issues can be linked to Modeselektor's roots in 1990s rave culture. Multiple formats and media must be kept in

---

11 Butler, *Playing with Something that Runs*, 25–64.

mind, also for the duo's releases—EPs, remixes, compilations, mixtapes, and so on, not to mention various online music formats: SoundCloud mixes, Spotify playlists, YouTube videos, and live-streamed DJ events. My emphasis on *network* aims to respond to these issues. Likewise, Modeselektor's considerable reputation as a live act and DJ-duo beyond their albums, EPs, and remixes will be kept in mind. Here, the duo's stage presence recalls a related idea from Reynolds's reflections on rave. He writes that rave's sparse use of lyrics, compared to rock, requires a "shift in emphasis" when considering the overwhelming sound of dance music:

> Where rock relates an experience (autobiographical or imaginary), rave *constructs* an experience. Bypassing interpretation, the listener is hurled into a vortex of heightened sensations, abstract emotions and artificial energies.[12]

He moves on to ask a fundamental question about this excess of dance music: "Is it possible to base a culture around sensations rather than truths, fascination rather than meaning?"[13] These experiences around which his ideas circle lie somewhere between audio frequency, intoxicated bliss, and party vibe— for me, it is also fundamentally a question of narrative rather than culture. His thoughts similarly reflect on a long tradition of *sound-system cultures*, or what scholars have described as "bass culture" in relation to a web of post–dub music scenes.[14]

---

12 Reynolds, *Energy Flash*, xxv.
13 Ibid.
14 Paul C. Jasen, *Low End Theory: Bass, Bodies and the Materiality of Sonic Experience* (London: Bloomsbury, 2016).

The experience of Modeselektor live is important here, presenting a performative link of pop and underground. This reputation was built across the 2000s and 2010s, in parallel with their releases. Like a production team on the bass assembly line, Szary often wears his factory-worker coveralls on stage. The duo's appearance on stage is a kind of 2000s rave twist on Kraftwerk or Daft Punk. Techno culture moves into everyday life, playing with banal day jobs in the bass excess. Rather than technopop robots, the duo appears as casual bass workers. Bronsert methodically works on the decks and audio equipment, and Szary hypes and energizes the crowd. Szary's presence on stage taps into the tradition of the goosebump quality of electronic music and the tactile low end, difficult to capture in language, and which has been recounted by scholars including Luis-Manuel Garcia and Paul C. Jasen[15]—that mix of excess and functionalism was part of the all-immersive experience at Movement's main stage in Detroit 2016.

Returning to Reynolds's discussion of bliss and inter-pretation, Modeselektor responds to these challenges of the "constructed experiences" of rave, involving a flood of hazy memories from the 1990s and beyond. These qualities have consequences for my narrative. *Happy Birthday!* as a full-length album can itself be described as a series of constructed experiences which display the tension between dance functionalism and album narrative.

---

15 See Jasen, *Low End Theory* and Luis-Manuel Garcia, "Beats, Flesh, and Grain: Sonic Tactility and Affect in Electronic Dance Music," *Sound Studies* 1 (2015): 59–76.

Related to such topics, we need an update to the questions of musical reception from the perspective of my 2017 Berlin trip and later. I am thinking here of the shifts to the online, mobile, and streaming worlds of music. There have been radical changes in the consumption of electronic music since the 2000s. Throughout this book, I thus explore how Modeselektor's albums also evoke, in contrast to their live performances, an *imagined party* for listeners—a blur of clubs, online consumption, and daily life—whose sounds can also be accessed at 35,000 feet. Such narrative shells or shards surround the overwhelming party experiences (real or imagined).

On the album, these stories are hinted at in a variety of ways: song titles, covers, samples, and insider winks. They hint at a compelling narrative about techno. Such practices could be said to merge the album network with the idea of constructed experiences. So let us just propose calling *Happy Birthday!* a "constructed network." Through collabs, covers, and comedic winks, the album practically functions as a bag of treats at the conclusion of a birthday party. Story and scene merge in this 2007 rave album, and this is reflected in my division of this book into two distinct parts (Part I and Part II).

Part I introduces and explores Modeselektor's music history by focusing on the following practices on *Happy Birthday*: their collaborations and associations with the Berlin scene. The international currents of Berlin electronic music in the 2000s, and Modeselektor's own international career and reputation, are also explored here—especially the British, Afro-Caribbean, and French collaborations and inspirations on the album relating to the work with Thom Yorke, Paul St. Hilaire, and TTC, among others. In fact, the variety of collabs on this album will be seen in the founding of Moderat—not to mention the rave collab with Otto von Schirach, saved for the second part of this book (Part II).

Indeed, the other side to this network, traced in Part II, will explore raves and festival culture in Modeselektor's music. Along with the party vibe that Modeselektor establishes, with inspirations from glitch to breakcore, the histories behind two covers of European dance hits from the 1990s are crucial—namely and notoriously, Scooter's "Hyper Hyper," which hit the German charts in 1994, and "The First Rebirth" by Belgian duo Jones & Stephenson, a track which rocked the rave scene in 1993. Modeselektor's covers will lead us on a history of Euro-rave scenes in the 1990s, crossing between Germany, Belgium, Spain, and beyond.

In considering those histories, I want to return briefly to some final musings about Reynolds. His writings will be an implicit inspiration in this book for two main reasons related to Modeselektor: first, Modeselektor's fundamental links to British electronica, hardcore, and post-rock music, from Aphex Twin to Radiohead, and second, the duo's intersections with hip-hop and rock, which move beyond the traditional club focus on disco, house, and techno traditions. In this spirit, I am not claiming *Happy Birthday!* as an artistic classic—it is a funny, functional, and emotional rave album integrated into an international dance scene.

Indeed, *Happy Birthday!* elicits the question of whether rave albums can be properly appreciated as enclosed artworks. Rather, the mix of styles, dance experiences, and moods invites multiple forms of "choose-your-own-adventure." When I think of the album again as a network, various groupings of tunes stand out—these can again be based on genre; on collabs; on covers; or on moods from party excess to melancholy. To these questions, a final point about networks needs to be highlighted. It concerns the network in its most obvious sense: *the online network*. Much of the writing of this book reflects new phases in the digital humanities with respect to music. While the classic worlds of vinyl and DJ culture remain important, I have primarily explored Modeselektor's music through the silver sheens of the laptop screen.

A mini-verse, if you like, has opened up for the exploration of musical context and meaning. In that spirit, my references to the track listing deal with the CD-digital version of the album; this has been the primary version that has circulated online. Accompanying the digital releases on Beatport and beyond, a system of online journalism has developed around European techno. Techno media outlets include *Electronic Beats* by Deutsche Telekom, the *Red Bull Music Academy* (RBMA),[16] *Resident Advisor*, and others. Such networks are important for the international transfer of knowledge and the reception of music from Germany. They provide the online program notes to so many dance events—not to mention being integrated into other databases and resources from *Discogs* to *Wikipedia* to *Pitchfork*, as well as the digital archives of the *Wayback Machine*.

---

16 See Guillaume Heugeut's account of Boiler Room: "When Club Culture Goes Online: The Case of Boiler Room," *Dancecult: Journal of Electronic Dance Music Culture* 8, no. 1 (2016): 73–87.

Modeselektor is now an online presence as much as it is a live act.[17] In fact, rave and hip-hop have both experienced profound shifts from their foundations in record cultures (vinyl-DJs, shops, and mixtapes) to online cultures of digital streaming and social networks—though each tradition still circles around the other. I recall such online developments happening around the time when *Happy Birthday!* was released, such as the rising role of social media after-parties (Facebook's exponential growth began at that time), not to mention that the iPhone was released during the same year: 2007. Thus, exploring *Happy Birthday!* will partly address the question of that transformation: What happens to rave and techno when it goes online?

As a scholar and writer, I feel it is my duty to try to connect the dots in ways that Modeselektor might not expect. I hope to do the duo justice. I am well aware that, like Modeselektor's inception and initial years on the periphery of Berlin, I occupy a space on a much greater periphery from Berlin. In properly geographic terms, I have interacted with the capital's techno scene only for intermittent periods. Though in digital, online, and jet-set terms, that number of encounters might be differently counted.

Like this "constructed network," perhaps that displacement can offer alternate sources of knowledge.

Now, on to the mix.

For that, we'll go back to Berlin.

---

17 For example, check out Modeselektor's RadioEins "Living Room" concert in 2020: https://www.youtube.com/watch?v=A9AYnNxKTdo.

Part I

Different Voices

1 The Former East

East Germany, communism, dusty air, "East Side."
BRONSERT AND SZARY

As an American scholar in the field of German studies, one of my responsibilities is to explain the networks of Berlin techno and so-called German techno—its multiple scenes and styles. Only in this way can we begin to understand the "constructed network" that I have proposed for understanding *Happy Birthday!* Yet, especially in Anglo-American popular music studies and journalism, comparatively little has been written on Modeselektor, let alone German techno history since the 2000s. To be sure, there has been a good deal of historical research in recent years, involving a new generation of musical and cultural scholars, such as can be found in the journal *Dancecult* and a variety of scholarly monographs.

In terms of American popular journalism and media since the 2000s, the most prominent introductions to Berlin techno have been a series of sensational exposés focusing on Berghain, a club often thought of as Berlin's "techno cathedral" and the main point of reference for the Berlin scene. This club has, in fact, been featured in both *The New Yorker* and *The New York Times*[1]—serving as an introduction into general scene

---

1 See Nick Paumgarten, "Berlin Nights: The Thrall of Techno," *The New Yorker*, March 24, 2014. http://www.newyorker.com/magazine/2014/03/24/berlin-nights,

histories, if not musical histories, that have elicited some of the main interests in Berlin techno since the 2000s.

Given the transatlantic fame of this club, and the transatlantic focus of my narrative, let's begin here. This singular club institution can serve as a gateway into the alleys of Berlin club history.

So, to explain:

Berghain was actually founded already in 2004, following its earlier history as the club Ostgut, housed at a nearby location. Like Berlin as icon, the name "Berghain" symbolizes the links of East and West Berlin. Similar to Moderat, Berghain is a techno portmanteau, drawn from the neighboring districts of Kreuz(berg), in the West, and Friedrichs(hain), in the East. The club was also key in retaining the foundational links between queer culture, house, and techno when it first emerged as Ostgut in 1998. With its place at the crossroads of Berlin's music history, Berghain has maintained a reputation from the late 2000s through the 2010s as one of the greatest clubs, and now a veritable club myth—on par with such clubs as Studio 54 and the Paradise Garage.

In terms of the Berlin club scene, it should be understood, however, that Berghain actually developed as part of the second stage of Berlin's post–1989 techno history. The club became the most prominent site on Berlin's *second club mile*, on that same border between Friedrichshain and Kreuzberg, involving such venues as the aforementioned RAW Tempel,

and Jon Pareles, "In Berlin, Still Partying in the Ruins," *The New York Times*, November 21, 2014. https://www.nytimes.com/2014/11/23/travel/in-berlin -still-partying-in-the-ruins.html.

Bar 25, and Maria am Ostbahnhof.[2] During the first stage of post–1989 techno, a variety of clubs were established closer to the center of Berlin (rather than the Friedrichshain/Kreuzberg mile to the southeast). These clubs included E-Werk, a 1990s "cathedral"[3] equivalent to Ostgut and Berghain. A practical playground hall with multiple floors,[4] E-Werk was one of many clubs to emerge in the fluid conditions of the post–1989 moment, when empty urban spaces allowed for the establishment of new clubs and music organizations. Other clubs on this original mile include Wahlfisch and, most importantly, Tresor. Founded in 1991, Tresor would establish close links between Berlin and Detroit techno, which would be inspirational for Modeselektor.

With the rise of the second club mile starting in the 2000s, an increasing global interest in the Berlin scene took place. This interest has looped back to a fascination with post–1989 club culture and the Fall of the Wall. The second club mile gradually developed following the closing of E-Werk in 1997, leading up to the opening of Berghain in 2004 and Tresor's 2007 move to a new address. Tresor's new location was at a power station, a.k.a. Kraftwerk Berlin, here a techno club rather than the famed electronic group. In fact, Ostgut had laid some of the foundations in this area, though it eventually had to be closed in 2003—a similar fate as the first club mile eventually

---

2 For an overview of this history and the two club miles, see Rapp, *Lost and Sound*.
3 See Felix Denk and Sven von Thülen, eds., *Der Klang der Familie: Berlin, Techno and the Fall of the Wall*, trans. Jenna Krumminga (Norderstedt: Books on Demand, 2014), 245.
4 Ibid., 245–64.

succumbed to Berlin's 1990s skyline of cranes and urban reconstruction.

Thus, before going deeper into *Happy Birthday!* as my selected "constructed network," I want to provide the specific context for how Modeselektor came of age in the wake of 1989 and within the mosaic of 1990s club culture. Modeselektor's trajectory intersects with some key histories of Berlin that became foundational to the city's later reputation as a global techno metropolis, which could allow for multiple collabs with international artists such as TTC. Modeselektor alludes to these Berlin moods and industrial club-mile experiences of the 1990s on the duo's early EPs and their first album. On *Hello Mom!* check out the tracks "Ziq Zaq," which provides an IDM atmosphere of rave serenity (leading to the hypnotic "Vote or Die"), and "Kill Bill Vol. 4," which features sounds from a warehouse rave, blissed-out Berlin babble, and a hard trance riff, the Morse-code symphonic arpeggio that soundtracked the 1990s.

Regarding their own 1990s biography, Bronsert and Szary actually grew up directly east of the city in the "Former East" state of Brandenburg, which surrounds Berlin. Brandenburg is one of five "New States" (*neue Bundesländer*) that originally comprised East Germany, or the German Democratic Republic (GDR). The designation of New States was given when the GDR was officially united with West Germany in 1990, which involved the merging of East and West Berlin into a new state and the new capital of what is now called the Berlin Republic. As mentioned, all of Berlin lies within the borders of Brandenburg. The towns in the immediate vicinity of the border, including Brandenburg's capital, Potsdam, are considered part of Berlin's greater metropolitan region.

In fact, much of the Brandenburg-Berlin border runs along the *less famous* sections of the Berlin Wall. As opposed to the iconic symbols of the Wall between East and West Berlin, such as Checkpoint Charlie and the Brandenburg Gate, the border between West Berlin and Brandenburg is located at the capital city's suburban and rural edges. Of course, there wasn't a national border or wall between East Berlin and Brandenburg, and regarding this more fluid border, Szary explains that the duo's roots lie in this area to the east with "the Berlin TV Tower always in sight—but Brandenburg."[5] To be precise, the duo grew up in two neighboring towns: Rüdersdorf (Szary) and Woltersdorf (Bronsert). To distinguish the towns, Szary describes the industrial Rüdersdorf as Brandenburg's "Manchester," since he worked in one of the town's factories, whereas Woltersdorf was a kind of vacation destination or "spa town."[6]

The industries of Rüdersdorf take on significance here: Szary actually worked in the same factory in the 1990s where, prior to 1989, limestone was mined and made into concrete for East Berlin, *including* the concrete for the Berlin Wall. Szary explains: "In Rüdersdorf limestone was mined and virtually all of Berlin was built with it, including the Berlin Wall. It was poured from the concrete. I learned a lot in the mines, where parts of the Wall were cast in the 1960s. It was crazy."[7] In a strange irony, he made good money from this work so that he was able to start

5 Modeselektor, interviewed by Torsten Schmidt, *Red Bull Music Academy*, 2018. http://www.redbullmusicacademy.com/lectures/modeselektor-2018.
6 *We are Modeselektor*, directed by Romi Agel and Holger Wick (Berlin: Monkeytown Records, 2013), DVD.
7 http://www.redbullmusicacademy.com/lectures/modeselektor-2018.

purchasing musical equipment—for what would eventually become an international jet-set career on the festival circuit.

Both Bronsert and Szary were, however, quite young when the Wall fell, so they came of age essentially in the transitional post-1989 era. Though the Fall of the Wall still fundamentally shaped their lives, they were too young to realize it. In a post-Wall irony, these childhood memories have now been shared on international online networks, such as in interviews with the Red Bull Music Academy. Bronsert's experience of the Fall drives home the point. For him, the Fall of the Wall simply revolved around one thing: a piano lesson that he hated. After all, he was only eleven years old, and during the week of November 9, 1989, he recalls being at the local church for his usual piano lesson. However, his teacher immediately left when it became clear that the borders were to be opened. His teacher simply disappeared. So after a while, little Bronsert went home alone and confused. Finally, he discovered the news about the Wall from his parents. Realizing that his teacher would not return, he reflected: "So I was just happy that I didn't need to go to the piano lessons anymore. So I was just, ok, cool, the Wall is down, and I am free now. . . . Thank you, Mr. Gorbachev."[8]

Similarly, Szary discusses how he (then aged fourteen) was in bed when the news of the Wall was heard by his family. His mother came in to tell him, and the first question that he asked was the following, of world-historical importance for any teenager: "Should I go to school tomorrow?"[9] She said yes,

8 http://www.redbullmusicacademy.com/lectures/modeselektor-2010.
9 *We are Modeselektor.*

and he went to school, but a good portion of the class was missing. That was his simple story.

These examples indicate the enormous variety of experiences of the Fall of the Wall, depending on age, place, and politics. They go far beyond the standard versions that CNN documentaries and TV features often report, with immediate celebrations in the center of Berlin. In fact, the Fall of the Wall is hardly mentioned in the duo's own official documentary released in 2013, *We are Modeselektor*. Rather, Szary describes their childhood as relatively idyllic: "Basically, you spent a lot of time out in nature: until techno arrived."[10] As with many techno enthusiasts, the access to new resources during the early 1990s—record stores and clubs—would become most important in these post-unification years. In other words, it was the later consequences of the Fall of the Wall that would serve as the key experiences for Bronsert and Szary.

Certainly, to tell the story of Berlin's techno transformation in the 1990s would take multiple books. Much research on this era has been published in recent years. For Modeselektor, what is key to relate here is the major shifts that took place across that decade, as partly recounted in the documentary *We Call it Techno: A Documentary about Germany's Early Techno Scene and Culture* and in the oral history, *Der Klang der Familie: Berlin, Techno, and the Fall of the Wall*, edited by Felix Denk and Sven von Thülen. Both accounts tell the history from a German perspective, however, which downplays some of the international currents already manifested at this time. This includes the links to Afro-Caribbean sound systems and

---

10 Ibid.

African-American club cultures, as well as the festival cultures in Ibiza and Goa—not to mention larger rave currents in Europe.

In the early 1990s, a gradual transformation and founding of institutions occurred that became key to Berlin club culture. For techno in Germany, the summer of 1991 is traditionally presented as a symbolic moment. At this time, local scenes from various cities, most prominently Frankfurt and Berlin, first encountered each other at the Love Parade. This was the third annual techno parade of its kind, taking place in the heart of West Berlin—the same parade that I was hearing about as a high school exchange student in 1995. The Love Parade would grow so large that, starting in 1996, it had to be moved to the main thoroughfare in Berlin's equivalent of Central Park, the Tiergarten, a major park that leads up to the Brandenburg Gate.

Following the unification, Szary and Bronsert slowly became integrated into a variety of these techno institutions in Berlin. They experienced much of the initial developments and clubs separately, though their musical paths eventually became firmly intertwined by the mid-1990s. One key inspiration for the duo was the aforementioned Tresor, the club originally located on Leipzigerstrasse in the former "no-man's-land" of the Berlin Wall. This location was near Potsdamer Platz, the urban center of prewar Berlin, which was an empty shell throughout the Cold War. Bronsert, starting at the young age of fourteen, would go each Wednesday to a club night called Headquarters, where he saw artists such as Detroit's Underground Resistance or Berlin-DJ Tanith. However, this was not the only important club experience: parties in Rauen and Frankfurt an der Oder, on the German/Polish border, are also mentioned, reflecting their youth spent on the periphery of East Berlin.[11]

In the spirit of life on the outskirts, radio was also key, as it was for many East German youth. Initially, the most important show on a local Berlin station was by radio-DJ Monika Dietl, who featured house and techno music. After the peak of Dietl's era, the show Dancehall (later called Rave Satellite) became legendary. This show was important especially for the regional East German scenes, as it was broadcast beyond Berlin.[12] The host of the show, Marusha, was later dubbed the "Rave Queen" of the 1990s, following her connection with Low Spirit, the most important Berlin label of the 1990s in terms of commercial success, about which more later. Marusha was eventually criticized, often in implicitly sexist terms, as responsible for the sellout of rave during the 1990s—made symbolic with her 1994 happy-hardcore cover of "Somewhere Over the Rainbow."[13] However, her influence in radio during the 1990s, and in DJing a version of rave and "arena techno" with high-energy stage presence, would be an important and sometimes unacknowledged legacy in Berlin.

Finally, beyond clubs and radio, *records* must be mentioned as formative interests in the early 1990s. The iconic Berlin record store Hard Wax, located in Kreuzberg, was crucial. Hard Wax was founded in 1989 by Mark Ernestus, a seminal figure who would also become a member of the equally iconic

---

11 Ibid.

12 Denk and von Thülen, *Der Klang der Familie*, 92–8.

13 Ibid., 265–70. This section exemplifies the logic of making this track representative of the commercial sellout of rave, even though many other artists and tracks could have been cited.

dub-techno duo Basic Channel, as well as a founder of a label by the same name.[14] Hard Wax established new distribution networks, partly through connections to the NYC disco scene.[15] To this day, the store has supplied the vinyl for many DJs from Berlin and beyond.

Bronsert highlights 1993 as the year when he first visited the store. He had already become obsessed with both Detroit and European techno, naming examples such as the Frankfurt hardcore icon Marc Acardipane, a.k.a. the Mover, and Detroit's Afrofuturist pioneers Underground Resistance.[16] By the time he first visited Hard Wax in 1993, however, he wanted to ask about a new British genre called jungle. Here, he came in contact with the English head of mail-order at the store, a guy called James who hardly spoke German, as well as DJ Pete, a.k.a. Substance. Very appropriately, Bronsert's first record purchased at Hard Wax was Aphex Twin—a foreshadowing of the British influences for Modeselektor. By the late 1990s, Bronsert himself was working at Hard Wax, and numerous contacts would result from this position.

But here, it's time for me to decenter some of this exclusively underground focus—and remind the reader of the parallels in pop and underground. These are also just some of the most legendary reference points for Berlin techno: hardcore, dub techno, Detroit techno, and jungle. When perusing interviews about the 1990s, sometimes you get the impression that everyone was only listening to Basic Channel and

14 Derek Walmsley. "Mark Ernestus: The Gene Genie," *The Wire*, February 2010: 34–8.
15 Denk and von Thülen, *Der Klang der Familie*, 87–8.
16 https://www.redbullmusicacademy.com/lectures/modeselektor-2010.

Underground Resistance. It needs to be mentioned, however, as with many techno fans and artists, that such inspirations often proceeded in steps across childhood and teenage years. For example, Bronsert, before this Hard Wax era, is kind enough to admit that as a youth, he was the proud owner of a record from Technotronic, the Belgian dance-act responsible for such legendary hits as 1989's "Pump up the Jam"—a key record for the rap-techno genre known as Eurodance.[17] Pop techno has always existed in parallel with the worlds of minimal and industrial techno. We'll explore these stylistic transformations and the crossovers between pop and underground later.

To return to local Brandenburg history: Bronsert and Szary knew each other already in elementary school, though their musical interests only gradually intertwined. Szary dropped out of school and focused on work in the factory. From the money he earned, he gradually was able to acquire equipment. As the older member of the duo, Szary was also the first to be inspired to organize a local party series in Rüdersdorf, his little "Manchester." While working at the factory, he saw some empty industrial buildings that he could use for a rave party. His party series was quite successful and became associated with its industrial surroundings, the *Seilscheibenpfeiler* (look up the meaning, if you dare). The multiple floors at the venues would reflect Modeselektor's interests in various genres: a gabber floor, a hardcore floor, a techno floor, and so on.

Bronsert, three years younger, was initially more focused on club-going than promotion. As a raver kid, he experienced those parties where Szary played the first live-PAs with the equipment he had collected. In these live sets, Szary also performed rave tunes under the name Fundamental Knowledge, the vast majority of which were unreleased. He would make a brief attempt at a label with one release in 1994, a label called *Seilscheibenpfeiler Schallplatten*. The global experience of techno parties in postindustrial sites was thus reflected in these Brandenburg outskirts to Berlin. From observing these local and regional developments, Bronsert would gradually become more devoted to DJing and production while practicing at home. By 1996, the duo was regularly interacting and exploring musical possibilities—and Bronsert eventually made the fateful move to Berlin in 1998. That same year, Szary became his neighbor. The periphery had moved to the center.

The move to Berlin also proved crucial, as the 2000s decade began, and the road to *Hello Mom!* and *Happy Birthday!* took shape. With new networks, the duo's career developed. This included links to their future label manager Marit Posch and the design/VJ collective Pfadfinderei. Following the Seilscheibenpfeiler and Rüdersdorf parties, a new era of weekly Berlin parties called Labstyle began, with visuals by Pfadfinderei. Labstyle continued the tradition of multiple stages for techno, hardcore, and jungle. Torsten Pröfrock of Hard Wax appropriately describes the duo's sets as follows: "They could play Bonzai Rave Techno and then abruptly switch over to Otto von Schirach types of noise, hip-hop or whatever."[18] These parties were also reported on by Berlin's

---

18 *We are Modeselektor.*

major techno magazine at the time, *De:Bug*.[19] Bronsert's and Szary's eclectic style as DJs and performers proved foundational, and their talents as producers continued to evolve through the extensive use of a studio at a youth center for musicians where they worked.[20] Such experiences at this studio reflect the fluid status of semi-professionalization and transitional work conditions for many Berlin artists.

But crucially, these music activities eventually led to the contact with BPitch Control, a key label headed by DJ/producer Ellen Allien. The contact came from Pfadfinderei, which was doing the design work for BPitch Control.[21] Allien, DJing in Berlin across the 1990s, had already become a representative Berlin star, cemented by such albums as *Stadtkind* (2001) and *Berlinette* (2003).[22] In fact, Modeselektor set up their professional recording studio in the same building as BPitch Control, practically confirming the BPitch era in literal architectural terms. Allien played a central role in establishing the duo as "Berlin artists." Their fame as live artists gradually evolved with these contacts, regularly performing with Allien at the BPitch events.

Considering this trajectory from the Eastern periphery to the Berlin scene, I want to return briefly to the fundamental idea of *networks* as we approach *Happy Birthday!* Namely, it is important to consider the networks of "Former East" DJs

---

19 See Sven von Thülen, "Willkommen in der Rappelkiste: Pfadfinderei, Visualtäter, Codec und Labstyle," *De:Bug*, 45, March 2001, 22.
20 In a blend of these transitional experiences to Berlin, the center was again located more on the outskirts of Berlin, in the southeast district of Treptow-Köpenick.
21 *We are Modeselektor.*
22 https://pitchfork.com/reviews/albums/411-berlinette/.

and promoters involved in the transformation of rave culture. Modeselektor is related to this history in some important ways. During the 1990s, a significant number of artists now considered part of the "Berlin sound" and scene were coming of age in various towns in the Former East. They include none other than Sascha Ring, a.k.a. Apparat, Marcel Dettmann, one of the key DJ residents of Berghain, René Pawlowitz, a.k.a. Shed, and Paul Kalkbrenner, who later starred in the techno film *Berlin Calling*. At the experimental edge, it also includes the Raster-Noton label in Chemnitz (a.k.a. Karl Marx Stadt). Raster-Noton artists include Carsten Nicolai and Frank Bretschneider, who have both been based in Berlin for many years.[23]

I point out these connections just to mark one important facet in the Berlin networks, from local to international. Links to the Former East were also present at Hard Wax, the definition of the record store as *network*. The links are exemplified here by Marcel Dettmann replacing Bronsert after he canceled his Monday shift due to the grueling tour schedule. Dettmann would focus on music distribution for Hard Wax, with Dettmann and Pawlowitz sharing responsibilities for the techno selections. But again, this Former East component is just one aspect of the store's history, as the staff have links across Europe, the UK, and beyond—and distribution networks from Tokyo to London. As Bronsert says, "It's a family thing; it's a pretty weird family thing going on."[24]

---

23 For an account of the Chemnitz history of Raster-Noton, see Nye, "Minimal Understandings" and Ben Borthwick, "Raster-Noton: The Perfect Strom," *The Wire*, December 2003: 40–7.

24 https://www.redbullmusicacademy.com/lectures/modeselektor-2010.

From Hard Wax to BPitch, Modeselektor was thus set for a rising career across the 2000s. The duo's approach certainly evolved by the time of the release of *Happy Birthday!* With the signing to BPitch, their role as producers of new music went into high gear. They released four EPs on BPitch Control between 2002 and 2004, leading up to the major success of *Hello Mom!* in 2005. As will be seen in the upcoming review of the opening four tracks on *Happy Birthday*, the duo's abilities to resonate with audiences far beyond Berlin continued to evolve. This album would point to a new stage in Modeselektor's career, involving a simple party greeting: Happy Birthday!

2 Title Track
Birthday Noise

The first track—and the title track—provides the appropriately cheeky beginning to Modeselektor's humor of the mid-2000s and their evolving production styles. It is a simple tune that recalls the childlike antics of the 1990s genre of pop-hardcore—rave riffs and DIY melodies. The melody on the first track also evokes the sly positivity of rave—a party with a wink. Minimal in its initial glitches, the track introduces us to styles not usually associated with 2000s Berlin. However, the mood of Modeselektor's "Happy Birthday," rather than just retro-rave, has a different form of humor. Namely, it is an intro to an album with more than an hour of musical delights. As an intro, it feels like one is entering a rave hall of mirrors: with a circus-like maze as you might get lost after downing the next pint or pill—but with a lightness that practically recalls polka.

Indeed, it begins with the sounds of an accordion glitch, like an 8-bit polka hiccup. With the gradual introduction of new sounds, the dance rhythm even recalls dub reggae and polka, if such a dance style could exist—a kind of East European spin on dubstep. This is retro not as a pop fad. It is retro as a nineteenth-century carnival—a circus clown or a jack-in-the-box, who is inviting you into the rave environment. It subtly reminds us of the fact that, with

Modeselektor, we are entering the "Former East," as the mood recalls artists like Gogol Bordello. And again, with its polka-like beats and accordion sounds, it provides a folksy sing-along in its simplicity. In short, it reminds us that before electronic music, there were mechanical instruments and wind-up toys, which is evident in the title of both the first track and the 2007 album.

Here, as plain as this reminder might sound, it needs to be mentioned with reference to the title: "Happy Birthday!" is, while a celebratory greeting, also about memories of childhood and juvenile fun. Birthdays are in fact a kind of apprenticeship in partying. They are the first parties most of us went to, or remember, as children. There is something educational in that dawn of entertainment, to which practically anyone can relate. The experience of birthday parties can be the start of silliness, of excitement, of rivalries, of sugar highs, and other fun adventures.

The traditions of presents and cake & ice-cream have also become common, to the point where some of these traditions have become transatlantic or even global. American birthdays have become technology marvels to the tune of Disney and Mattel, while in Germany, precedents have been set from classic toy designers to Haribo's Gummy Bears. Germans sometimes play with these American influences, which involve the pop-neon versions of birthday parties. In fact, this play takes the form of the pop brevity of English as a language. Modeselektor's title *Happy Birthday!* already calls up an international party in Berlin. Instead of saying the drawn-out German form of happy birthday, "*herzlichen Glückwunsch zum Geburtstag,*" Germans often have fun with American influences by wishing "Happy Birthday!"—or in its playfully accented written form: "Häppie Börsday."

Modeselektor's use of English indicates here an obvious fact about post–1989 techno culture, though it is often forgotten since it is such a part of everyday life: unlike Kraftwerk's famous 1970s foregrounding of German lyrics and identity, or Rammstein's heavy metal German, post–1989 German techno culture relies heavily on international English, or more specifically EU-English, in its networks. Let me invite us then to take the English language in German electronica just as seriously as the German lyrics of Kraftwerk (or Rammstein).

By 2007, Modeselektor was already moving cleverly between multiple cultural registers: from Berlin to (East) German, British, Afro-Caribbean, European, and international or global contexts. Within these registers, the figure of the East, as East German and East European, not to mention Berlin as a global brand, will be important. Part of Modeselektor's, and later Moderat's, success has been its ability to move between these multiple registers of cultural and musical reference, while being accessible to diverse audiences. At one moment, Modeselektor can be strikingly European in reference, and at other times, its references seem to closely resemble British or other international acts—to the point where you might forget that the title of *Happy Birthday!* could have any significance at all. It is so internationally nonchalant.

Still, Modeselektor's success in America has arguably been limited in a variety of ways due to the duo's playful engagement with German techno histories and its distinct Europeanness, one that is intertwined with Anglophone popular culture in Europe in ways that do not necessarily register for Americans.

But here, let us also address the album's title beyond the title track. "Happy birthday!" as greeting also takes the form of that excruciating song, that damn simple melody to which children across the world are now introduced: "Happy birthday to you!" This tune has itself become streamlined as an international product. It is sung in various forms of English, and it has even been translated into other languages, including German: "Zum Geburtstag viel Glück . . ." Fortunately, the actual melody of "Happy Birthday to You" is not heard. In traditional terms, the wishing of happy birthday is about family and community experiences.

Who wishes you happy birthday? Friends and family—and now Facebook. But the question of techno generations is also implied in this title. In truth, *Happy Birthday!* intersected with a particular biographical occasion for both Szary and Bronsert: they both became fathers that year. *Happy Birthday!* thus is both a nonchalant title—but also part of a bigger celebration. It was named on account of the coincidence of parenthood. So, in essence, *Happy Birthday!* is a shout-out to the kids. And rather than the excruciating photos of celebrity children, it is here simply the rave fathers wishing the kids "Happy birthday"—while nodding to the traditions of rave juvenilia. Here, the title is an adult flip on Bronsert's and Szary's first album as "Gold Star" youthful achievement: *Hello Mom!*

As productions, artworks are often compared with children. Here, the work of art linked up with having children. That biographical link bears some implications for electronic music. Techno culture tends to avoid discussions about personal life experiences. Electronic music is replete with cyborgs images, from Kraftwerk to Daft Punk. Yet with *Happy Birthday!* we have another example of "human after all." The announcement of parenthood is a reminder that DJs and techno producers also have basic responsibilities: relationships, chores, and sometimes, parenthood.

Happy Birthday! was also a reminder, in 2007, that the Rave Generation had aged. Well, the *Second Rave Generation* had aged. After all, Bronsert and Szary were not the original DJs at the clubs in post-1989 Berlin. They were *the kids* partying to the DJs. Bronsert was only thirteen during his first visit to the clubs; he had repeated opportunities to sneak in through connections with friends. Thus, the kids from the 1990s techno era are gradually having their own kids. The cover of *Happy Birthday!* introduces this experience of parenthood in 2007: Bronsert's head is photoshopped onto a mother's body, and Szary appears as the whining baby. In the spirit of rave, here is the juvenile humor of dudes satirically representing family life and fatherhood.

The duo's confused faces recall the dry humor from one of Modeselektor's key inspirations: Aphex Twin. Indeed, Richard D. James's immortal rave smile echoes Jack Nicholson's psychotic grin on *The Shining* and elsewhere. Aphex Twin's countenance challenged such conventions of authority, role models, and stardom. Extending this, Modeselektor plays with family life and parenthood as everyday life—arrested development in the rave age. Moreover, family life is not celebrated as natural and traditional. Rather than an eternally godly institution, the techno duo appears on the cover as a blundering rave Madonna and child. Whether this imagery still intersects with dude humor and traditional masculinity is another matter.

International humor is present as well—or rather, you could say that the cover of *Happy Birthday!* is an international example of hipster humor. The parodies on the album artwork continue with the silly masculinity of raver dudes on the inner covers. A rave tryptic presents the following images: the Garden of Eden with the forbidden fruit; rave angels in heaven; and hip-hop hellfire with full gangster swag. To compare these poses, this satirical style recalls a new, international cartoon generation, educated on shows from *The Simpsons* to *South Park*—and *Monty Python.* In sum, the cover and the images inaugurate multiple themes on the album: techno and everyday life; the fancy and prosaic; and humor and excess.

In this connection, I'll begin tracing the international music collabs and associations by comparing Modeselektor's opening track to another duo. This duo is now often forgotten in the selective memories focusing on cultural cachet. I am thinking of the humor of the British husband-and-wife duo of Lee Newman and Michael Wells, a.k.a. Technohead. The duo was one of the rave acts that developed a dual soundtrack during the 1990s: from dance-pop to rave excess. While most famous for 1995s "I Wanna be a Hippy," Newman and Wells produced a practical cottage industry of monikers: from Church of Extacy to John + Julie. Newman and Wells even had a 1996 tune and music video as Technohead that was called, "Happy Birthday."[1] Rave humor is certainly present on that music video: the impatient pounding of forks; spoiled cake fights; and various other antics.

---

1 https://www.discogs.com/Technohead-Happy-Birthday/master/80860. Certainly, if one wants to go further back in time to the post-punk era, the Birthday Party also practically heralded a new dissonant take on birthdays.

Technohead's "Happy Birthday" has a retro 8-bit vibe with a simple sing-along melody and choo-choo train sounds; one of many 12"s lost in the flood of 1990s music releases—although to be sure, the style and humor of Modeselektor takes things in a different direction in 2007. The comparison with Technohead is just a loose and fun angle to consider.

Indeed, already with *the second track* on the album, we are presented with the complexity and contrast of Modeselektor's music. A shift in mood takes place. We begin to get a hint of why Modeselektor have been able to move between both the anonymity of techno and the emotional expressions of pop and ambient. The opening cheekiness of the title track moves into the more reflective "Godspeed." That shift is foreshadowed in the title track with its hall-of-mirrors invitation—a more subtle version of humor. "Godspeed" begins with a simple ping-pong theme, but gradually, a windswept drone returns—again and again—with a swooping cadence that sounds like you're being swallowed up. As this drone returns with each cadence, variations of glitch-hop breakbeats are introduced—variation upon variation, teasing by the end at IDM or glitchcore. Toward the end, the calm and fading echoes of religious chants hint at why the track might be called "Godspeed." The wind gives an atmospheric setting to the moods that will follow.

With that shift in mood, we begin to see the intertwining of party and reflective moods. And these moods will twist through the album like a double helix, even as it plays with rave fireworks and a collage of genres. Such reflective melancholy is revisited again and again on tracks from "Em Ocean" to "Edgar" to "B.M.I."

To address those many and multiple moods, we need to move into some of the finer details of genres in electronic music. The mix of "Happy Birthday" and "Godspeed" already provides an intriguing audio contrast. We will gradually begin to grasp those excesses of emotion that occurred across the 1990s, while continuing to explore the regional and transnational networks of *Happy Birthday!* The third track already boldly explores some of these links with a move to hip-hop. It also features the first of many surprising collabs. As a reminder, the key themes in Part I are the Berlin scene and Modeselektor's multiple collaborations—both regional and international. In this spirit, the particular collab on track 3 is with a French hip-hop group called TTC.

3 The 200000 Decade
Russian Crunk, Or Genre Fun

It's revenge, it's punishment, it's techno in the cathedral
It's the Gothic rave party, take out your glowsticks,
it's the black metal
It's revenge, it's punishment, it's techno in the cathedral
TTC, with Modeselektor, "2000007."
(GOOGLE TRANSLATION)

Following these 1990s foundations, what happened in Berlin during the 2000s? And how did Modeselektor's music transform in this era, leading up to the releases of *Hello Mom!* and *Happy Birthday!*? Moreover, how might these transformations link up with the third track on the album?

Well, one way to answer this is to say that, following the 1990s pop excesses of the Love Parade and Low Spirit, Berlin experienced a variety of digital refinements—from the continuing influence of glitch, to glitch-hop, to microhouse, and more.[1] Much of this was locally filtered through the record shelves at Hard Wax. Reflected in the sound design of dance productions, the Berlin scene was also gradually

---

1 See Philip Sherburne, "Digital Discipline: Minimalism in House and Techno," in *Audio Culture: Readings in Modern Music*, ed. Christoph Cox and Daniel Warner (New York: Continuum, 2004), 319–26.

professionalized in a variety of ways. A tech industry, with major firms such as Native Instruments and Ableton, now developed in parallel with Berlin dance music. Techno culture in the 2000s did indeed go digital in a number of respects, despite the repeated celebrations of Berlin vinyl culture and analog hardware, whether at Hard Wax or at club performances.[2] We'll explore these examples of glitch and noise on Modeselektor's early LPs in Part II—suffice to say, Modeselektor was by the time of *Happy Birthday!* well aware of this context.

Modeselektor's track with the French hip-hop group TTC, "2000007"—the album's third track—appropriately plays with digital data as glitch and represents the album's year of release, spelling it out in the lyrics: "2.0.0.0.0.0.7." Marking that year, it should be mentioned that the vinyl version of *Happy Birthday!* actually has "2000007" as the first track on the album (record 1, A-side). Replacing "Happy Birthday" as opener, this choice is arguably appropriate given Modeselektor's previous collab with TTC on *Hello Mom!* The group was originally featured on "Dancing Box," the debut album's opening track. "Dancing Box" begins with some cool French-accented mic checks, in preparation for the onslaught of glitch-hop: "Yo! . . . Tell me . . . One, two . . ."—as compared to "2000007" with "Check yo, TTC, Modeselektor . . . 2.0.0.0.0.0.7." The work with this French hip-hop group thus remained prominent, though Modeselektor decided to mix the tracks up to tell a new story on *Happy Birthday!*

<hr>

2 *RA Exchange*, ep. 176. "Berlin Vinyl Culture," November 29, 2013. https://www.residentadvisor.net/podcast-episode.aspx?exchange=176.

As a challenge to genre limits, the impressive variety of collabs has been one of Modeselektor's signature practices across their career. Certainly, the collab tradition reveals the Berlin duo's distinctive links with hip-hop culture. For *Happy Birthday!*, French hip-hop is just one example. The rap references are reinforced by "Dark Side of the Sun" with Berlin group Puppetmastaz. Here, the pop playfulness of glitch-hop represents style in the digital age. "Dark Side of the Sun" proved to be such a banger that it received its own 12″ release that year, with Paul Kalkbrenner and Siriusmo remixing "2000007" in 2009.

In truth, these tracks most closely represent Modeselektor's witty invention of the genre "Russian crunk," among other inventions. It has been no secret that Modeselektor has aimed to challenge genre definitions. Most prominently in an interview around the time of *Happy Birthday!* (and which has spread across the internet, even to the duo's Wikipedia page), Szary answered the question about genre as follows: "Happy metal, hard rap, country ambient, Russian crunk. We don't like it if people tag us as being of a certain style, or school, or scene or whatever."[3] This witty approach aims to play the style game rather than the genre game, offering an updated twist to rave excess—as well as tapping into the early history of rave culture before such clear genre definitions.

Still, Modeselektor can't break totally free from genre associations. Even Russian crunk, for example, hints at the East

---

3   *Northernlights: Manchester Clublistings*, "Modeselektor Interview," November 7, 2007. https://web.archive.org/web/20080429143548/http://northernights.co.uk/listings.php?id=662.

Berlin, and more generally East European, hip-hop heritage, while reflecting the global spread of hip-hop culture. The many collabs do, however, help the duo break free from a strictly Berlin or East German context. During their career, Modeselektor's (and Moderat's) collaborations with MCs and rap artists alone have crossed from Los Angeles to Tallinn: TTC, Sasha Perera, Paul St. Hilaire, Puppetmastaz, Busdriver, Antipop Consortium, Seeed, Flohio, and Tommy Cash.[4] As Modeselektor evolved over the 2000s, their performance style and their refusal at genre references certainly stood out from minimal techno.

At the same time, Modeselektor was primarily linked to the techno scene in terms of club venues, the festival circuit, and their own label/producer networks. Their work with hip-hop artists and dub MCs is lodged within a transnational representation of styles that is distinct from the German hip-hop scenes primarily expressive of minority experiences and critique of German society, which can include major rap stars. The use of French and English-language hip-hop, including with Berlin-based groups like Puppetmastaz, keeps Modeselektor linked to an international circuit that places them as part of global Berlin.

In this focus on the international collabs, the main issue is one that continues to run through the techno scene: the relative scarcity of collaborations with local hip-hop artists or hip-hop scenes in Germany. In this respect, transnational

---

4 For an analysis of Tommy Cash, see Matthias Pasdzierny, "'Produced by Some Chemical Waste and Cum': TOMM¥ €A$H and His Concept of Signifying 'Post-Sovietness.'" *Res Music* 10 (2018): 29–40.

hip-hop resembles Berlin techno's over-identification with Detroit.[5] Still, Modeselektor's practice of international collabs, especially after the Fall of the Wall, is an understandable trajectory. The shock for many Americans, in particular, could be to realize that Modeselektor's roots are even in the Former East. In this sense, their achievement has been to forge a mix of global and local, following a youth in provincial Brandenburg. This achievement continues a practice described by Tony Mitchell as hip-hop "syncretism," or the combination of local influences and African-American hip-hop—this time in the direction of electronic music.[6]

Here it is crucial, especially for Americans, to update cultural associations of popular German and electronic music. Twenty-first-century associations of Berlin culture have already been reconfigured within the global currents of clubs and festivals. With the constructed networks of *Happy Birthday!* and other releases, listening to Modeselektor (and Moderat) can draw one into new scenes and generations of electronic artists, which hopefully moves beyond standard representations of Germanness. Modeselektor explores here a form of international humor with a mix of techno and hip-hop.

Given their celebration of musical styles of the Black Atlantic and transnational techno, while playing with identity in names like Russian crunk, I'll admit here that I practically

---

5 Reynolds, *Energy Flash*, 503. See also Melanie Schiller's account of German identity and techno in *Soundtracking Germany: Popular Music and National Identity* (London: Rowman & Littlefield, 2018), 181–220.
6 Tony Mitchell, "Introduction—Another Root: Hip-hop Outside of the USA," in *Global Noise: Rap and Hip-hop Outside the USA*, ed. Tony Mitchell (Middletown: Wesleyan University Press, 2001), 1–12.

view Modeselektor, especially for the American reception of East German artists, as the antipodes to Rammstein. To be sure, Bronsert and Szary sometimes play with East German origins, such as the technological origins of their name—but still, certainly never on the Teutonic level of Rammstein. Indeed, it is time to reveal the origin of the name "Modeselektor": their name actually derives from a control called the "mode selector" on the Roland RE-201: Space Echo—a key piece of equipment in their studio.[7] For example, on the 2019 compilation *10 Years of Monkeytown*, the duo revisited their love for the tape-echo unit on "My Friend the 201," a direct reference to the Space Echo. "My Friend the 201" is itself an epic track that could practically be called cosmic techno in the tradition of Krautrock.

But let's explain the name "Modeselektor" a bit further. The "mode selector" control was the inspiration for the name, and the duo playfully Germanized it by making it one word and adding the K: Modeselektor. The name thus appeared to have a cheekily German and technical origin. And yet, the twist is that, while admitting their German identity, the use of *selector* proves to have a double origin. Namely, it draws up obvious associations with the Jamaican term for DJ: the selector. This name is key because it celebrates the role of the disc jockey as the *selector of records*.

Thus, at the opposite of German excess, Modeselektor provides a shout-out to the Black Atlantic histories of Jamaican sound-system culture in the context of Berlin. At the same time, the reference to selector clearly shows the British heritage of rave—as the Afro-Caribbean heritages of London rave culture

---

7 http://www.roland.co.uk/blog/the-roland-re-201-space-echo-story/.

would likewise give toasts to the "selector" in the tradition of dub sound systems. In a sense, the name Modeselektor is thus an appropriate expression of Bronsert's and Szary's dual roles as producers and DJs. As "selectors" of original and surprising styles, Modeselektor could playfully challenge Berlin-techno expectations.

The surprise of Modeselektor's style in the 2000s, and in the context of minimal techno culture, can be recounted on *Speaking in Code*, an American documentary released in 2009. Directed by Amy Grill, the film focuses a good deal on German electronic music. A hybrid mix of music documentary and personal travel narrative, Grill's film explores German and American techno in a transatlantic story about the 2000s, emphasizing club-festival links between the United States, Germany, and Spain. German techno artists are featured throughout: the Wighnomy Brothers, Robert Henke, a.k.a. Monolake, Wolfgang Voigt, Ellen Allien—as well as Modeselektor.

This 2009 context captures an American longing for Radio Free Europe in the fearful mood of post–9/11 America. In the United States during the 2000s, club culture suffered significantly,[8] and many North American artists, from Magda to Richie Hawtin to Adam X, moved to Berlin—a shift with lasting consequences for American dance culture. DJ/promoter David Day, a key narrator in the film and also Grill's partner at the time, expresses such feelings of 2000s national rejection from the struggling position of Boston's club scene: "Electronic music

---

8 See tobias c. van veen's review of *Speaking in Code* in *Dancecult: Journal of Electronic Dance Music Culture* 2, no. 1 (2011): 111–14.

seems totally foreign; totally un-American." He also engages in German-centric hyperbole, emerging from a feeling of crisis in American dance culture: "When you think of Germany as the source of most of the world's electronic music, you're pretty much right on." *Speaking in Code* thus captures a variety of sentiments at a moment prior to the EDM boom in the United States, which will cause its own set of problems for American club culture.

Modeselektor is also presented as a key representative of this new generation of German artists. It is clear from the selection of artists that Day and Grill are particularly interested in a new generation of electronic artists associated with minimalist refinement—an underground analog to the hi-tech industry. Berlin's focus on minimal techno, tech house, and microhouse during the 2000s was appropriate here.

However, the documentary captures Modeselektor's playful role as an exception in its parodies of genres and professional attitudes. In one scene at their studio, Bronsert and Szary play with the current styles of Berlin. Bronsert explains to Day: "Right now we want to show you the *typical Berlin minimal music* [ironic tone]. It's like this . . . . No, no, no, it's like this!" He starts to mix some beats that are quite industrial and intense. Bronsert then says, "That's the music which Ricardo Villalobos and Richie Hawtin are playing." Villalobos and Hawtin are two DJ-producers who were key representatives for 2000s minimal music and Berlin's international status. *But then*, defying this statement, Modeselektor speeds up the beat and adds some freaky-303 acid lines. Day is quite confused, and he remarks: "That doesn't sound very minimal to me," and Bronsert concludes: "No, that's the new style . . . called maximal."

The reference to maximalism at this moment has a couple of connotations. On the one hand, minimal represents serious club culture and design, with maximal being a kind of satirical punk attitude. It enjoys humor and refuses claims to serious art. But this also is not so simple. Modeselektor still show a reverence for the roots of minimal techno, in particular the traditions of Detroit techno. Rather, maximal just means a willingness to play with styles, implying a maximal number of references with a love for electronic music. Maximal represents the "Russian crunk" attitude about genre from the year "2000007." This maximal playfulness, as mentioned, is driven home by the loose narrative in the album structure of *Happy Birthday!*

With the idea of track listings as narrative in mind, I should mention the following: so far, I've been exploring the album in the logical order of the track listing—having methodically addressed the first three tracks. However, with the fourth track, a particular collab will be addressed without further ado, and one that immediately moves far beyond the album's own horizons. Indeed, it is time to address the origins of the most sustained collaboration for Modeselektor, namely as the supergroup Moderat. This collaboration will drive home the full force of Modeselektor's links to the international networks of electronic music, and their later representation of the Berlin scene. At the same time, this collab will begin an intricate journey—through festival culture, rave histories, sound systems, and transatlantic histories of Berlin.

Here I will introduce a final twist to Bronsert's history with Hard Wax. It is as follows: in interviews, Bronsert has uncovered some of the hidden hip-hop history of this iconic institution of electronic music. In terms of hip-hop, Bronsert claims that the secret hip-hop fandom at Hard Wax was an inspiration for him: "Everyone working in the store was so much into Neptunes and Timbaland productions."[9] This crossover between electronic music and rap is captured on Modeselektor's track "The Rapanthem" on *Hello Mom!*, a perfect mix of rap and ambient-trance. Thus, the hip-hop links of Modeselektor have stronger Berlin-techno roots than might be imagined. Yet, it was Modeselektor that challenged the distinctions of these worlds in a variety of ways—by choosing to also bring the private fandom of hip-hop, along with a variety of genres, especially British electronica, into the public arena. We'll see how that unfolded in the next chapter.

9 Modeselektor, interview with Mark Smith, *RA Exchange*, ep. 459. Podcast audio. May 23, 2019. https://ra.co/exchange/459.

4 Moderat Beginnings

The supergroup known as Moderat practically requires its own book. A longtime project with Sascha Ring, a.k.a. *Apparat*, as mentioned in the Introduction, this collab meant the group name took the form of a techno portmanteau: Modeselektor + Apparat = Moderat. These playful name games have even left some fans confused as to who is who. I have had a number of conversations with American fans who are still trying to figure out the differences between the groups. Despite the confusion, this trio went on quickly to become the most famous electronic supergroup from Berlin, achieving an extensive American reception with three albums: *Moderat, II,* and *III.* To be sure, this success was built partly on the separate followings already established by Modeselektor and Apparat.

The generational experiences of the Former East come into play here again. Sascha Ring has also been based in Berlin since 1998, although he is originally from the town of Quedlinburg. Born in 1978, the same year as Bronsert, Ring was likewise devoted to electronic music despite the provincial surroundings. To be sure, Quedlinburg lies significantly further away from Berlin than Woltersdorf or Rüdersdorf, as it is located southwest of Magdeburg in the state of Saxony-Anhalt. Across the 1990s, Ring's interests crossed the spectrum of electronic music—from hardcore rave to experimental music.

Like Modeselektor, Ring would also become fascinated with Radiohead (we will explore Modeselektor's collaboration with Thom Yorke in the next chapter). Ring's interest started late, however, as he was resistant to exploring the most popular stars of the 1990s. Radiohead finally captured his fascination with the album *Hail to the Thief* in 2003.[1] This interest is not so surprising, however, because Ring was already following British electronica from Autechre to Boards of Canada.[2] The influence of experimental groups as represented by Sheffield label Warp Records can be seen in Apparat's initial releases.

Following the move to Berlin, Ring quickly integrated into the new network of labels. He became co-manager for a period of the influential label Shitkatapult, headed by Marco Haas, a.k.a. T-Raumschmiere, with Apparat releasing multiple albums on the label in the early 2000s. Obsessed with extreme sounds from techno to gabber in the 1990s, this interest led to the experimental, fucked-up IDM soundscapes of his first album for Shitkatapult, *Multifunkstionsebene* (2001). In his follow-up album, *Duplex* (2003), this trajectory would lead to more glitch distortion, but also the beginnings of his experimentation of various emotional states through vocal textures.

Apparat was at this time coming into the orbit of Modeselektor. In 2003, he started to release records on BPitch Control, and in 2006, he released, together with BPitch icon Ellen Allien, the popular and critical success, *Orchestra of Bubbles*. Through these multiple connections at Shitkatapult and BPitch, Apparat was developing an extraordinary following

---

1 Apparat, interview with Tom Breihan, *Pitchfork*, October 28, 2010. https://pitchfork.com/news/40516-5-10-15-20-apparat/.
2 Ibid.

as part of the new generation of Berlin producers. However, given that the first Moderat album was not released until 2009, it would seem that Moderat developed a couple of years after *Happy Birthday!* It might indeed be presumed that the supergroup was formed only after the careers of Modeselektor and Apparat had fully developed.

But this is not so simple.

In fact, the collaboration began in parallel, and quite early on in the careers of both Modeselektor and Apparat. Bronsert, Szary, and Ring first met in Berlin in 2002. From sharing studio time, a lovely EP resulted in 2003: *Auf Kosten der Gesundheit.* One might thus describe Moderat as an ongoing and parallel collaboration, except for the fact that a multiyear hiatus followed this release. As indicated by the title, which can be translated as "At the Cost of Health," it appears that the initial collaboration proved difficult. The early EP also reveals little of the pop sensibilities of Moderat; it is fully in the glitch and IDM phases of their respective careers, and there is no use of Ring's distinctive vocals.

The trajectory from this obscure 2003 moment to the momentous 2009 release of *Moderat* thus seems to have been a long one. But once again, there is a fascinating link that returns us to *Happy Birthday!* For, in 2007, Moderat was already re-introduced to the music world in a subtle way. "Let Your Love Grow," the fourth track on Modeselektor's album, is in truth the one track not credited to "Modeselektor." Rather, the credits are listed as *Moderat, feat. Paul St. Hilaire.* Thus, hidden on the album, we find essentially the beginnings of Moderat, announcing a new era of collaboration and one that would have significant success on the electronic stage. This moment drives home my point that *Happy Birthday!* is the ultimate transitional album

Indeed, it would actually be with *Happy Birthday!* that the implicit future of what would become Moderat as pop icon developed. "Let Your Love Grow" is strikingly different in style from *Auf Kosten der Gesundheit.* The pop sensibilities of future Moderat are on full display; indeed, it is one of the most popular songs on the album. At the same time, the song is more reflective and subdued than the other Modeselektor tracks, one that foreshadows the somber moods in the later Moderat albums. A kind of rave anthem as dirge, "Let Your Love Grow" features a descending melodic line. And rather than glitch IDM, we have ambient and bass music, featuring the careful use of the vocals by Paul St. Hilaire. Originally from Dominica in the West Indies, St. Hilaire has also had a multidecade career as one of the key MCs of the Berlin-techno scene.

These collaborations between Apparat, Paul St. Hilaire, and Modeselektor are key in contemplating the significance of this track. The track further anticipates the international success of Moderat and its links to British and Afro-Caribbean electronica. We will further see important networks resulting from international tours, which circle back to local fame. For example, in answering a question about Moderat's possible international plans connected to their rising fame, Bronsert provided an intriguing perspective: "We have always been more internationally popular than we have been here in Germany. It's just that we are now getting the attention here that we already had in other countries."[3] As we will see in Chapter 5, this boomerang effect of transnational fame can

____

3 "Modeselektor's Gernot Bronsert on the Evolution of Moderat," *Electronic Beats,* April 11, 2016. https://www.electronicbeats.net/modeselektors-gernot-bronsert-on-the-development-of-moderat/.

practically be traced to the British and German exchange of Krautrock and post-punk in the 1970s.

Beyond the UK, the transatlantic career of Modeselektor, Apparat, and Moderat (not to confuse the names again) are fascinating. An obvious litmus test for the reception of international artists in the United States is coverage in American online media. It should be noted here that Modeselektor and Apparat were, early on, in a special class of German electronic artists who were regularly reviewed on platforms such as *Pitchfork*. Given the online magazine's esteem for the traditions of Krautrock and post-rock,[4] *Pitchfork*'s selection of German electronic artists to review implies the continuation of this tradition. As with Berlin artists like Ellen Allien and Ricardo Villalobos, *Pitchfork* and other online media have led American readers into these techno worlds, while introducing a new generation of readers to 1970s groups such as Can and Cluster. In this context, Moderat achieved an even greater presence in American music journalism. Here we will see how this new network built on what Sean Albiez has called a "sonic futurescape" of British-German musical exchange.

Moderat's distinct trajectory of dub music, electronica, and pop vocals helped to establish the trio in truly transatlantic fashion. If artists like Autechre and Aphex Twin were the main British reference points for the early careers of Modeselektor and Apparat, Moderat would slot into a new generation of British producers such as Four Tet, Jon Hopkins, and Burial. At the same time, these tunes recall some of Paul Kalkbrenner's

---

4 See Ulrich Adelt, *Krautrock: German Music in the Seventies* (Ann Arbor: University of Michigan Press, 2016), 170–4.

ambient techno from the soundtrack to *Berlin Calling*, a 2008 film feature that represented the Berlin scene for mainly European audiences. However, it can be said that Moderat's productions as a trio resulted in subtler dub music than Kalkbrenner's *Berlin Calling*. Sascha Ring's new role as vocalist on the 2009 album resulted in memorable hits such as "Rusty Nails" and "Out of Sight." These are examples of the trio's new art of producing *singles*, with this initial success being followed in 2013 by their signature classic "Bad Kingdom."

A comparison with Burial helps to comprehend these ongoing links to British electronica and dub music, as well as the subtle shifts in styles pioneered by Moderat. The track "Out of Sight" most clearly shows the distinctive dubstep influence of Burial, combined with Ring's vocals. The Moderat albums are steeped in moods of melancholy, with increasing use of reverb to provide a practical sense of being underwater. Beyond the trio's respective contributions to the music, their collabs widened the sonic possibilities on the album. Indeed, there is a direct artistic link in terms of collabs between *Happy Birthday!* and the first Moderat album: namely, Paul St. Hilaire.

The collabs between St. Hilaire and Modeselektor were ongoing, for St. Hilaire had already been featured on *Hello Mom!* with the excellent track "Fake Emotion." Two years later, on "Let Your Love Grow," these dub influences were reinforced. Moderat's 2009 debut featured yet another standout piece with St. Hilaire: "Slow Match" (effectively a third collab between St. Hilaire and Modeselektor). "Slow Match" leans more into the style of Burial, bringing the dub hypnosis to full fruition. Here, Modeselektor and Moderat's music with St. Hilaire can be compared to the Bug's collabs with Killa P & Flowdan or Burial and Kode 9's collabs with The Spaceape—classic examples of electronica and dub or grime in the late 2000s.

But it's also important not to emphasize only these specifically British dub comparisons—for the work with St. Hilaire also emerges out of specifically Berlin histories. St. Hilaire had moved from Dominica to Europe already in the early 1990s, eventually settling in Berlin.[5] Starting in 1995, he began a long collaboration with Basic Channel legends Moritz von Oswald and Mark Ernestus, mentioned earlier as the founder of Hard Wax. This brought St. Hilaire iconic status in dub techno, as he became the MC for their project Rhythm & Sound. With this example, the musical links at Hard Wax prove, indeed, to have hip-hop and dub-techno facets. As opposed to the minimal dub of Rhythm & Sound, the pop sensibilities of Moderat brought out a kinship to British stars such as Leftfield, a comparison that Jon Hopkins would make when discussing the trio.[6] This blended and collab approach only carried Modeselektor further away from orthodoxies of so-called German techno or Berlin minimal techno. This work, together with St. Hilaire, made Afro-Caribbean and Black British histories explicit in a Berlin context, already implicit in the reliance of events like the Love Parade on the history of sound-system culture.

I also read "Let Your Love Grow" as a kind of tribute to the MCs who were so prominent in British hardcore rave during the 1990s. Dutch gabber would likewise bring in hip-hop

---

5 See CTM Festival website: https://archive.ctm-festival.de/index.php?id=8492.
6 "Jon Hopkins Meets Moderat," *Electronic Beats*, March 26, 2015. http://www.electronicbeats.net/youtube/eb-tv-slices-feature-jon-hopkins-meets-moderat/.

MC references, though in Germany, these MC links proved less explicit. If there is a comparison I would make with hip-hop and reggae vocalists in Germany specifically, it could be with this perhaps surprising example: Eurodance. Dub techno and electronica could be seen here as the ghostly and underground B-side to the commercial A-side of pop-hardcore and Eurodance. St. Hilaire was thus one of the multiple voices emphasizing the Black Atlantic history of electronic music in Germany, at a time when some of these roots were essentially forgotten by the mid-1990s, partly through the discourses of electronic music and "Tekkno," a point which Alexander Weheliye has made and critiqued in his historiography of German techno.[7]

In fact, hardcore rave and Eurodance are both genres that harken back to memories of 1990s dance culture and its roots in dub and hip-hop. Working with St. Hilaire follows this logic of *Happy Birthday!*, highlighting the connections of German techno and British rave. Modeselektor's and Moderat's inspirations from British electronica and dub cannot be discounted, and in this context, I would view the most explicit stylistic inspiration on "Let Your Love Grow" to be Leftfield. Indeed, it was these British connections that would also lead to arguably Modeselektor's work with its most famous collaborator: with none other than Thom Yorke, though for this collab, we will need to jump ahead on the album track list.

---

7 Alexander Weheliye, interview with Annie Goh, "White Brothers with No Soul—Untuning the Historiography of Berlin Techno," *Un Tune, CTM 2015*, 40–3.

5 Radiohead Stardust

*Since the late 1980s artists have returned time and time
again to the creative and sonic sources of the 1970s
in electronica, drum and bass, HipHop and techno as
well as in "progressive" areas of contemporary rock (e.g.,
Radiohead).*

SEAN ALBIEZ

It is perhaps the ultimate example of DJ cheekiness, though
also a nice expression of nonchalance, that there is lodged
late on *Happy Birthday!*—and specifically track 15, after
many club bangers—a little collaboration that proves to be
quite big. It is Modeselektor's first collab with Thom Yorke,
world star and frontman for Radiohead. The track is entitled
"The White Flash," and it is this tune that would inaugurate
Modeselektor's multiple collaborations with Yorke. In this
sense, *Happy Birthday!* proved a milestone for Modeselektor.
Yorke had professed fandom for Modeselektor's music
already in 2003, in an interview on German TV that brought
the duo new attention and a change in direction.[1] Meetings

---

1 The show was called "Fast Forward," hosted by Charlotte Roche, on
the German music channel Viva, and it took place on July 10, 2003.
https://www.youtube.com/watch?v=DWSH3P7YSKc. Yorke has also repeatedly mentioned Modeselektor, including in American contexts such as this
Pitchfork: Thom Yorke, interviewed by Scott Plagenhoef, *Pitchfork*, August 16,
2006. https://pitchfork.com/features/interview/6402-thom-yorke/.

with Yorke followed, and even before "The White Flash," Modeselektor provided a remix for Yorke's "Skip Divided" in 2006. Following "The White Flash" on *Happy Birthday!*, the duo would go on to collaborate with Yorke again in 2011 on "Shipwreck" and "This," both featured on the album *Monkeytown*.

That an artist such as Yorke was interested in collaborating with Modeselektor certainly bears consideration, not just for the duo, but for the transnational links and crossovers of post-rock and electronic music. Questions of future trajectories are important, because this collaboration with Yorke anticipated in my view the later success of Moderat two years later—arguably the closest Berlin techno has come to a band that has the status of Radiohead. As mentioned, Sascha Ring was himself inspired by Yorke and Radiohead.

"The White Flash" is also the closest to Modeselektor's album theme of fatherhood, though thankfully it is not a power ballad. The lyrics are minimalist and only vaguely linked to childhood and time. It includes Yorke's isolated use of the word "teeth," as well as his primary line, repeated as a mantra:

You have all the time in the world.

The line practically caresses the listener, with an ambient-breakbeat accompaniment produced by Bronsert. In more subtle fashion than TTC or Puppetmastaz, the vocals are chopped up. The texture of the voice becomes more important than the lyrics, and Yorke's tone and cries are as important as his words.

These stripped-down lyrics continue the trajectory of Yorke's vocal performance and Radiohead's musical production following *Kid A*. Beyond these post-rock and electronic crossovers, the British-German links could not be more apparent. This lush ambient song shows once again the inspiration of Aphex Twin. Modeselektor's production recalls Twin, and the melody and sound appear as echoes of Twin's "Alberto Balsalm" from . . . *I Care Because You Do* (1995). One is allowed to meditate on "The White Flash," lodged somewhere between track and pop song, sleep and dance—Yorke's post–Kid-A style intersects so well with the beats of Modeselektor. It is at once a celebration of new life, and a calm dirge to time passing.

Obviously, Modeselektor's profile was raised through these collaborations with Yorke. The song certainly reflects the established process where artists become noticed in other countries through collaborations with international stars. The significance of such moments for European pop culture and techno in the 2000s has not been truly explored by scholars. To give some historical context, I would compare Modeselektor's work with Thom Yorke to the original transnational links that were established in the 1970s. To drive home the importance of these exchanges in the twenty-first century and the international Berlin scene, let's be so bold as to compare the Radiohead/Modeselektor/Moderat links to a prior German-British exchange: I'm thinking here of none other than David Bowie's praise of Kraftwerk and Neu! Bowie's engagement with Krautrock, together with artists such as Brian Eno and Iggy Pop, proved to be a definitive 1970s expression of the rock-electronic crossover in Europe. In terms of pop iconicity,

Bowie and Yorke are comparable, and most especially, Yorke's and Bowie's move toward experimental electronica and dance culture can be compared.

To give expression to these links, I want to highlight here the writings of British scholar Sean Albiez. His research and historiography provide key tracings of such networks, for Albiez highlighted the significance of German-English exchanges in electronic and rock music. In his 2003 article, "Sounds of Future Past: From Neu! to Numan," Albiez states that in the 1970s, "a predominately Deutsch-Englisch creative network of musicians forged a *sonic futurescape*."[2] The German translation of "German-English," or "Deutsch-Englisch," seems to indicate the West German settings of many of the collaborations. Transnational exchanges were key in these developments, stretching across Krautrock, post-punk, and synthpop, with the aforementioned links of artists like David Bowie, Brian Eno, Kraftwerk, and Neu!

The sonic futurescape not only featured collaborations but also common interests in instrumental experimentation and production. Likewise, there was a shared interest in countercultures, psychedelia, and science fiction. Albiez delineates what he sees as two primary traditions in this sonic futurescape as it was forged in the 1970s: *machine rock vs. the oceanic rock*.[3] In these broad traditions, we can see, on the one hand, the early foundations of industrial and techno as linked to machine rock, and, on the other hand, ambient and

---

2 Sean Albiez, "Sounds of Future Past: From Neu! to Numan," in *Pop Sounds: Klangtexturen in der Pop- und Rockmusik*, ed. Thomas Phleps and Ralf von Appen (Transcript: Bielefeld, 2003), 129.
3 Ibid., 141–7.

post-rock represented by Albiez's oceanic rock. While these two wings of rock remain crucial, I'd like to consider how these 1970s Deutsch-Englisch networks have continued to evolve across Afro-Caribbean bass and breakbeat music, and techno, dub, and industrial music. In the European context, it should be noted that since the 1970s, there have also been significant influences on this futurescape from areas such as France, Holland, and Belgium.

Here, the collaborations between Yorke and Modeselektor could be described as symbolic of a new German-British network that has evolved since the exchanges of Bowie and Kraftwerk. Indeed, the Yorke-Modeselektor collab can be seen as a pop symbol of the migration of many British artists and DJs to Berlin since the 1990s—stylistically and geographically. Mark Reeder, founder of MFS records, was arguably the pioneering figure in this tradition, reflected in a unique documentary that focuses on his life as an expat: *B-Movie: Lust and Sound in West Berlin, 1979-1989*.

Some of these British-German trajectories have been reversed, however, in the sense that the music of Modeselektor and Moderat could be described as a sort of "reverse Bowie." I mean by this that Modeselektor and Moderat, as Berlin-techno representatives with strong links to the United Kingdom and the United States, have been disseminating ideas of British rave and American glitch-hop for new generations of European audiences in the 2000s. This has been done in comparable fashion to how Bowie was processing and disseminating Krautrock themes for Anglo-American audiences in the 1970s. After all, it was arguably already Modeselektor's stylistic interests in British electronica that predetermined Yorke's praise of the duo.

As indicated by the epigraph to this chapter, Albiez identifies the long heritage of these futurescape networks in the 1980s, 1990s, and into the 2000s. *And crucially*, he highlights Radiohead as a singular example in the heritage of the sonic futurescape. In his article, the final section is focused on a review of Radiohead. Albiez writes, "Radiohead's *Kid A* and *Amnesiac* explored a similar sonic and musical space to that negotiated by the musicians of the Deutsch-Englisch alliance in the late 1970s and early 80s, and the post-rock bands of the 1990s."[4]

As Albiez was writing these lines in 2003, he could not have known that this history would develop new Deutsch-Englisch networks, including among Modeselektor, Moderat, and Radiohead. There are clear echoes of this sonic futurescape in the present era. The magazine *Dazed*, for example, would highlight Yorke as a transatlantic representative of rock-electronic crossovers. The magazine describes Yorke's collaborations with Modeselektor, along with Four Tet and Flying Lotus, as marking him as "a true EDM renaissance man."[5] As mentioned, Yorke's citing of Modeselektor in 2003 was comparable, if arguably less age-defining, to Bowie's citing of Kraftwerk.

Modeselektor would later become the opener for some of Radiohead's concerts. The year 2008 was key in this respect, with Modeselektor playing at Radiohead's Berlin concert at the Kindl Bühne Wuhlheide on July 8, as well as a concert in Barcelona on June 6 and a series of six concerts in Japan in

---

4 Ibid., 149.
5 http://www.dazeddigital.com/music/article/15601/1/splitting-atoms-thom-yorke.

October[6] (Moderat would follow as an opener the next year). One could see these 2008 moments as echoes of Bowie's insistence on playing Kraftwerk's music as openers during his tours in 1976 and 1977. The exposure to new fans through concert performances should not be discounted, although this is more symbolic, as Modeselektor was already integrated onto a massive festival circuit during the 2000s.[7]

Sean Albiez would later expand on these ideas about German-British histories in his article, "Europe-Nonstop: West Germany, Britain, and the Rise of Synthpop, 1975–81."[8] In this refinement of his ideas, he focuses on a network of German-British musicians between Krautrock, post-punk, and synthpop. These networks go beyond the singular focus on Kraftwerk, and here, beyond Yorke, it should be mentioned that Modeselektor's final song on *Happy Birthday!* is with a British band—Maxïmo Park. The track, "(I Can't Sleep) without Music" demonstrates that these networks involve multiple artists. This collab intriguingly reflects Albiez's focus on synthpop,

6 https://de-bug.de/musik/radiohead-live-in-der-wuhlheide-berlin/ https://livemusicblog.com/news/radiohead-announce-full-2008-tour-dates/ https://www.residentadvisor.net/news/9632.

7 As EDM pop was expanding across the United States at the beginning of the 2010s, Thom Yorke even joined Radiohead in Coachella in 2012. His appearance could be described as an underground supplement to Radiohead's headlining of Coachella that same year. This partly shows that interest in German electronic music continued to be a niche fascination, as Anglo-American pop and rock remained dominant across the 2000s and into the 2010s. See the reports on the following websites: https://www.nme.com/news/music/thom-yorke-37-1276194 https://latimesblogs.latimes.com/music_blog/2012/04/coachella-2012-thom-yorke -djs-til-dawn-at-the-parker-hotel.html.

8 Sean Albiez, "Europe Non-Stop: West Germany, Britain, and the Rise of Synthpop, 1975–81," in *Kraftwerk: Music Non-Stop*, ed. Sean Albiez and David Pattie (London: Continuum, 2011), 139–62.

with Maxïmo Park and Modeselektor tapping into some retro-Depeche Mode.

If we were to update Albiez's histories with the electronic links that intersect in Berlin today, one could highlight further examples. Indeed, one might cite dub/ambient and techno as updates. Modeselektor's links to Yorke and Maxïmo Park can be compared here to other collaborations between British and German producers and labels: for example, the music of the Orb and Thomas Fehlmann in the dub/ambient tradition, and in the techno tradition, the releases of Surgeon, the Advent, and James Ruskin on Tresor—not to mention remixes exchanged between Moderat and Jon Hopkins.

Modeselektor's DJ mixes and remixes beyond *Happy Birthday!* are similarly expressive of this futurescape spirit. Not only did the duo remix Yorke's "Skip Divided" in 2006, but also Radiohead's "Good Evening Mrs. Magpie" (2011). As an expression of the post-rock links across Europe, their double remix for Björk's "The Dull Flame of Desire" (2008) should also be highlighted. On the flip side, the numerous remixes of their own tracks by artists such as Rustie, Shackleton, and SBTRKT reinforce these networks. The founding of Monkeytown, next to labels like BPitch Control and Tresor, helped establish these networks as Berlin answers to the likes of Warp, Mute, and Ninja Tune.

And here, a final point on DJ culture, before we turn to the adventures of rave culture: the duo's *Modeselektion* series of curated albums has only brought home these bass networks connecting Europe, the UK, and North America. It is this crossover of electronica, rock, and DJ culture that has been a mark for Modeselektor and related artists in this new futurescape. If these musings help to explain their most famous official collab with Thom Yorke, it also shows how the constant partnerships can create a plethora of names and portmanteaus, as intertwined as Modeselektor, Apparat, and Moderat.

Part II

Rave Chronicles

6 Arena Techno Heritage

If we got asked to play at the Super Bowl,
I would order one million stroboscopes
and all the fog machines they have in the USA.
And I would pitch-black the whole stadium—
and strobe, and fog, and 30 minutes gabber.
GERNOT BRONSERT

Modeselektor's establishment in the Berlin scene in the mid-2000s came at a timely moment, and not only with respect to the global status of Berlin that brought on collabs and crossovers with post-rock and electronica. Specifically, the duo came up around the time of several profound shifts in Berlin techno—shifts that made certain aspects of 1990s rave culture feel like distant memories. A number of topics related to Berlin and European history thus need to be addressed, beyond the duo's famous collabs and genre games at the height of minimal techno. In particular, I would like to argue that Modeselektor's impact involved, specifically with their first two albums, a distinct tradition that was on decline in Berlin during the 2000s decade—rave massives.

This designation was reflective of the popular status of techno in Germany. The soundtrack to rave events involved a variety of subgenres loosely placed under the moniker of "rave music." In this sense, one might describe it as electronic music's answer to arena rock, though rave music involves multiple approaches. Most closely associated with acid house, hardcore, and breakbeat music, these styles became popular in both Britain and Germany between the late 1980s and early 1990s. A key group from Britain, the KLF, pioneered a particular vision for this future with their genre coinage of "stadium house." Across the decade, groups associated with the arena crossover also came primarily from the UK. Most famous were arguably the "Big Beat" groups of the Prodigy, the Chemical Brothers, and Fatboy Slim, but there were also great electronica acts from Orbital to Underworld. This rave music, now ranging from stadium house to Big Beat, usually involved shorter sets, greater stage presence and spectacle, and crossovers with rock and hip-hop. At the same time, the rave scenes in the Netherlands, Belgium, and Germany were immersed in evolving styles such as gabber, new beat, hardcore techno, and trance—with the bouncing echoes of Roland 909s filling numerous warehouses.

The continuation and refinement of such arena traditions in live music can be seen during the 2000s, and prominently in French house acts like Daft Punk and Justice, among other examples in house and trance from the UK, Holland, and Scandinavia. However, Germany—*and 2000s Berlin, especially*—did not develop the same prominence of electronica bands and international stars in what would eventually become the moniker of "EDM." How Modeselektor functioned in this transitional context of rave needs to be understood carefully.

A few Berlin rave institutions first require explaining: specifically, the Love Parade and an annual rave known as Mayday. Nothing said massive rave festivals during the 1990s quite like these two events. The Love Parade, which could be described as a hybrid of sound-system block party, Carnival, and Pride Parade, became the largest and most famous techno event in Berlin across the 1990s. It began as a small musical protest event, conceived by Dr. Motte, a Berlin DJ in the acid house scene. Its first motto was similarly humorous in cheeky rave fashion: "Peace, Joy, Pancakes." Yet after this small event, the Love Parade grew to become the most popular techno event in Europe, reaching in excess of *one million attendees* in the late 1990s.

However, the commercial excess of the event resulted in a gradual backlash. In 2003, the Love Parade was held by the original Berlin organizers for the last time, before it was canceled in 2004 and 2005. In the meantime, a major fitness chain took over the financing of the Love Parade. The parade would be held just once more in Berlin in 2006, before taking on a new and ultimately tragic history in the Ruhr Valley. The final Love Parade, held in the industrial city of Duisburg in 2010, suffered from severe organizational failures and overcrowding, which resulted in a stampede that led to the deaths of twenty-one people and hundreds of injuries—a horrific end to the most representative mass event for European techno in the 1990s.

If the Love Parade was the most famous "techno parade" event of its type, the most famous indoor "rave massive" in Germany during the 1990s was the Mayday. This event became symbolic of mass commercial raves during the era.

First held in Berlin in December 1991, the event took place in a number of cities before moving permanently to Dortmund in 1997, where it has been held annually ever since. Aside from the inaugural party, the most notorious Mayday held in Berlin was a multiday extravaganza called "The Raving Society (We are Different)" in November 1994. Broadcast live on *VIVA*, Germany's version of MTV, this event was representative of the heights of arena raves in the 1990s, and it proved to be the largest Mayday in history.

Yet, with the move of the Mayday to Dortmund, rave massives in Germany eventually became closely associated with metropolitan areas in the Rhine region. Event organizations, especially I-Motion, host multiple festivals in the area. I-Motion would even take over the management of the Mayday. Moreover, these I-Motion festivals such as Nature One intersect with an established mass festival culture in the Netherlands and Belgium. Parts of these festivals transformed into what Fabian Holt has described as a new network of "EDM pop."[1] Most famously, these festivals have been represented by Tomorrowland in Belgium, which has regular attendance in the hundreds of thousands. ID&T, the promoter behind Tomorrowland, is, together with Q-Dance, a key festival operator in Holland and Belgium. These promoters are comparable to I-Motion, which has its headquarters near Koblenz. As maximalist events, these festivals have continued

1 Fabian Holt, "EDM Pop: A Soft Shell Formation in a New Festival Economy," in *Weekend Societies: Electronic Dance Music Festivals and Event-Cultures*, ed. Graham St. John (London: Bloomsbury, 2017), 25–44.

traditions of rave music from hardcore to trance, as well as more recent styles such as electro house and EDM pop.

To return to Berlin, with the Love Parade and the Mayday, it should be clear that by 2003 both events had become distanced from the Berlin scene. Rave culture in Berlin transformed into a focus on club cultures and more circumscribed open-airs. The scene aimed here at a consolidation and reigning in of pop tendencies, and Berlin techno was made more professional and international. The new coordinates of "Berlin minimal"— techno, house, and electro—were thus understandable responses to the excesses of rave music—or what became satirized in its worst examples as *Kirmistechno*, a.k.a. Funfair Techno.

At the same time, a new system of music festivals gradually developed around the larger Berlin region, which focused more on techno, house, and experimental electronic music, often including alternative rock and hip-hop. Thus, festivals such as Melt and the Fusion Festival, just a couple hours away from Berlin in the "Former East," became important events during the 2000s. Moreover, these events were closely linked to a new network of festivals across Europe. As presented in the documentary *Speaking in Code*, one of the key European festivals—if not *the* key festival—is Sónar in Barcelona, well established on the international stage by the beginning of the 2000s.

Modeselektor's—and Moderat's—performance styles tapped into this new generation of festival experiences that would gradually become part of a new international network. At the same time, however, their roots in Berlin clubs and underground rave culture were foundational. Modeselektor certainly draws much inspiration from this history. At the same time, Moderat, as a supergroup in its more subdued performance style, could be described as the ideal Berlin answer to this arena-need during the aging of techno. Indeed, Moderat's style is practically a Berlin stamp on Kraftwerk's ideal of technopop. Yet aside from Moderat's pop vocal style, I would say that the more exuberant performance style of Modeselektor slots into the ongoing interest in rave music.

So let us return to the legacies of Berlin rave in the 1990s, specifically with the Mayday. I will highlight here a major label and artist, with which I will contrast Modeselektor and techno in the 2000s—specifically as concerns the history of Berlin events. I am thinking here of the label Low Spirit and Maximilian Lenz, a.k.a. Westbam, who was the biggest Berlin techno and rave star of the 1990s. He and Low Spirit were linked to the Love Parade and Mayday across the decade.

Low Spirit was founded in 1985, and the label helped to established house and breakbeat music in Berlin during the late 1980s—and pop-rave culture in the 1990s. However, changes in Berlin during the 2000s proved crucial. There was *a decline* in Low Spirit's tradition of raves in an era of renewed commitment to Berlin club culture. The year 2006 could be seen as symbolic. As mentioned, a final Berlin Love Parade was held in 2006 following its two-year cancellation and transfer in ownership. Moreover, the Low Spirit label had been in decline since the late 1990s, and in 2006, the label went defunct— perfect timing for a new generation of Berlin artists to grasp the new space and possibilities in techno.

With respect to Berlin raves, it should also be stated that New York City had fundamental influences on East and West

Berlin—from the hip-hop of the Bronx, Queens, and related boroughs, to the disco and club culture of Manhattan, to the rave culture of Brooklyn. Westbam himself was one of the few to emphasize the hip-hop links—for example, in the classic electro on his 1997 album, *We'll Never Stop Living this Way*, and in his collabs with NYC DJ Afrika Islam as the duo Mr. X and Mr. Y. Yet, as discussed in Part I, in the focus on international artists of the Black Atlantic, there was a scarcity of collaborations with local hip-hop artists.

The East Berlin encounter with hip-hop was already established in the 1980s, with the reception of films like *Beat Street* resulting in an eighties breakdance scene behind the Wall.[2] NYC graffiti also became an inspiration for postindustrial Berlin, with graffiti found on structures from the Wall to U-Bahn stations. These histories point to a more variegated reception of electro and hip-hop in Berlin, beyond the emphasis on the "techno alliance" of Berlin and Detroit. The specific Detroit focus was successfully propagated by Tresor, which released numerous records by Detroit artists starting in the early 1990s. The underground practices of Tresor and related techno labels were also understandable responses to the pop excesses of rave. Still, compared with Berlin's emphasis on techno and house, Modeselektor has retained this hip-hop history in the 2000s, as featured on the collabs with TTC and the Puppetmastaz. Modeselektor thus operates as a corrective to overly simplistic separations of hip-hop and German techno.

The balance of inspirations from hip-hop and techno has been a marker of the duo's multiple heritages. While retaining

___

2 See Denk and von Thülen, *Der Klang der Familie*, 20–1.

musical refinement in the heritage of Detroit techno, their presence on stage as hype performers with hipster cool represents this new generation. In establishing this style, Modeselektor have mentioned that their performances responded to a new generation of *laptop performers*. Bronsert mentions the Austrian group Farmers Manual, stating that the group performed around a table, with "10 guys and 12 laptops probably . . . like seeing a bunch of guys having an internet conference."[3] He and Szary loved Farmers Manual's music, but they could not stand this tech-office performance style. The duo thus tried to get away from the laptop-DJs through a more dynamic engagement with the audience, while working to refine their visuals with Pfadfinderei.

This new generation of international festival practices is nicely captured in their documentary *We are Modeselektor*. Thaddeus Herrmann, the former editor of *De:Bug* (the Berlin magazine that reported on the Labstyle parties), aptly refers to Modeselektor's anticipation of new styles of what he terms arena techno, as an appropriate Euro-variation on stadium house. Herrmann states, "With their development they have anticipated so much that in the context of Arena-Techno is day-to-day routine now."[4] He adds, "They managed to create a sound that is compatible for the masses and that is still musically exciting, and that is what I find sensational."[5]

The documentary reflects Modeselektor's constant play with the sensational and everyday experiences in digital life.

---

3 Modeselektor, *RA Exchange*, 2019.
4 *We are Modeselektor*.
5 Ibid.

The film's narrative, for example, is certainly a study in the contrast of small-town rural life in Brandenburg versus the intense tours on the international festival and club circuit. Their playful performance style as bass workers in the new Berlin is representative here. Most recently, it was represented in a great series of promotional photos for their album *Who Else*—involving pictures of the duo looking rough around the edges and sitting on a bench at a nondescript Berlin park, reading the newspaper and drinking coffee.

That mix of the sensational and everyday life is reflected in contemporary digital media and party events such as *Boiler Room*, a series of DJ parties live-streamed on the internet. During their sets, the mix of the populist roots of 1990s Euro-rave and the online party series is on display. Modeselektor's sets have included references to Euro-rave for a new generation of online listeners and clubbers. For example, in their 2012 set, and to bring this discussion full circle, Modeselektor even offered a climactic conclusion by referencing Mayday. They played a track by Members of Mayday, a moniker for Westbam and producer Klaus Jankuhn that created annual anthems for the iconic rave. During the Boiler Room set, Modeselektor concluded with the Members of Mayday's first "Mayday Anthem" from the year 1992. Obviously, Bronsert and Szary knew about these trends at the same time as they were following the techno currents of Hard Wax. Such a play with the rave era in their DJ sets has only reinforced the references that appeared on their own albums from the mid-2000s, and associated DJs like Ellen Allien and Marcel Dettmann make repeated reference to this rave heritage in their sets as well.

And as mentioned, this included, beyond collaborations, *covers* of a particular sort. To continue the historical exploration of the 1990s, and this divide of pop arena and underground, it is time to move to the covers themselves. For, beyond the playful spinning of Members of Mayday, one of the most surprising examples for many, specifically in the context of 2007, was Modeselektor's reference to Scooter. With this reference, we'll be able to explore the pop-rave 1990s in new—and shall we say, excessive—ways. And in truth, Modeselektor's cover of Scooter circles back to the KLF roots of stadium house in all its manifestations. This brings out Modeselektor's sly humor in all its glory—though to maintain the confusion, their devotion to Detroit techno and British electronica remained constant throughout.

But now, it must be done—we now turn to a group known as Scooter.

7 Cover I
Scooter Studies

Love, peace, and unity
Siberia, the place to be.
The K the L the F and the -ology
Hallelujah!
SCOOTER, "RAMP! (THE LOGICAL SONG)"

Scooter, to say the least, has had enormous popular success in Europe, though they remain quite an enigma on the other side of the Atlantic. So let us first explain Scooter in transatlantic terms. Many Americans, whether involved in rave culture or not, might not realize that they may have heard the music of this notorious German dance-act. The transatlantic encounter would likely have taken the following form in the 2000s, specifically in 2009, with none other than Sacha Baron Cohen's outrageous mockumentary, *Brüno*.

Produced by "Üniversal," this film features a gay Austrian fashionista who moves to Los Angeles in order to become "überfamous," and in the process he causes scandal across America. The appropriate loss of all Western values is the result—a flood of Euro-rave as total pop disaster. And appropriately for Brüno's überpop identity, a good part of the soundtrack features Euro-techno, from Crazy Frog's Eurotrash hits to the underground Dutch gabber of 3 Steps Ahead (the moniker of legendary producer Peter-Paul Pigmans).

Yet—most prominently—the title sequence features Scooter, specifically the group's 2002 dance hit "Nessaja." This banger introduces Brüno in all his outrageous glory, mixed to flashing disco lights. The scandal of Eurotrash is put on full display; the rise and fall of Brüno's queer-as-shock tactics follows in the movie, as he traverses America in his quest to become "überfamous." To be sure, when viewing the title sequence at the time, Europeans would have been more familiar with the reasons why Scooter was used. "Nessaja" was one of Scooter's biggest European hits.

A hard trance banger, "Nessaja" samples a moment in Euro-pop history. Scooter raves up the melody and lyrics from a 1983 Kinderlied, a.k.a. children's song, of the same name. The original "Nessaja" was by Peter Maffay, a bestselling German music star who traversed pop and rock. In live performance, Maffay's "Nessaja" practically turns Kinderlied into power ballad, the culmination of an album with a title as grand as a romantic novel: *Tabulaga oder die Reise zur Vernunft* (*Tabaluga or the Journey to Reason*). Maffay's fairytale album (it's about the education of a little dragon) could be understood here as the Euro-pop prelude to a more well-known fantasy film from 1984, *The NeverEnding Story*, with the title song by Munich-disco godfather Giorgio Moroder (also later covered by Scooter).

Now—this is a roundabout way of saying the following: Americans should realize that Scooter has had such pop success to be referenced by everyone from Sacha Baron Cohen to Modeselektor. Scooter's references to pop and

Euro-techno will be important for addressing Modeselektor's own 1990s winks to Euro-rave culture. So, we need to answer: Who is Scooter? And, what does Scooter have to do with Modeselektor?

Let's return to the 1990s and Scooter's formation. It should first be understood that, to produce chart-topping hits, Scooter covered or interpolated many artists. The dance-act was particularly adept at utilizing Euro-pop—from rock to synthpop. Yet, Scooter was also notorious for sampling underground rave tracks. In this sense, Scooter is often described as the scandalous Eurotrash version of the KLF, the "stadium house" group in England that aimed to conquer the charts with efficient DIY means. In fact, the KLF published a punk instruction manual to achieve this, entitled *The Manual (How to Have a Number One the Easy Way)*. But far beyond the chart successes of the KLF, Scooter's strategy would result in the following singular achievement: *Scooter became the most commercially successful dance-act from Germany.*[1]

The Hamburg-based act was founded in 1993, led most prominently by its superstar MC, H. P. Baxxter (Hans Peter Geerdes). Originally from East Frisia, a coastal region on the Dutch border, Baxxter has a striking star appearance as a tall, blond star (one might describe his style as a German-rave update to synthpop and new wave, inspired by artists like Billy

---

1 Their total sales have exceeded thirty million albums according to multiple press sites. See also https://www.dw.com/en/the-top-10-electronic-dance-acts-from-germany/g-18644267. In April 2021, Scooter's monthly listeners on Spotify were also listed at 4,077,000, compared to 535,000 for Modeselektor and 1,013,000 for Moderat. See also Max Dax, *Scooter: Always Hardcore* (Hamburg: Edel, 2013).

Idol—he even covered "Rebel Yell" once). Baxxter gradually developed a star quality that was located somewhere between playboy and hooligan, with his signature-spiked blond hair. Indeed, Baxxter achieved fame through his performance presence, as well as his British-accented MCing, which borrowed heavily from the traditions of rave.

Though Baxxter is the face of Scooter, the music productions of Rick J. Jordan (Hendrik Stedler) have also been key. Jordan and Baxxter met in Hannover in 1986, initially founding a synthpop band, Celebrate the Nun, which lasted until 1992. The chart potential of synthpop was in decline, and at this time Baxxter began to have new inspirations when attending raves. By 1993, they decided to form Scooter and jump on the rave train. Jordan built up their music studio, before transferring operations to Hamburg in 1995. For the next twenty years, Jordan crafted Scooter's music.[2] Scooter's success was also managed by Jens Thele, founder of the Hamburg dance label Kontor and Sheffield Tunes, the label for Scooter's releases. These were sublabels of Edel Records, founded in 1986 as an independent label and now a major company. Hamburg thus became, along with Munich, Frankfurt, Cologne, and Berlin, a key center for dance-pop—from Eurodance to trance—aside from its underground house and techno scenes.

Scooter was designed as an act responding to rave trends— and success came quickly. Here, the link to Modeselektor is

---

2 Jordan departed in 2013, though it should also be noted that Scooter has always been presented as a trio. Baxxter and Jordan were accompanied by a variety of supporting producers and performers, the most famous being cofounder Sören Bühler, Baxxter's cousin, who was a member of Scooter from 1993 to 1998.

gradually coming into focus, for just months into its proper founding, Scooter rose to stardom in 1994 with a chart-breaking hit: "Hyper Hyper"—the track that Modeselektor would cover. "Hyper Hyper" took the form of a trance cover of a Scottish hardcore anthem from 1993, UltraSonic's "Annihilating Rhythm." The exploitation of rave trends was thus crucial to Scooter's earliest chart-topping singles.

Since "Hyper Hyper," Scooter's presence at the border of dance-pop and Euro-rave has been secure. Initially, this presence was supported by regular coverage in Germany's most prominent teen magazine, *Bravo*.[3] As a rave act, Scooter also became distinguished from the previously mentioned 1990s trends of Eurodance. The most popular form of 1990s dance-pop, Eurodance mixed rap with hi-NRG, Italo disco, or techno, featuring a vocal mix of African-American male rappers, usually former GIs stationed in West Germany, and female singers.[4] Key Eurodance examples include Snap! and Culture Beat, which featured GI rappers Turbo B and Jay Supreme. As the "Euro" in Eurodance implies, the genre was also popular across Europe. Holland and Belgium were likewise prominent, featuring groups like 2 Unlimited, Twenty 4 Seven, and Technotronic (the group that had young Bronsert as a fan).

While retaining MC elements, Scooter was distinguished from these groups by focusing on happy hardcore, trance, and hardstyle, along with occasional EBM and synthpop. Again, rather

---

3 See Sean Nye, "Techno in der BRAVO: Eine wahre Geschichte," in *50 Jahre BRAVO*, ed. Archiv der Jugendkulturen (Berlin: Verlag Archiv der Jugendkulturen, 2006), 210–25.
4 For accounts of the avoidance of Eurodance in techno historiography, see Weheliye, "White Brothers with No Soul," 41–3.

than a dance-act, Scooter could be more accurately described as a *rave act* in the tradition of groups like Dune. Scooter also played with white Euro-masculine performance that at its most extreme could be described as the dance-pop answer to Rammstein. The rave act approached pyrotechnic metal on hits like "Faster Harder Scooter" (1999), although Scooter never played with Rammstein's über-deutsch provocations. Rather, Scooter retained a playfully Anglophone spirit where Baxxter's MCing became a witty mix of sound poetry and pop gabber.

However, Scooter's multidecade stardom was by no means clear at the time of "Hyper Hyper." Few would have predicted their durability. Back in 1994, "Hyper Hyper" was primarily received in rave culture as an exploitative novelty track. It was the lyrics, rather than the sampling of UltraSonic, that drew the most attention. The song concluded with a notorious series of shout-outs to key DJs in Europe, supposedly showing respect. With these shout-outs, "Hyper Hyper" simulated their star status. In this sense, the track could be described as a German techno version of the Sugarhill Gang's "Rappers' Delight." Just as the Sugarhill Gang had no status in NYC hip-hop, though they boasted of having original style and fame, Scooter had no status in the German techno scene. In a sense, Baxxter turned rave fandom into stardom, and Jordan supported this simulated status by borrowing from a technique pioneered by the KLF in their "stadium house" trilogy: the use of crowd noises and cheering to give a sense of size and spectacle. Baxxter humorously describes this strategy as "staged megalomania."[5]

____

5 Max Dax, "Auf der Suche nach einer eigenen Kunstsprache: H.P. Baxxter," *Spex*, September 1, 2008. https://spex.de/auf-der-suche-nach-einer-eigenen-kunstsprache-hp-baxxter-scooter-interview/.

This arena atmosphere eventually led to the notorious DJ shout-out. Scooter's list of DJ luminaries proved to be a snapshot of 1990s European rave culture. Anyone familiar with rave music would know how crucial these artists were. It could be described as a Wiki version of 1990s Euro-techno. I will thus take a brief regional tour through these names and explain the West German context of Scooter's rave inspirations. We will then see why "Hyper Hyper" matters to Modeselektor.

Here is Scooter's notorious list, shouted out by H.P. Baxxter at one of the song's peak moments:

> We want to sing a big shout to U.S. and to all ravers in the world!
> And to Westbam, Marusha, Steve Mason, The Mystic Man, DJ Dick, Carl Cox, The Hooligan, Cosmic, Kid Paul, Dag, Mijk van Dijk, Jens Lissat, Lenny Dee, Sven Väth, Mark Spoon, Marco Zaffarano, Hell, Paul Elstak, Mate Galic, Roland Casper, Sylvie, Miss Djax, Jens Mahlstedt, Tanith, Laurent Garnier, Special, Pascal F.E.O.S., Gary D., Scotty, Gizmo... and to all DJs all over the world!

The regional features of this list are important. Berlin rave music is of course highlighted. The most prominent DJs are the Low Spirit stars Westbam, Marusha, and DJ Dick, along with Tanith, Cosmic, Mijk van Dijk, Kid Paul, and Special. Other prominent regions that Scooter highlights are Frankfurt (Sven Väth, Dag, Sylvie, Mark Spoon, Pascal F.E.O.S.), the Rhine-Ruhr (Roland Casper, Mate Galic, The Hooligan), and Munich (Jens Lissat, Hell). While focused on German techno, the international dimensions of rave culture are also represented. This includes the Dutch scene (Paul Elstak, Miss Djax, Gizmo), along with luminaries from Britain (Carl Cox), France (Laurent Garnier), and the United States (Lenny Dee).

While I don't have the space to discuss the influence of all these artists, suffice to say that these DJs were prominent in the spreading of rave music across Europe in the post-1989 moment, representing styles including acid house, trance, and gabber. Certainly, Scooter relied on the cachet of these DJs to promote its own brand. In terms of Scooter's specific musical inspirations, however, two artists from the list are key to their regional influences in Hannover: Steve Mason and the Mystic Man. In fact, Steve Mason and the Mystic Man were an influential British DJ and MC duo, particularly in Northern Germany. Beginning in 1991, Mason spread rave music on the radio airwaves, namely via the British Forces Broadcasting Service (BFBS), along with the Mystic Man, who was one of the MC inspirations for Baxxter himself.

It is thus appropriate that their names appear early on in Scooter's list. Indeed, "Hyper Hyper" is partly modeled on the radio show, The Steve Mason Experience.[6] Together with the Mystic Man's MCing, Mason would often have a mix of British rave and trance in his sets—a comparable mix that Baxxter and Jordan would then feature as Scooter. It is indicative here that Hannover, as well as Hamburg, were located in the British Occupation Zone, so the influence of the BFBS is logical. Thus, Scooter is actually a late and surprising example of the influence of military radio in West Germany—across the Cold War and into the post–Cold War 1990s.

---

6 Baxxter also emphasizes these links. Ibid.

This influence of British rave and trance, along with synthpop, continued for Scooter, with the sampling of underground hits such as Shut Up & Dance's "Raving I'm Raving" (1992). However, many Euro-pop fans would not have known of these origins. These covers thus amounted to a covering up of history. So it was a statement in 2007 when, from the emergence of the Berlin underground, Modeselektor decided to cover "Hyper Hyper." This track was produced together with Otto von Schirach, the Cuban-Floridian breakcore artist mentioned in the intro—and in fact, "Hyper Hyper" proved to be the perfect mix of cover and collab. Von Schirach provided the vocals and the Miami-bass experience to make "Hyper Hyper" a more proper expression of transatlantic hip-hop and electronica— and this collab began a fruitful partnership with von Schirach, as we'll explore in the next chapter.

Von Schirach replaces Baxxter as MC, and he repeats the entirety of the lyrics, including the shout-outs to all the 1990s DJs. His vocals are chopped up and approach glitch-hop. On Modeselektor's and von Schirach's version, Scooter's 4-on-the-floor kick drum is no more. The sequenced and symphonic trance elements are toned down, with the introduction of a distorted Roland-909 and acid 303s following the parody of Scooter's classic line, "we need a bass drum!" The track could thus be described as an impossible hybrid of breakcore, acid house, and trance—an updated post-rave style for the 2000s.

Eventually, in a form of poetic justice, many international Modeselektor fans would listen to "Hyper Hyper" without any knowledge of Scooter. It could be said that if Scooter instigated the process of rave exploitation, Modeselektor contributed to the rebooting of underground history by covering Scooter. The emphasis on the breakcore and hip-hop elements also serves to place the track in the hardcore continuum of rave styles. Modeselektor and von Schirach invite a playful return to a transnational history of the rave underground.

Still, a point regarding the history and the status of Scooter needs mentioning: 2007 is an intriguing year for the release of this track. Even if many international fans might miss the reference, Modeselektor's "Hyper Hyper" points to Scooter's enduring stardom.[7] At this time, the surprise at Scooter's pop longevity was relatively fresh. Gradually, an ironic—and sometimes genuine—appreciation of Scooter unfolded in the 2000s. This was confirmed by a 2008 interview with Scooter that was published in *Spex*, the German equivalent to *Rolling Stone* or *NME*.[8] Such an interview would have been unheard of in the 1990s. It could be argued here that techno coolness in 2000s Berlin seemed to forget some of the rave euphoria; Scooter at least played with the era in its own comedic way. The timing of Modeselektor's cover was also appropriate, for Scooter was reaching new heights of success. Their 2007 album, *Jumping All over the World*, had a particular achievement: it was their first number-1 album in the UK. The album notoriously knocked Madonna off the top slot early in 2008, its success guaranteed by Scooter adapting to new trends. Here, "jumping" refers to jumpstyle, a popular 2000s hardcore dance for teens that looks like a raving Riverdance.

---

7 H. P. Baxxter and Modeselektor would later meet each other. See Max Dax, "H.P. Baxxter meets Modeselektor," *Electronicbeats.net*, December 15–17, 2012.
8 Dax, "Auf der Suche nach einer eigenen Kunstsprache: H.P. Baxxter."

Scooter had also refined its sense of humor. By this time, Baxxter's wordplay had become sillier and more nonsensical. In KLF spirit, this trend had been famously inaugurated with their 1998 hit, "How much is the fish?"—and Scooter paid homage to KLF's tactics, also in the year 2007, with yet another chart hit: "The Question is what is the Question?"

Ultimately, the lesson from Modeselektor's and von Schirach's cover of Scooter in 2007 involves the following: it recalls a different version of the 1990s. As mentioned, at its cool peak in mid-2000s Berlin, you got the impression that the 1990s only consisted of underground clubs. Even if Modeselektor was firmly entrenched in the Hard Wax avant-garde, it must be said that for many people Hard Wax was not the first exposure to techno. Modeselektor's "Hyper Hyper" was a memory of the silly 1990s, recalling the reception of pop techno in provincial contexts. Modeselektor thus engaged here in the unspoken pop-Eurodance that was an influence on so many Euro-teens, whether reading *Bravo* or watching VIVA. Still, media consumption was experiencing major transitions in the 2000s. Youth culture was transforming in new digital directions, and the standard German teen venues of *Bravo* and VIVA were in steep decline, as pop culture ushered in an era of glitch overload.

Let us not forget that the first iPhone was released the same year as *Happy Birthday!* In the spirit of these rave themes, let us now turn to another 2000s digital genre, breakcore, which was particularly active in Berlin.

8 Interlude
What about Breakcore?

Is there a message?
It's sort of a mix of finding everything shitty,
and everything great.
GERNOT BRONSERT

With the selection of "Hyper Hyper," Modeselektor once again expertly traversed the line between underground and pop reference—both in the covers and collaborations. Beyond the collab with Otto von Schirach, quite the underground contrast to Thom Yorke, there is a particular significance to the choice of Scooter in the engagement with musical genres. It takes this form: with "Hyper Hyper," Modeselektor made an appropriate selection that touched on the genre tradition known as breakcore, which responded to the rave 1990s in its own satirical ways. Indeed, one can scarcely find a more apt reference than Scooter. As a dance track, Modeselektor's "Hyper Hyper" practically mixes breakcore and pop-rave hit, providing a more accessible, cheeky enjoyment rather than total breakcore shredding. In other words, their remix is a pop echo of breakcore—inviting one into the genre's history.

In truth, this reference to breakcore takes us back to Modeselektor's own roots. The duo has had a complex relation with breakcore. The "Hyper Hyper" cover links up with Modeselektor's early career, and with the history of breakcore as it evolved in the 2000s. After all, at the same time as Modeselektor was developing, a new breakcore generation was becoming firmly established in Berlin, to which Modeselektor was partly related. The collaboration with von Schirach is the most direct example.

Breakcore's roots in Berlin are long and deep. The label Digital Hardcore, centered around Alec Empire of Atari Teenage Riot, practically confirms Berlin's claim to be one of breakcore's originators. Empire's 1996 album *The Destroyer* provided an overwhelming beginning to the genre as an album form. In its extremity, the album is at the antipodes of Modeselektor's and von Schirach's accessible collab. *The Destroyer* could be described as the radical shock of new style—at its noisy extreme, the album is the breakcore answer to Lou Reed's *Metal Machine Music* as pop feedback.

Following Empire's inception of the genre, breakcore's links to culture and politics became more complicated. A variety of approaches to the genre developed. An evolving transnational network of labels took shape in subsequent years, including Planet Mu, Peace Off, Tigerbeat6, Cock Rock Disco, and in Berlin itself, Ad Noiseam and Praxis. Breakcore also developed a variety of approaches during the ominous political situation of the post-9/11 era.

In the context of transnational networks, it should be noted here that the migration of electronic artists to Berlin did not only include techno and house artists. It also included breakcore producers. Artists based in Berlin in the late 2000s included Kid606 of Tigerbeat6 and DJ Donna Summer of Cock Rock Disco. Artists from Venetian Snares to Enduser had also moved to Europe and were in the Berlin orbit at this time.[1] Around the time of *Happy Birthday!,* there was a breakcore scene in Berlin that was becoming as active as minimal techno, albeit as a more confined subscene. One important center for the scene was the record store Dense, and the record label Ad Noiseam, headed by Nicolas Chevreux. The scene extended around industrial D 'n' B and IDM-ambient producers such as Current Value The Panacea and Hecq (Ben Lukas Boysen). The transnational links continued to Holland and Belgium, represented by artists like DJ Hidden and Bong-ra, and an active UK scene was reflected in the traditions of hardcore electronica represented at the Bang-Face parties.

Even at Berlin's techno-cathedral Berghain, breakcore was played. During the late 2000s and early 2010s, weekends did not just involve techno and house nights, though the signature club nights from late Saturday through Monday remained. As Berghain developed links to experimental electronic music scenes, Friday nights could feature parties that explored the full spectrum of bass music and electronica. For example, one major night in 2009 featured Venetian Snares, Current Value, and Larvae, and in 2011, Ad Noiseam hosted a ten-year event featuring DJ Hidden, Enduser, Hecq, and related artists—not to mention numerous dubstep events at Berghain, most prominently Scuba's Sub:Stance series from 2008 to 2013.

---

1 Kid606's 2009 album has an appropriately Berlin breakcore title: *Shout at the Döner.*

Clubs such as Maria am Ostbahnhof and WMF were also key venues at this time, including for Modeselektor. To be sure, Shitkatapult and BPitch Control artists hosted many nights at these venues as well.

Indeed, the networks of this scene involving breakcore, dubstep, and IDM would again require its own book. For our purposes, Modeselektor's engagement with these styles in the context of minimal and microhouse Berlin is intriguing. As Simon Reynolds states, in its 2000s context breakcore could almost be considered as the "riposte to microhouse," involving all the styles that don't belong in the minimal and microhouse universe: "jungle, gabba, dancehall, Miami bass, gangstarap, etc."[2] Breakcore often strips rave of naive euphoria, though at the same time, its intense rhythms invite a physical euphoria in dance that comes from a refinement of the cerebral beats of IDM.

In terms of humor, breakcore and glitch in the Modeselektor vein could be described as a satirical and ironic take on rave. Reinvigorating the spirit of punk, some of its tendencies, especially in pop reference and satire, are practically the rave equivalent to *South Park*. Rather than 'ardcore and happy hardcore, which feature witty wordplay as pop-psychedelic bliss, breakcore cheekily engages samples and covers in a mix of satire, trash, and zonked intoxication—and sometimes bliss. Indeed, the links are almost too perfect in that, around the time of *Happy Birthday!,* one of the most popular breakcore party series in Berlin, hosted by DJ Donna Summer, was called *Birthday Party Berlin*—replete with balloons, confetti, and other

---

2 Reynolds, *Energy Flash*, 507.

adornments.[3] *Happy Birthday!* is thus also a breakcore title as pop echo.

Modeselektor's records from the early 2000s reflect some of these breakcore roots. In fact, all of their early EPs could be described as combinations of IDM and glitch, with echoes of breakcore. Such tracks include 2002's "We do it Too" on *In Loving Memory*, their first EP, as well as "Das Claudia Wolkey Massaker," "Panaria in Bukarest 2002," and "Death Medley" on their second EP, also entitled *Death Medley* and released that same year. But in most prominent fashion, breakcore was featured on their third EP, 2003's *Ganes de Frau*. This EP features not only a trash-swag photo of Bronsert and Szary in electro-punk spirit but also the glitch and breakcore tracks "Die Tekknoprostitutionsmaschine (Von Bohlen Empfohlen),""Don't Panic," and a remix of Ellen Allien's "Trash Scapes."

The first title requires, well, careful translation. As might be imagined, it is Modeselektor's most breakcore-maximalist title, for it could be roughly translated as: "The Techno-Prostitution-Machine: Recommended by Bohlen." Aside from the "Techno-Prostitution-Machine," the latter half of the title is a perfect German-pop reference as breakcore satire. Bohlen refers to Dieter Bohlen, member of the bestselling duo Modern Talking, which released epic Euro-hits during the 1980s such as "You're My Heart, You're My Soul" (1984) and "Cheri, Cheri Lady" (1985). The duo features the classic falsetto and camp performance by singer Thomas Anders, with song-writing, production, and witty smiles provided by Dieter Bohlen.

---

3 See this example on the Wayback Machine: https://web.archive.org/web/20080901101621/http://www.birthdaypartyberlin.com/.

The release of "Die Tekknoprostitutionsmaschine" in 2003 was also timely. In 2002, Bohlen had inaugurated a new pop era in Germany. For he gained a reputation as the super-critical, prickly judge on *Deutschland sucht den Superstar*—the German version of *American Idol* or *Pop Idol*. In effect, Bohlen became the German answer to Simon Cowell. Needless to say, it would have been quite a pop accolade in 2003 to have "A Bohlen Recommendation." Here, Modeselektor references pop in classic breakcore fashion, taking the piss out of stardom with a little Bohlen sample and following it with a retro-hardcore sample from the hoover-synths of rave. In short, its parody of Bohlen could be thought of as a breakcore prelude of their parodic anthem of "Hyper Hyper."

To return to Modeselektor's and Otto von Schirach's "Hyper Hyper," this track can be seen as a window into breakcore's transnational history in the 2000s. As a kind of gateway, Modeselektor was providing breakcore echoes on the mass festival circuit—a pop window into the relatively small scene of breakcore devotees. In fact, von Schirach was the mashed-up Miami-bass representative of the breakcore scene, and Modeselektor had repeated collabs with von Schirach. The collabs include the banging electro of "Evil Twin" on *Monkeytown*, as well as "I am Your God," on 2019's *Who Else*—not to mention that von Schirach released *Supermeng* on Monkeytown in 2012.[4]

Modeselektor's references to breakcore have continued to the present. Following the early EPs, Bronsert and Szary ultimately returned like a boomerang to breakcore on *Who*

---

4 https://www.monkeytownrecords.com/artist/otto-von-schirach/.

Else. Following "I Am Your God," *Who Else* would conclude with an epic breakcore tribute: "Wake Me Up When It's Over." The track features mashed Amen-breaks mixed to what sounds like Auto-Tune humming in the Kanye West-era. The title represents the full sense of breakcore's satire of pop pleasure, art, and politics. Here is the digital age as hardcore hell—a return to the shredding spirit of breakcore's rage. Considering the political context in 2019, Modeselektor has also made clear their stance on transnational Europe, against rightwing turns taking place across Europe, especially in the "Former East." The album proves to be one of the many electronic soundings of political crisis in the late 2010s. With breakcore and glitch, music still hurts.

9 Cover II
Rave Rebirth

Thoughts running through my head,
Some are good, some are not . . .
Thoughts running through my head,
Some are good, some are not . . . bad.
SHED, "DAY AFTER."

. . . but between breakcore, happy hardcore, and many other -cores—there was also once a subgenre that emerged in the 1990s, which received a special reference on *Happy Birthday!* It could be called trancecore, or simply hard trance. Here, I turn to the second cover of rave music, for, as a reminder, there are *two covers* on this album. While the cover of "Hyper Hyper" is the more famous of the two, there is in fact another interesting cover on *Happy Birthday!* known as "The First Rebirth."

What is this title referring to?

"The First Rebirth" is a reference to one of the trancecore anthems from the 1990s. The original "First Rebirth" was by a Belgian duo called Jones & Stephenson. It was released in the distant year of 1993, a year prior to Scooter's "Hyper Hyper." Lodged quietly near the album's end as track 14, Modeselektor's "First Rebirth" is, compared to "Hyper Hyper," a rave cover as B-side. It subtly reinforces the album's multiple references to Euro-rave from the 1990s. The choice of Jones & Stephenson is intriguing, although it is less surprising. After all, compared to "Hyper Hyper," "The First Rebirth" is a revered track in the rave scene, and it has been remixed dozens of times. Its 2003 reissue alone included a compilation of twenty remixes.

And yet, Modeselektor's inclusion of a trancecore cover in minimal Berlin in the year 2007 remains another interesting move in the spirit of post-rave references. With this choice, Modeselektor taps into another transnational history; the duo arguably updates Sean Albiez's sonic futurescape as a transnational ravescape across Europe during the 1990s. These exchanges involved constant crossovers between the techno and DJ scenes of Belgium, Holland, France, the UK, Germany, Italy, and more—with Belgium's scene being quite central.

Belgium was in fact poised to enter the rave scene in the early 1990s in a variety of distinctive ways, with established disco and soul scenes in the 1970s, and New Beat and EBM in the 1980s. To mark some of the punk features of the Belgian scene, producer CJ Bolland nicely sums up his critical feelings regarding Kraftwerk and English synthpop: "a lot of robots; but no rebellion."[1] While there was certainly rebellion in some senses in the music of Kraftwerk and British post-punk and synthpop, you know what he means if you know Belgian music. New Beat and EBM in the 1980s, most famously with groups like Front 242, helped to bring punk energy into electronic music.

A club scene, as recounted in the 2012 documentary *The Sound of Belgium*, was established in the 1980s. As the scene

---

1 *The Sound of Belgium*, directed by Jozef Deville (Brussels: Visual Antics, 2012).

developed, the label R&S Records, founded in Ghent in 1984, became the basis for a Belgian network of electronic producers from New Beat to rave—a network that became transnational. Club scenes had also been established via the new highway networks in the country, from the Popcorn club during the soul/disco era, into the New Beat and rave era with the clubs Cherry Moon, Extreme, and perhaps most famously, Boccacio.

Belgian techno and rave evolved in the early 1990s, with new labels and producers developing at this time. The producers behind "The First Rebirth," Jones & Stephenson, come from Antwerp. Consisting of Franky Jones (Frank Sels) and Axel Stephenson (David Brants), the duo was inspired by German-rave culture. Jones & Stephenson was itself conceived as the Belgian answer to Jam & Spoon, a famous trance duo from Frankfurt.[2] "The First Rebirth" was released on Bonzai, an influential Belgian label founded in 1992. Franky Jones was a key force behind Bonzai, and he would go on to release EPs such as *Trance-O-Logic* (1994). These styles slot into the intensity of hardcore trance.

As a hard trance track, "The First Rebirth" is a thrilling but nightmarish trip. It features a gradual swirling and ascending alarm that feels like one is entering a vortex of rave hypnosis. Modeselektor's cover plays with such thrilling aspects of this era. Indeed, these Belgian references might have been expected, given the duo's rave and breakcore roots. A prelude to "The First Rebirth" can be found on "Kill Bill, Vol. 4" from *Hello Mom!* with its relentless Morse-code trance riff, not to mention some EBM/techno influences in Modeselektor's club bangers.

---

2 Ibid.

It is important to consider, however, that Modeselektor elected to have covers of two very different examples of Euro-rave from the mid-1990s—one celebrated, the other the subject of parody. But together, with the dual links to Euro-rave, "Hyper Hyper" and "The First Rebirth" engage European constructions of hardcore techno and dance music, while providing a ravescape that merges these tracks with the breakbeats and bass pressure of the Black Atlantic. In other words, breaking with the relentless four-on-the-floor kickdrum, these remixes restructure European raves in a way that situates the cultural flows in Black Atlantic contexts from dubstep to hip-hop—another variation on Albiez's sonic futurescape.

At the same time, a remix like "The First Rebirth" acknowledged Berlin's location within the European networks of rave, at a time when it felt like the general attempt was to make Berlin the hipster center of club culture, with ongoing processes of gentrification. At the height of the minimal 2000s, it was a statement to be directly referencing one of the trancecore anthems of the 1990s and acknowledge its influence. In short, in its mix of British bass music and Belgian trancecore, it was a reminder that Berlin remained a rave intersection.

"The First Rebirth" is also an intriguing cover. Rather than a functional dance remix, Modeselektor elects to go subtly meditative. In this sense, in bringing out new possibilities in the track, it is a kind of ambient inverse to their banging and funny celebrations on "Hyper Hyper." I'll drive home the uniquely quiet nature of this track in the following way: beyond the surprise that both Scooter and Radiohead have direct links to *Happy Birthday!*, one would not expect that their remix of "The First Rebirth" would lead into the next track on the album: Thom Yorke's ambience on "The White Flash." And yet, it works so well here.

Modeselektor turns on some intoxicating, but not overwhelming, bass pressure; the half-time rhythm restructures this trancecore track as subdued dubstep, with many of the trance elements retained, but only as distant Morse-code signals that border on ambient echoes. It resituates dubstep again as the ultimate post-rave genre of the 2000s. Its reflective mood even approaches the melancholy of "Edgar," one of the great meditative tracks on *Happy Birthday!* These tracks feature haunting drones and reverb in the same year as the release of Burial's *Untrue.* Again, one could say that this is an appropriate update on Euro-hardcore, and this time, Belgian hard trance is updated and transformed for the dubstep era.

In the context of these covers and remixes, however, and to return to my exploration of the album as a *constructed network*, I'd like to make one more point. It concerns format, because a format comes to mind with respect to "The First Rebirth" that is important to consider: the compilation—and specifically, the CD-compilation. It is a format often forgotten in the reverence for classic DJ mixes and albums, though it was crucial for the spreading of rave across the 1990s. "The First Rebirth" draws up these memories.

Closely related to mixtapes, the CD-compilation was central to the spreading of 1990s dance music. *Happy Birthday!* approaches this format in its "choose-your-own-adventure" model of covers and collabs. Its selection of rave memories in the context of 2007 remains fascinating. After all, the flood of curated musical memories on social media has only increased since the release of this album (one final reminder that the iPhone was released that same year).

In that spirit, let's bring this into a contemporary context.

For me, the role of the compilation and the iconicity of "The First Rebirth" recall a key component of social media and music curation. I am thinking here of the endless procession of retrospective lists of favorite music (and films and literature) that have been posted on Facebook and other platforms across the last decade. These would take the form of various prompts that quickly went viral. In 2017, one prompt thus came up that was arguably social media's equivalent to *33 1/3*:

List the Top 10 Albums of Your Teenage Years.

Countless online friends immediately jumped at this opportunity to trade musical knowledge, many realizing the chance to curate their teenage tastes on cyberspace. Here, many friends emphasized refined tastes with only classic albums and cool, acceptable artists. At the same time, many online friends would challenge and satirize these photoshopped examples of digital memory.

But, when confronted with this Top-10 list, I was left at a double loss, involving taste and format. As a young raver, my musical life had not revolved around albums during my teenage years in the mid-1990s—and especially during the high school exchange in Braunschweig in 1995 and 1996. I was essentially absorbed in DJ culture before album culture. Only by the end of my teenage years did the love for albums truly blossom, bleeding into the rock and electronic classics.

These experiences with formats return us to an introductory reflection: namely, to Simon Reynolds's musings on dance formats, as well as Mark Butler's analysis of the work-concept. As a reminder, for dance music, Reynolds views the following distinctions as key: "the anthemic track rather than the album, the total flow of the DJ's mix, [and] the alternative media of pirate radio and specialist record stores."[3] These alternate formats provide insight, but one would want to add the *compilation* to this list—as the mass-pop equivalent to the specialist record store. Next to the car mixtape, the unmixed CD-compilation was the 1990s dance fan's most beloved form of extended listening. It invited options for budding DJs to explore tracks as DJ tools.

And so, in recalling this idea, and in response to the Facebook request for one's Top-10 albums, my answer was to display some sonic skeletons in double fashion. I did not list a series of classic albums, and I did not list traditional albums—*only compilations*. Moreover, some of the compilations consisted of glaringly commercial Euro-pop and dance music. However, when listing these, I was also pleasantly struck by the variety of techno styles and trends featured on these compilations. Many of these I bought during my exchange year. Germans at this time similarly found such compilations at standard shops such as *MediaMarkt* and *Saturn*.

Posted in 2017, my compilation list included, for example, volumes 10 and 14 from *Techno Trax*, a series by one of Germany's definitive independent labels, *ZYX*. This label, a pioneer in the compilation format, had already been crucial

---

3 Reynolds, *Energy Flash*, xxi.

to the dissemination of Italo disco compilations in the 1980s. The *Techno Trax* series led listeners to a variety of techno styles, including gabber and hard trance. Other examples include ID&T's *Thunderdome* series, based on the famous Dutch gabber party, to Eurodance and trance compilations. At its most embarrassing moments the list also had hits from the compilation series released by Germany's teen magazine, *Bravo*—where Scooter was prominent. Beyond these, many other compilations could have been listed—from *Trance Nation* to *RaveBase*.

Since I posted this list, I have been thinking about the multiple influences of CD-compilations, and the slight inferiority complex that the compilation-obsessed have compared with the album-obsessed. The CD-compilation does represent a specifically 1990s teen-raver subjectivity that, again, is ultimately reflective of the DJ-listener in training. In terms of rave compilations, these links reinforce the transnational influences of the Rhine region (both the Rhine-Ruhr and the Rhine-Main), France, Holland, Belgium, Italy, and beyond.

This legacy of the rave compilation continues to this day. It still functions in representing various scenes, though in altered fashioned in the digital age. In fact, Modeselektor has also engaged in this tradition. Beyond their constant collabs, Modeselektor actually revisited compilations in the online era primarily through the *Modeselektion* series. Beginning in 2010, and now consisting of four volumes, *Modeselektion* represents a particular approach to the art of the compilation. Original pieces were solicited from diverse artists and curated by Modeselektor. The duo emphasizes here the importance of curation in an era of digital consumption, with an accompanying party series or tour taking place with each release: in effect, a compilation tour rather than an album tour.

In this sense, *Modeselektion* is one example of how the art of the compilation as scene experience has transformed in the digital era. It reflects the ways in which Modeselektor has worked to invigorate and support the Berlin scene in its multiple roles as producers, curators, and label owners. With the labels Monkeytown and 50Weapons, the duo maintained the function of labels as scene support in the digital era—bringing together artists such as Siriusmo, Mouse on Mars, FJAAK, Funkstörung, and Shed into new networks of digital distribution. It is Berlin focused, yet the labels and the scene are transnational as only Berlin techno can be.

10 Arena Techno to Anti-EDM

The past is a light train
To unknown trash scapes.
ELLEN ALLIEN

My story here is gradually winding down. However, one aspect has been missing in this tour through 1990s hardcore and rave history. In my focus on the collabs and covers of *Happy Birthday!*, I have not focused on Modeselektor's self-produced dance tracks—aside from my introductory remarks about "Happy Birthday!" and "Godspeed." The duo's strictly instrumental electro and techno tracks that pepper the album, from "Sucker Pin" to "The Black Block," provide the most direct party anthems. "Déboutonner," feat. Siriusmo also provides a special sonic experience in the form of a *producer* collaboration. As with Apparat, this collaboration with Siriusmo represents the networks of Monkeytown and 50Weapons. Functional and banging, Modeselektor constructs truly updated expressions of "arena techno." The tracks are themselves crossovers between EBM and techno, the banging electroclash of early 2000s Berlin, and even the French house of Daft Punk.

This reference to Daft Punk invites yet one more—final—comparison for me. As we approach the end of this album tour,

I will conclude with my boldest claim, or at least comparison, with respect to pop and underground. It is as follows: I would say that, as an electronic duo between festival scene and underground, Modeselektor is to Berlin techno what Daft Punk is to French house. I don't mean by this to compare the two in terms of fame and impact. Daft Punk has attained a singular position here. But, I also don't mean to reduce this final comparison to the simple fact that both are electronic duos—in this sense, Modeselektor are closer to such British inspirations as Autechre and Orbital, not to mention their Monkeytown colleagues Mouse on Mars and Funkstörung.

Rather, there are historical implications in this comparison. The example of Daft Punk reminds me of a reflection from the intro, to which I now return. In the context of the release of *Happy Birthday!* in 2007, I pointed out an intriguing feature of that historical moment: namely, that the maximalist albums of Daft Punk's *Alive 2007* and Justice's *Cross* appeared that year. At the same time, multiple releases in the British and German scenes were presenting reflections on the ghostly past.

Happy Birthday! occupies a middle ground here; the album provides a maximalist soundtrack for banging 2000s Berlin, but at the same time, in "The First Rebirth" and its melancholic tracks from "Em Ocean" to "Edgar," it offers some ghostly moments. Here, the double helix of party emotions that I described in Chapter 2 returns. We find specific musical postures related to both East German and Berlin cultural history, situated within the transatlantic currents of electronic music.

In truth, this is a reminder that, despite the duo's parody of minimal during the 2000s on *Speaking in Code*, Modeselektor has retained a refined and restrained Berlin maximalism.

Indeed, Modeselektor remained a Berlin act to the extent that the reception of Detroit techno, as well as Berlin minimal, still informed their approaches. The breadth of inspiration did not exclude minimal. As a result, the caricatured maximal-to-excess approach of what became known as EDM remains a distant world. Such resistance is already obvious on *Hello Mom!* and subdued tracks like "Fake Emotion" with Paul St. Hilaire.

This distinction returns me to the challenges in explaining the transatlantic musical histories of electronic music. To be sure, both *Hello Mom!* and *Happy Birthday!* were released prior to the EDM boom in the United States. Like Daft Punk, Modeselektor anticipated some of the EDM-maximalist successes while later shying away from them. My sense here is that the strange juggernaut of EDM in the United States makes Modeselektor—as well as Moderat—feel like a pre-history or distant European echo of the American festival scene. In 2016, Bronsert explained such a perspective, following Modeselektor's and Apparat's American successes in the 2000s: "The USA is a special case. We had a solid base there. We had fans. But six or seven years ago, when EDM started, we lost interest because the whole electronic music world we knew just evaporated, and only now is it slowly starting again."[1]

This explosion of EDM toward the end of the 2000s resulted in some complex transatlantic dynamics. In a certain sense, electronic dance music finally obtained mass appeal in the United States with major festivals from Ultra in Florida to Electric Daisy Carnival and the casino club mile in Las Vegas.

---

1 https://www.electronicbeats.net/modeselektors-gernot-bronsert-on-the-development-of-moderat/.

A new generation of American and Canadian artists such as Skrillex and Deadmau5 supported an American festival circuit that also involved European crowd–pleasing stars—David Guetta, Calvin Harris, Swedish House Mafia, Tiësto, and so on. A split in techno and EDM could be witnessed, or what Fabian Holt has theorized as a "soft shell" formation of EDM pop as a festival economy.[2]

Reflecting this split, Modeselektor in a sense pioneered a popular spirit of arena techno but recoiled from the populist spectacle of EDM. During these transatlantic developments, the duo did perform, for example, at Coachella in 2008 and 2012 (and in 2017 as Moderat), though they have steadfastly avoided EDM festivals and bottle-service clubs. Bronsert said frankly in 2016: "We want to go the classic old-school way, and we don't really want to play Las Vegas and the like. Honestly, we've been to the United States enough already, and we all have families now."[3] He has been highly critical of what one might call the bad populism of EDM pop: "You can look at what is going on in the U.S. right now and draw your own conclusions about that kind of thing—but we don't like to talk about 'EDM.' If we're going to talk about EDM we might as well sit here and talk about Las Vegas or Disneyland."[4]

Given this post-2007 debate, and in the context of techno heritage, let me return here to my transatlantic experience of seeing Modeselektor perform in Detroit in 2016. While driving

---

2 Holt, "EDM Pop."
3 https://www.electronicbeats.net/modeselektors-gernot-bronsert-on-the-development-of-moderat/.
4 Alex Gwilliam, "Modeselektor," *Crack Magazine*, May 10, 2013. https://crackmagazine.net/article/news/modeselektor/.

through the city to the various events at Movement, I was struck by the divides in techno and EDM as represented by the Detroit cityscape. With its economic struggles as capital of the Rust Belt, Detroit has some isolated examples of neon nightlife amid the postindustrial bleakness. These pockets of lights usually are from casinos. Relatively modest in size, these casinos were opened after Detroit legalized gambling in 1996. With these isolated casinos, Detroit appears like the postindustrial, working-class inversion of the firework glories of Las Vegas and its club nightlife—and yet, in terms of musical culture, the bright lights of Vegas actually reflect an impoverished culture of conspicuous consumption and pathetic bottle-service clubs. Here was the height of the cynical appropriation of dance music—*the drop and the fury*.

Modeselektor's media presentations as a duo are strikingly distinct from EDM stars. As opposed to stardom in the form of social media, which provides a false sense of intimacy (with no hint of class dynamics), Modeselektor constantly reminds one of everyday struggles. Their masks are off, and they play as normal guys. Bronsert simply states, "We are a well-balanced couple. This is so to speak my second marriage."[5] As bass workers with the masks off, they emphasize the banal aspects of life.[6] In this sense, they are presented as the everyday duo that is distinct from Daft Punk's robot performance style, now integrated into Tron Disneyland. While iconic, the robot image of Daft Punk has become reduced to the logic of the EDM

---

5 *We are Modeselektor.*

6 Sebastian Szary reminded fans of such everyday challenges with a subdued photo book of backstage rooms: see Sebastian Szary, *Backstage Tristesse* (Berlin: Monkeytown Music, 2014).

mask as a corporate brand: from Deadmau5 to Marshmello. It was not a surprise then that Daft Punk, in a different reaction than Modeselektor, would on *Random Access Memories* (2013) explore traditional musical values away from maximalist excess.

Let's close with the discussion of this working-class and everyday spirit as represented in the album's final tracks. In truth, "The Wedding Toccata Theme" always felt to me like the conclusion of the album. The song with Maxïmo Park, "(I Can't Sleep) Without Music," though listed as the concluding track, feels like a bonus mix. A synthpop homage with some lyrical clichés, it is emotionally less interesting than "The Wedding Toccata Theme." This track, by contrast, is the subdued, drained inversion of the opening track, "Happy Birthday"—taking the epic rave journey to its hung-over end. Following the jazz ambience of "Late Check-Out," which leads into the track, it feels like "The Wedding Toccata Theme" is an 8-bit, drunken slog home to one's apartment (perhaps on the U-Bahn)—a Berlin-glitch version of Burial's "Night Bus." It also is a melancholic tune that leans toward an 8-bit experience of computer game love—arguably the 2007 melancholic dirge to Kraftwerk's "It's More Fun to Compute."

A fitting conclusion to the variegated representation of transnational and local Berlin with, again, the maintenance of Modeselektor's presentation of working-class, everyday life—amid the party fun, club tourism, and ongoing gentrification of the city.

With this slog home, it should be reminded: even after exploring Modeselektor, it remains a long journey in obtaining a sense of the culture of Berlin—its surrounding regions and transnational currents. In that spirit, this book remains but an introduction to the city's history and "Former East" music history—and in considering this fact, I will return to that definitive city image of the Berlin Wall. Recalling the international fascination with the Wall, I'll conclude with, as opposed to Szary's and Bronsert's childhood memories, the perspective of my American experience as a tourist at the Berlin Wall. This final scene will take place on the edge of the "American Sector," as it once existed in Berlin.

Postlude
Wall Ghosts

The Berlin Wall continues to fascinate nearly every tourist who visits the capital. However, it must be admitted, there are concerning trends with this fascination. One example consists of two little words: Checkpoint Charlie—the formerly famous checkpoint between the American sector and East Berlin. This spot has become one of the ultimate pop moments on standard Berlin tours. When you arrive at Checkpoint Charlie, you realize the unfortunate forms that tourism can take.

At the gates of the Checkpoint, like a postmodern caricature of *Woyzeck*, play-soldiers now march up and down, guarding the tourist trap. You may have pictures taken with the soldiers—and the iPhoto and selfie celebrations follow. The black-and-white photography of Cold War authenticity is everywhere to be seen along the block, with museums and gift shops surrounding the mock guard house. Yet also stuck between these museums are examples of global consumerism: McDonald's, KFC, and Starbucks. After all, this entertaining spectacle is now supported by the usual need for refreshments.

It almost had to be. Checkpoint Charlie has become a banal monument to the Cold War. For American tourists, the fixation with 1989 as eternal victory is on display, with the assumed links to Ronald Reagan and other triumphant visions. The markers of fast-food and coffee convenience appear universal and timeless. In other words, American shops securely frame the historical entertainment. The convenience reminds me of how Americans often use the term "fast forward" when moving between historical periods—historiography as a remote control. Or rather, history becomes a movie theater, with refreshments.

I must admit here that while living in Berlin between 2008 and 2011, in the wake of *Happy Birthday!*, I would occasionally work at precisely that Starbucks by Checkpoint Charlie. There, while reading and writing in a quiet corner, I could observe the stream of tourists enjoying lattes, coffee, and muffins following the viewing of Checkpoint Charlie. The sounds of sipping and slurping, the pulling out of cell phones, and the usual banter would follow.

As the countless containers and plastic cups were thrown into the trash, I'd hear the usual comments about the lessons of how bad communism was. And in my dark moments, I'd conclude that American individualism can now be defined as the love of single-use items—the cups, one after another, into the trash. Like so many American expats, I was struggling at that moment with the state of the country during the Iraq War and in the wake of George W. Bush. The tourists would then move on to the next stop on the Berlin tour—perhaps involving another example of Past Existing Socialism.

I have not been back to Checkpoint Charlie since the election of Trump (and certainly not since the pandemic), though it would be intriguing to know how these visits have been affected by the discursive shift in American politics to an actual discussion of "Walls." Usually, or at least across the

2000s, American politicians claimed to want to build a "fence" or "strengthen security" on the border with Mexico. I always assumed that "fences" was a deliberate euphemism to avoid the repeated use of the term *wall*, with the consequences of the Berlin Wall still fresh during the 1990s and 2000s.

With Trump, the direct call for the building of walls was finally made. Even if the total Wall is never built, American history is now stamped with a political victory built fundamentally on the ideas of walls. Sadly, it seems that the Berlin Wall has become a caricature along with Checkpoint Charlie. It has been provided its proper frame and refreshment stand. The breaking up of such fixed perspectives might thus be necessary.

As with my historical exploration of Modeselektor from the Brandenburg periphery to the center of Berlin, a unique document of the Berlin Wall's past could be paired here with this study: the fascinating 1988 documentary *Cycling the Frame*. In a comparable mix of underground and pop culture, it features Tilda Swinton cycling the entire border of the Berlin Wall, and it features quiet and rural scenes on the periphery of Brandenburg. It thus offers much more than the CNN icons of the Brandenburg Gate and Checkpoint Charlie. In fact, Swinton returned in 2009, on the twentieth anniversary of the Fall of the Wall, to film a sequel, *The Invisible Frame*—traversing the fragments of an empty border on a new bike tour.[1]

Similarly, my decision to focus on musical practices from the 2000s, and the rave and techno webs of Modeselektor,

---

1 Toward the end of this 2009 tour, she has a brief scene of confused observation upon her arrival at Checkpoint Charlie. At that moment, two pedal pubs full of drinking revelers are biking across the former border.

returns me to that desire—a need—that the understanding of German histories and music be renewed, along with understandings of Berlin in the context of Europe and other political frames. In other words, this little book aims to be an update that deepens rather than distances historical understanding. In a small sense, the study of the bizarre, witty, and modest practices of Modeselektor hopes to carry our perspective in that direction.

Bibliography

Adelt, Ulrich. *Krautrock: German Music in the Seventies*. Ann Arbor: University of Michigan Press, 2016.

Albiez, Sean. "Europe Non-Stop: West Germany, Britain, and the Rise of Synthpop, 1975–81." In *Kraftwerk: Music Non-Stop*, edited by Sean Albiez and David Pattie, 139–62. London: Continuum, 2011.

Albiez, Sean. "Sounds of Future Past: From Neu! To Numan." In *Pop Sounds: Klangtexturen in der Pop- und Rockmusik*, edited by Thomas Phleps and Ralf von Appen, 129–52. Bielefeld: Transcript, 2003.

Borthwick, Ben. "Raster-Noton: The Perfect Strom." *The Wire*, December 2003, 40–47.

Butler, Mark. *Playing with Something that Runs: Technology, Improvisation, and Composition in DJ and Laptop Performance*. Oxford: Oxford University Press, 2014.

Dax, Max. "Auf der Suche nach einer eigenen Kunstsprache: H.P. Baxxter." *Spex*, September 1, 2008. https://spex.de/auf-der-s uche-nach-einer-eigenen-kunstsprache-hp-baxxter-scooter -interview/.

Dax, Max. "H.P. Baxxter meets Modeselektor." *Electronicbeats.net*, December 14–16, 2012. http://www.electronicbeats.net/h-p- baxxter-meets-modeselektor-part-1-its-the-haircut-i-guess/; https://www.electronicbeats.net/h-p-baxxter-meets-modes elektor-part-2-every-audience-loves-pyro; https://www.ele ctronicbeats.net/h-p-baxxter-meets-modeselektor-the-hate -wears-off-part-3/.

Dax, Max. *Scooter: Always Hardcore*. Hamburg: Edel, 2013.

Denk, Felix and Sven von Thülen. *Der Klang der Familie: Berlin, Techno, and the Fall of the Wall*. Translated by Jenna Krumminga. Norderstedt: Books on Demand, 2014.

Dierikx, Marc. *Clipping the Clouds: How Air Travel Changed the World*. Westport: Praeger, 2008.

Feser, Kim and Matthias Pasdzierny, ed. *Techno Studies: Ästhetik und Geschichte elektronischer Tanzmusik*. Berlin: B_Books, 2016.

Garcia, Luis-Manuel. "Beats, Flesh, and Grain: Sonic Tactility and Affect in Electronic Dance Music." *Sound Studies* 1 (2015): 59–76.

Gwilliam, Alex. "Modeselektor." *Crack Magazine*, May 10, 2013. https://crackmagazine.net/article/news/modeselektor/.

Heuguet, Guillaume. "When Club Culture goes Online: The Case of Boiler Room." *Dancecult: Journal of Electronic Dance Music Culture* 8, no. 1 (2016): 73–87.

Holt, Fabian. "EDM Pop: A Soft Shell Formation in a New Festival Economy." In *Weekend Societies: Electronic Dance Music Festivals and Event-Cultures*, edited by Graham St. John, 25–44. London: Bloomsbury, 2017.

Jasen, Paul C. *Low End Theory: Bass, Bodies and the Materiality of Sonic Experience*. London: Bloomsbury, 2016.

Jelavich, Peter. "The *Wrapped Reichstag*: From Political Symbol to Artistic Spectacle." *German Politics and Society* 13, no. 4 (1995): 110–27.

Matos, Michaelangelo. *The Underground is Massive: How Electronic Dance Music Conquered America*. New York: Dey St., 2015.

McCaskill, Clark. "Moderat Chats About Their Tour, Their New Album, Gentrification, and Thom Yorke." *Earmilk*, 2016. https://earmilk.com/2016/04/09/moderat-chats-about-their-tour-their-new-album-gentrification-and-thom-yorke-interview/.

Mitchell, Tony. "Introduction - Another Root: Hip-hop Outside of the USA." In *Global Noise: Rap and Hip-hop Outside the*

USA, edited by Tony Mitchell, 1–38. Middletown: Wesleyan University Press, 2001.

Nye, Sean. "Love Parade, Please Not Again: A Berlin Cultural History." *Echo: A Music-Centered Journal* 9, no. 1 (2009): no page.

Nye, Sean. "Minimal Understandings: The Berlin Decade, The Minimal Continuum, and Debates on the Legacy of German Techno." *The Journal of Popular Music Studies* 25, no. 2 (2013): 154–84.

Nye, Sean. "Techno in der BRAVO: Eine wahre Geschichte." In *50 Jahre BRAVO*, edited by Archiv der Jugendkulturen, 210–25. Berlin: Verlag Archiv der Jugendkulturen, 2006.

Pareles, Jon. "In Berlin, Still Partying in the Ruins." *The New York Times*, November 21, 2014. https://www.nytimes.com/2014/1 1/23/travel/in-berlin-still-partying-in-the-ruins.html.

Pasdzierny, Matthias. "'Produced by some chemical waste and cum': TOMM¥ €A$H and His Concept of Signifying 'post-Sovietness.'" *Res Music* 10 (2018): 29–40.

Paumgarten, Nick. "Berlin Nights: The Thrall of Techno." *The New Yorker*, March 24, 2014. http://www.newyorker.com/magazine /2014/03/24/berlin-nights/.

Rapp, Tobias. *Lost and Sound: Berlin, Techno, und der Easyjetset*. Frankfurt: Surhkamp, 2009.

Reynolds, Simon. *Energy Flash: A Journey though Rave Music and Dance Culture*. Berkeley: Soft Skull Press, 2012.

Reynolds, Simon. "Maximal Nation: Electronic Music's Evolution toward the Thrilling Excess of Digital Maximalism." *Pitchfork*, December 6, 2011. http://pitchfork.com/features/articles/8 721-maximal-nation/.

Schiller, Melanie. *Soundtracking Germany: Popular Music and National Identity*. London: Rowman & Littlefield, 2018.

Sherburne, Philip. "Digital Discipline: Minimalism in House and Techno." In *Audio Culture: Readings in Modern Music*, edited by Christoph Cox and Daniel Warner, 319–26. New York: Continuum, 2004.

Szary, Sebastian. *Backstage Tristesse*. Berlin: Monkeytown Music, 2014.

van veen, Tobias C. "Review of *Speaking in Code*." *Dancecult: Journal of Electronic Dance Music Culture* 2, no. 1 (2011): 111–4.

Von Thülen, Sven. "Willkommen in der Rappelkiste: Pfadfinderei, Visualtäter, Codec und Labstyle." *De:Bug* 45 (March, 2001): 22.

Walmsley, Derek. "Mark Ernestus: The Gene Genie." *The Wire*, February 2010: 34–38.

Weheliye, Alexander, interview with Annie Goh. "White Brothers with No Soul – Untuning the Historiography of Berlin Techno." *Un Tune, CTM 2015*, 40–3.

Westbam, with Rainald Goetz. *Mix, Cuts & Scratches*. Berlin: Merve, 1997.

Filmography

Berlin Calling, directed by Hannes Stöhr. Berlin: AV Visionen GMBH, 2008.

B-Movie: Lust and Sound in West Berlin, 1979–1989, directed by Jörg A. Hoppe and Heiko Lange Berlin: DEF Media, 2015.

Cycling the Frame, directed by Cynthia Beatt. Berlin: Sender Freies Berlin, 1988. https://www.youtube.com/watch?v=RU_1nA33 2ws.

The Invisible Frame, directed by Cynthis Beatt. Berlin: Filmgalerie 451, 2009.

The Sound of Belgium, directed by Jozef Deville. Brussels: Visual Antics, 2012.

Speaking in Code, directed by Amy Grill. San Francisco: Microcinema, 2009.

We Call It Techno! A Documentary about Germany's Early Techno Scene and Culture, directed by Maren Sextro and Holger Wick. Berlin: Sense Music & Media, 2008.

Online Techno and Rave Sources

Arte

Modeselektor feature, *Arte TRACKS*, December 6, 2007. https://www.youtube.com/watch?v=WHDtlvVcNZI.

Modeselektor & Corey Scott-Gilbert, *Work – ARTE Concert*, April 9, 2021. https://www.youtube.com/watch?v=56--MBTTg5k.

Boiler Room

https://boilerroom.tv/recording/modeselektor-live-in-the-boiler-room-2 (2012).

https://boilerroom.tv/recording/modeselektor-60-min-mix (2013).

https://boilerroom.tv/recording/modeselektor (2017).

Electronic Beats

We are Modeselektor, directed by Romi Agel and Holger Wick. Berlin: Monkeytown Records, 2013), DVD. http://www.electronicbeats.net/youtube/we-are-modeselektor-documentary/.

H.P. Baxxter meets Modeselektor. http://www.electronicbeats.net/h-p-baxxter-meets-modeselektor-part-1-its-the-haircut-i-guess/; http://www.electronicbeats.net/h-p-baxxter-meets-modeselektor-part-2-every-audience-loves-pyro/; http://www.electronicbeats.net/h-p-baxxter-meets-modeselektor-the-hate-wears-off-part-3/.

Jon Hopkins meets Moderat. https://www.electronicbeats.net/vid
eo/jon-hopkins-meets-moderat-eb-tv-feature/.

"Modeselektor's Gernot Bronsert on the evolution of Moderat."
https://www.electronicbeats.net/modeselektors-gernot-br
onsert-on-the-development-of-moderat/.

"Otto von Schirach: The Mutant behind the Music." https://www.
electronicbeats.net/otto-von-schirach-the-mutant-behind-
the-music/.

Pitchfork

https://pitchfork.com/news/40516-5-10-15-20-apparat/.

https://pitchfork.com/features/guest-lists/7671-moderat/.

https://pitchfork.com/reviews/albums/5671-hello-mom/.

https://pitchfork.com/reviews/albums/10675-happy-birthday/.

https://pitchfork.com/reviews/albums/15867-modeselektor-
monkeytown/.

https://pitchfork.com/features/grime-dubstep/7805-grime-
dubstep/.

https://pitchfork.com/reviews/albums/411-berlinette/.

Red Bull Music Academy

Modeselektor (London 2010) / Red Bull Music Academy. Interview
with Torsten Schmidt: http://www.redbullmusicacademy.com/
lectures/modeselektor-2010.

Modeselektor (Berlin 2018) / Red Bull Music Academy. Interview
with Torsten Schmidt: http://www.redbullmusicacademy
.com/lectures/modeselektor-2018.

"A Guide to the Discography of Paul. St. Hilaire / Tikiman." http://
daily.redbullmusicacademy.com/2013/09/paul-st-hilaire-tiki
man-guide.

"Interview" Teki Latex" (of TTC). https://daily.redbullmusicacad
emy.com/2013/03/teki-latex-interview.

Resident Advisor

Real Scenes: Berlin. September 6, 2011. https://ra.co/features/
1405.
RA Podcast, no. 173: Modeselektor. September 21, 2009. https://
ra.co/podcast/173.
RA Exchange, no. 180: Ellen Allien. December 27, 2013. https://ra.
co/exchange/180.
RA Exchange, no. 459: Modeselektor. May 23, 2019. https://ra.co/
exchange/459.

Diverse Websites

Modeselektor and Monkeytown features: https://crackmagazine
.net/article/news/modeselektor/; http://dasfilter.com/sounds
/es-reicht-nicht-mehr-nur-gute-musik-zu-machen-label-portr
aet-10-jahre-monkeytown.
The Steve Mason Experience, Steve Mason & MC Mystic Man –
June 18, 1994: https://www.youtube.com/watch?v=W5LE
eUJioml.

Index

3 Steps Ahead   66
50Weapons (label)   xxiii, 91, 92

Ableton   27
Ad Noiseam   77–8
Afro-Caribbean links   xxxi, 9, 20, 31, 39, 48
Albiez, Sean   40, 43, 47–52, 84, 86
Allien, Ellen   15, 32, 37, 40, 63, 80, 92
Aphex Twin   xviii, xxxii, 12, 22, 40, 46
Apparat (Sascha Ring)   xiv, 16, 36–40, 45, 52, 92, 94

Baron Cohen, Sacha, *see Brüno*
Basic Channel   11–13, 42
Baxxter, H.P. (Hans Peter Geerdes), *see* Scooter
Belgian Techno   13, 83–7
Berghain   3–5, 16, 78
   breakcore parties   78
   Ostgut   4–5
Berlin
   Berlin Wall   xix, 6–10, 30, 98–102
   breakcore scene   78–9
   Checkpoint Charlie   7, 99–102
   Club Scene   xxv–xxvi, 4–6, 90–1
   Friedrichshain/Kreuzberg   xvii, 4–5
   tech industry   26–7
   Wrapped Reichstag   xvi
birthday parties   19–21
Birthday Party   23
Black Atlantic   31, 42–3, 61, 86
Bohlen, Dieter   80
Boiler Room   xxxiii, 63
Bonzai Records, *see* Jones & Stephenson
Boysen, Ben Lukas, *see* Hecq
BPitch Control   xxiii, 15–17, 37, 51, 79
Brandenburg   6–7, 10, 13–14, 30, 36, 63, 101
   Rüdersdorf   7, 13–14, 36
   Woltersdorf   7, 36
BRAVO (youth magazine)   69, 75, 90
breakcore   76–82

British Forces Broadcasting
    Service (BFBS)   72
Brüno   65–6
Burial   xiv, xx, 40–2, 87, 97
Butler, Mark   xxii, xxiv, xxviii, 89

CD Compilations   87–91
Christo and Jeanne-Claude   xvi
Coachella   xxi, 50, 95
constructed network, *see*
    networks
Current Value   78
Cycling the Frame   101

Daft Punk   xxi, xxx, 21, 59,
    92–7
    Alive 2007   xxi, 93
Deadmau5   95, 97
De:Bug   15, 62
Depeche Mode   51
Detroit
    city history   95–6
    contrast with Las Vegas   96
    Detroit techno   xv, xviii, 12,
        34, 61–2, 64, 94
    Movement Festival   xv,
        xvi–xvii, xxx, 96
    Tresor links   5, 61
Dettman, Marcel   16, 63
*Deutschland Sucht den
    Superstar*   81
digital media   xxvi–xxxiv

DJ Donna Summer   78–9
    Birthday Party Series   79
dubstep   18, 41, 78–9, 86–7
dub techno   12, 42–3
Dune (rave act)   70

East Germany, "Former
    East"   xvi, xix–xxv, 3–17,
        19, 30, 36, 59, 82, 98
    East German DJs   15–17
EDM criticism   95–8
EDM pop   50, 58–9, 95
EDM stars   95
Electric Daisy Carnival   94
Electronic Beats   xxxiii, 39, 41
Empire, Alec   77
    The Destroyer   77
Enduser   78
Energy Flash, see Reynolds,
    Simon
Ernestus, Mark   11–12
Eurodance   13, 43, 69, 75, 90
    GI Rappers   69

Farmers Manuel   62
"The First Rebirth", *see* Jones &
    Stephenson
Four Tet   40, 49
French House   xxi, 56, 92–3

gabber   37, 43, 55, 56, 66
Garcia, Luis-Manuel   xxx

German Democratic Republic
(GDR), *see* East Germany
German techno   xix–xxi,
xxv–xxviii, 20, 42–3, 70–1
English language   19–20
Gogol Bordello   19

Happy Birthday!, *see also*
Modeselektor
cover design   21–3
title   19–21
hard trance, *see* trancecore
Hard Wax   11–13, 16, 17, 26–7,
34–5, 42, 63, 75
Hecq   78
hip-hop   xxxii, xxxiv, 14, 23,
25–35, 42–3, 61, 70, 86
French hip-hop   xxxi, 25,
27–9
Puppetmastaz   28–9, 45,
61
Sugarhill Gang   70
Hopkins, Jon   40, 42, 51
"Hyper, Hyper", *see* Scooter

I-Motion   58–9

Jasen, Paul C.   xxix, xxx
jet set   xiii, xxxiv, 8
Jones & Stephenson   xxxii,
83–8, 93
Justice   xxi, 56, 93
Cross   xxi, 93

Kalkbrenner, Paul   16, 28, 40–1
Berlin Calling   16, 40–1
KLF   56, 64, 67, 70, 75
Kraftwerk   xxviii, xxx, 5, 20, 21,
46–50, 60, 84, 97

Las Vegas   94–6
Leftfield (band)   42, 43
Love Parade   xv, 10, 26, 42,
57–60
Low Spirit (label)   11, 26, 60, 71

Maffay, Peter   66
"Nessaja"   66
Maria am Ostbahnhof   5, 79
Marshmello   97
Marusha   11, 71
Mason, Steve and the Mystic
Man 71–2
influence on Scooter   71–2
maximalism   xxi, 33–4, 58, 80,
93–4, 97
Mayday (rave)   57–60, 63–4
minimalism (minimal
techno)   xxi–xxii, xxv,
13, 18, 26, 29, 32–4, 42,
59, 78–9, 84, 86, 93–4
Moderat   xxiii–xxiv, xxvii–xxxii,
4, 20, 29–30, 34, 36–43,
45–52, 60–1, 94–5
Modern Talking   80
Modeselektor, *see also Happy
Birthday!*

bass workers   xxx, 63, 96

British influences   xxxi–xxxii,
        12, 31, 39–43, 47–8,
        50–1, 86, 93

early EPs   80–2

Hello Mom!   xxiii, 6, 14, 17,
        21, 27, 35, 41, 85, 94

Modeselektion series   51, 91

Monkeytown   xxiii, 81

name origin   31–2

satire/humor   xxi–xxiii,
        22–4, 30, 34, 64, 79–82

Who Else   xxiii, 63, 81–2

youth   11, 13

Monkeytown (label)   xxiii, 31,
        81, 91–3

Mystic Man, *see* Mason, Steve

Native Instruments   27

networks   xxiv, xxvi, xxix,
        xxxi–xxxiv, 3, 6, 15–16, 29,
        47–52, 58–9, 77–9, 85–6

    constructed network   xxxi,
        xxxiv, 3, 6, 87

online culture   xxix, xxxi,
        xxxiii–xxxiv, 8, 40, 63,
        88, 90

Ostgut   4–5

Pfadfinderei   14–15, 62

Pigmans, Peter-Paul, *see* 3 Steps
        Ahead

Radiohead, *see* Thom Yorke

Rammstein   xx, 20, 31, 70

rave culture   xxvi–xxxiv, 11,
        13–14, 16, 18, 21–4, 43,
        55–64

Red Bull Music
        Academy   xxxiii, 7–8

Resident Advisor   xxxiii

Reynolds, Simon   xx–xxi,
        xxxvii–xxx, xxxii, 79, 89

Rhine region   58, 71, 90

Rhythm & Sound   42

Ring, Sascha, *see* Apparat

St. Hilaire, Paul   xxxi, 29, 38–43,
        94

Scooter   xxvi, xxxii, 64–76, 83,
        86, 90

    Baxxter, H.P.   67–8, 70–5

    British Forces Network
        (influence)   72

    founding   68

    "Hyper, Hyper"   69–75

    "Nessaja"   66

    "Raving, I'm Raving"   73

Shed   xxi, 16, 83, 91

Shitkatapult   37, 79

Siriusmo   28, 91, 92

Skrillex   95

Social Media (Facebook)   xxxiv,
        21, 88–9

Sónar Festival   59

South Park   23, 79

Speaking in Code   32–3, 59, 93
Swinton, Tilda   101
synthpop   50–1, 67–9, 84, 97

Technohead   23–4
Technotronic   13, 69
Thunderdome   90
tourism   xiii, 99
trancecore   83–7, 89–90
Tresor   xxii, 5, 10, 51, 61
Trump, Donald   xviii, 100–1
TTC   xxxi, 25, 27–9

Ultra Festival   94
Underground Resistance   10,
    12–13

United States
    American rave culture
        xx–xxi, 32–3, 50, 94–5
    Modeselektor's relation to
        94–5

VIVA (TV channel)   44, 58, 75
Von Schirach, Otto   xvii–xviii,
    xxxii, 14, 73–7, 81

Westbam   60–1, 63, 71

Yorke, Thom   xxxi, 37, 44–52,
    86–7
    "The White Flash"   44–6,
        87

9 781501 346248